PLAYING
DEAD

PLAYING DEAD

CHOOSING LIFE

ANNETTE L. EASTIS

TATE PUBLISHING
AND ENTERPRISES, LLC

This book is designed to provide accurate and authoritative information with regard to the subject matter covered. This information is given with the understanding that neither the author nor Tate Publishing, LLC is engaged in rendering legal, professional advice. Since the details of your situation are fact dependent, you should additionally seek the services of a competent professional.

The opinions expressed by the author are not necessarily those of Tate Publishing, LLC.

Published by Tate Publishing & Enterprises, LLC
127 E. Trade Center Terrace | Mustang, Oklahoma 73064 USA
1.888.361.9473 | www.tatepublishing.com

Tate Publishing is committed to excellence in the publishing industry. The company reflects the philosophy established by the founders, based on Psalm 68:11,
"The Lord gave the word and great was the company of those who published it."

Book design copyright © 2015 by Tate Publishing, LLC. All rights reserved.
Cover design by Bill Francis Peralta
Interior design by Jomar Ouano

Published in the United States of America

ISBN: 978-1-68187-464-7
1. Religion / Christian Life / Women's Issues
2. Religion / Christian Ministry / Counseling & Recovery
15.09.04

Acknowledgments

Derek Baker, for persevering through helping me to edit this book. Larali Boal, who has always been honest and real with me. Jim Boyer, who helped me put this story together in chronological order and provided valuable insights and feedback. Diana Boyer, who encouraged me with unconditional love and soft smiles. Greg Getz, who I have heard it was confirmed was raised by wolves, flooding me with encouragement, endlessly pressing me forward and at the same time frustrating me. Sara Getz, who has proved the marriage theory of "opposites attract." She has been an incredible prayer warrior and best version of the scripture which speaks about iron sharpening iron. Joe Himes, for being a faithful prayer warrior. Jim and Marcia Hyland, who portrayed God's love in incredible ways. Linda and John Oelze, who God sent at just the right time. Bob and Sherry Reeve, whose truth at times has been hard to digest, yet, have diligently been honest with me, which has been worth its weight in gold. Eddie

Rivera, who has since the day I met him made me laugh. Renee Rivera, who has more compassion than blood running through her veins. Diane Rodocker, who was willing to help me make my final edits in time to get this book published. Mary Schofield, who could hear my soul and give wise counsel. To the Missionary Church, Inc., who has provided educational opportunities as well as opportunities to meet incredible persons who have changed the trajectory of my husband's life and mine forever. To my precious children and adored grandchildren, who constantly remind me of the future. To my supportive family members, who recognized why I had to share this story of hope and healing. To John, my lovable husband and best friend, the one who has believed in me since day one. Even on days when miscommunication seems endless and I am incredibly irritated, I do dearly love you and always will. Our journey has been wonderfully wild, and I'm all in for another thirty-five years! And of course to God, Jesus, and the Holy Spirit, who I owe my life to. Thank you.

Contents

Preface

For years it was unthinkable for Christians to admit to having a problem with alcohol or drugs, let alone talk about their struggle. Thankfully times have changed. Today people are slowly opening their hearts and lives to reveal to others the sins they've been harboring or have lived through. Yes, sin exists whether we want to acknowledge it or not. The sins mentioned in my story here are not commonly discussed in "respectable" circles and will make most readers uncomfortable. However, denying these sins exist is not an option. God wants to deliver us from all sin, even the unspeakable ones.

As the story unfolds, some may question my salvation experience. Let me assure you that though putting my confidence in Jesus Christ as my Lord and Savior was the beginning of an incredible personal relationship with God, it did not make me perfect. It was the first step in an unending journey.

Life can be incredibly messy. With built-in survival instincts, we sometimes turn to false gods (little *g*) to make it through tough times instead of trusting the one true God (big *G*) to meet our needs. As a Christian, I never intended to put a small-*g* god in God's place in my life, yet I blindly did just that. Without thinking, I latched onto whatever addictions, habits, or behaviors could provide quick relief from stress and anxiety, whatever allowed me to regain control.

Though some sins have become "acceptable" in today's society, all sin is equally hideous in God's sight.

My story is not pretty. Nothing is hidden from your scrutiny apart from graphic details of sexual abuse. My story may be your first encounter with sexual abuse. It may mirror your own past all too well. Wherever you, my reading friend, find yourself, I want you to know that there is hope. I have been hurt by sexual abuse, physically beaten, and worse, betrayed by those whom I thought loved me most. My life was supposed to be beautiful like a lovely glass vase, and I felt at first my vase was cracked, then smashed, and then finally, trampled upon with pieces kicked to faraway places, never to be made whole again. Never. However, God took my glass shards—though so sharp, tiny, and tossed about—and made me better than whole. He made me something so priceless and precious. My friend, may you find in the proceeding pages God, the true Healer of the brokenhearted.

Because He lives!
Annette L. Eastis

1

Playing Dead

The first prayer I can ever recall saying was asking—no, begging—God to take away Shadow Man.

Late at night, when I was around four years old, someone came into my bedroom and woke me from a sound sleep, gently tugging on my pajamas to undress me. All I could see in the pitch-black room was the mere shadow of a grown man, so without any other way to describe him, I thought of my attacker as Shadow Man. The person molested me. His wordless silence actually scared me more than his painful touching.

I just lay there perfectly still because I was surprised and so scared I could barely breathe, let alone move. I thought if I simply pretended to be dead, like the actors I'd seen on television, I could block out the physical and emotional trauma during the whole painful experience, including the unnerving fear of dying at the hands of this masked, in-the-shadows stranger. Thoughts of dying, because I tried to move or cry out in pain, consumed me. I kept telling myself to get up and run or scream for Mom and Dad, but my body betrayed me. A frightened little girl can only imagine the worst, no matter how unrealistic. I only wanted to survive!

After Shadow Man finished with me, he redressed me and left my room. I waited until it felt safe to move before heading to the nearest bathroom to vomit and then continue to my parents' bedroom. I stood beside their bed crying and shaking uncontrollably. My mother awoke to my sobbing and sleepily asked if I had had a bad dream. I had no words to describe what just happened, so I answered yes. Mom made a spot for me in the king-size bed, and I happily crawled in. I was still barely able to breathe, yet the warmth under the protective covers and the security of having my parents so close soothed my soul. I knew I was safe and eventually fell asleep.

As a child, I knew my mother loved me very much and would come to my rescue if I got hurt, so I tried to tell her the next day about the man in my bed. "He came in, woke me up, and took off my clothes," I began. "And then—"

She immediately stopped me to say, "A young lady never speaks of such things. You have very dirty thoughts."

Her words ripped an enormous gash in the core of my soul! I felt like I was standing before my mother bleeding, but she just couldn't see my gaping wound. I wanted to be a good girl, not dirty. I walked away, feeling so confused by her failure to listen or help. It was a feeling of being tossed to the side, like a soiled rag. I knew intuitively that if I did not want to be thought of as "dirty," I could never speak of the "dirty" events that happened in my bedroom that night.

To my horror, Shadow Man returned. He didn't come every night, but he came again and again to do what he wanted to my body. Sometimes weeks or months passed between his visits, yet his startling presence on my bed always filled me with the same paralyzing terror. I always wore pajama tops and bottoms plus panties to bed each night. Shadow Man unbuttoned my top all the way down and pulled it open. I felt exposed lying there half naked and had to press my arms into the mattress to keep myself from closing it. He then removed the bottoms and my panties. Oddly, him opening my shirt proved more embarrassing than when he removed the rest of my clothing.

His hideous routine only escalated. He violated my most private body areas with groping, penetrating fingers, and eventually, he rubbed himself against my body until he ejaculated. After these later episodes, he washed in the bathroom next to my bedroom then returned to clean me with a cold, wet cloth. Plus, he sprayed my delicate skin with bathroom disinfecting air freshener before redressing me. The burning sensation was incredibly painful, but I would never flinch! My goal was to remain dead on the outside no matter what. My child's mind screamed inside with condemnation. Apparently Shadow Man saw me as a dirty little girl too and felt the need to clean away my cooties, my filthiness, when he finished abusing me.

Once I awoke before Shadow Man had completely undressed me, so I took a chance on moaning and rolling from my back to my belly, thinking he could not get to my front private areas to touch. This was a huge mistake because he simply accessed my rectum to please himself. The pain in the lower part of my body was so great I clawed my head with my nails and bit the inside of my mouth. After his backside attack, I dirtied my pajamas before reaching the bathroom and again went crying to my parents for help. My father scolded me for acting like a baby, and my mother cleaned me. I was so ashamed. I vowed *never* to turn onto my stomach for Shadow Man again!

Each time my bedroom door quietly closed at his retreat, I breathed deeply, feeling safe to be alive again. Feeling "alive" is really a nice way to put it! I would roll around in bed, scared, sweating, and needing to vomit. Shadow Man never stayed very long, but even just thirty minutes of pure torture seemed like forever! I felt like I was living in a dream where I was running full speed from some sort of evil, only never gaining any ground from my pursuer. It felt as if Shadow Man were slicing away a part of me on each visit. It's hard to explain, but part of me was missing or torn off. I knew I was not completely whole. The hopeless resignation of knowing it was only a matter of time before the night of paralyzing fear would start anew left me desperate to gain some control over my world in whatever ways I could manage.

2

Grandpa

Before Shadow Man came into my life, there was Grandpa. As a toddler, I could be soothed in his strong warm arms, listening to his deep, rich voice sing melodious Spanish tunes. I didn't understand a word he sang, yet my eyelids easily grew heavy in his care. One day, as he sang me to sleep, his hand found its way into my panties and began causing me great pain. His eyes changed from those of a loving grandfather to someone I had never seen before. His piercing eyes sent the instant message to my mind to take action and flee. Squirming and crying loudly got me an immediate release, and I don't remember relaxing in his arms ever again.

Growing up, my cousins and I loved playing horsey with Grandpa, where he bounced us on his lap as if we were riding a fast horse. I was usually excited for my turn on the horsey and eagerly climbed onto his lap, giggling and laughing along with the rest of the family. I think I could have ridden that make-believe horse forever, but one day, Grandpa suddenly slid his hand underneath and inside my panties while I bounced, causing awful pain. I squirmed and cried this time too until I was released to run off. My parents were probably embarrassed at times because I would not sit still to let my grandpa hold me, but I was unwilling to get closer because of my experiences with him.

My experience with my grandpa affected me in many ways. I could not understand why my parents did not protect me from his reach. It caused me to be wary of my uncles and men in general. It was as though men in my mind were unsafe. One minute they were fun to be with, and the next they could hurt you. This caused me to cling to my mother's side a lot when we went outside our home. I was considered to be a moody child, which was a small price to pay in order to be safe and not to be on the lap of someone who was going to hurt me.

3

Escaping

Unsure when Shadow Man might visit, I often hid in my closet during the days after a nighttime attack. Even in the middle of the afternoon, my mother could find me playing in the closet, light on and door closed. Though hiding made me feel safe, fear sometimes choked me as I imagined Shadow Man right outside my closet door! I would break out into a sweat, my heart racing, and a trapped feeling would overwhelm and petrify me. It seemed to be a no-win situation.

Mom walked through the house one time calling my name and searching for me while I hid safely in my closet. I dared not answer, imagining Shadow Man nearby. My mother, when entering my room looking for me, must have seen the closet light on and opened the closet door quickly and turned off the light. I screamed in fright because I thought it was the Shadow Man. In turn, my mom screamed because I scared her, for she did not expect to find someone in the closet. I always had an excuse for playing in the closet. She simply asked me to leave the door open so I wouldn't overheat. Grateful for such escape opportunities, I ran outside to play. Hiding was proving less effective.

Like I said earlier, I grew up in a large family and have two younger siblings, yet I always found a way to sleep in my parents' bed. Alone in my bed at night after the attacks began, an unexpected noise would send me flying to their room. This habit drove Mom and Dad absolutely nuts, and I knew it, but nothing beat the safety of their bed. I could not take a chance that the sound I heard in the house was Shadow Man coming down the hall or turning the doorknob to enter my room.

Hiding was only a way to physically be safe, but I needed something more in order to control the fear and pain that raged within my soul. My hair was pretty straight as a child, but Mom or an older sister would frequently curl my hair using curlers for special occasions, like Sunday mass, weddings, or parties. After taking the curlers out, they would brush my hair then spray it with hair spray. The hair spray would cause my scalp to burn at the nape of my neck, for I had developed a tic/habit of scratching it, causing an open wound. When the hair spray would hit my raw skin, the pain was worse than the pain in my soul; and though it may be incredibly hard to believe, it took my mind off my soul pain. Of course, with any bad habit, it had to increase in order to be more effective, and so regularly I would end up with my hands bloody from too much scratching. My hair camouflaged my actions. Though

I was so young, I could understand it was I who controlled the amount of pain I would experience when I scratched my head. It gave me control in a world I lived that seemed to spin out of control and in which I had no power. This power of control helped me drown out the shame, humiliation, and fear that tried to smother me.

My uncle, who came regularly to cut our family's hair, once noticed a large scabbed area on the back of my head while cutting my hair. When asked what happened, I had no words to explain, so I said I got hurt and it itched a lot. Both my uncle and my mother were displeased and advised me not to touch the area so it could heal. They insisted that peeling off my skin could lead to infection or eventually result in permanent hair loss and scarring. Uncle's discovery pressed a huge panic button inside me! I now made sure to watch the calendar for haircut appointments so there was time for my head to heal. However, I would naturally lose track of time, being a youngster, and eventually I had to start clawing or scratching other parts of my body to hide any sign of self-abuse.

I was *so* embarrassed that someone uncovered the secret damage I had caused, but what I feared the most was revealing *the* secret. What if someone discovered the awful, ugly, dirty things Shadow Man was doing to me? What if someone saw my life was abnormal? No matter how much I tried not to dig my nails into my skin, I could not stop nor, to be honest, did I want to stop. Whether right or wrong, these self-mutilating actions brought more relief than harm, so my goal focused on avoiding being caught in the act or leaving noticeable traces.

From the very first Shadow Man attack, my desire to die right there on that bed was huge. I decided to "will" myself to die. Holding my breath came naturally from the fear and dread I felt, and blacking out proved a helpful bonus. If I awoke before Shadow Man was finished, it took extra-mental strength, but I tried holding my breath to black out again.

As the Shadow Man's attacks continued, I began sensing that playing dead was not enough to mask the mounting pain and emotions I felt while being molested. I feared I might mess up, and who knows what that might mean! I don't know exactly when I figured it out, but I mastered shutting out the bedroom and the assault while dashing off to one of two imaginary places: sheets or beaches.

At first I imagined an invitation to visit wonderful, beautiful faraway places. Since control of my will evaporated any time Shadow Man pulled the covers toward the end of the bed, I soon gave my will completely to exploring and embellishing these fantasy getaway spots. I totally immersed myself in the refuge of those worlds, leaving the painful reality behind until I heard the bathroom-sink water running, which signaled the approaching end.

Sheets was a place where fresh laundry hung to dry in the lazy warm summer sunshine, billowed by a steady, invigorating breeze. The clean smell of a recent washing and the coolness of the fabric against my cheeks were calming and refreshing.

I would stand, eyes closed, in the middle of circular spinning lines of bedsheets blowing gently in the wind. I would walk or run along the lines of snapping sheets, holding my hands wide to comb through delightful sensations. Other times I would run into the inviting sheets, basking in the joy of something so thrillingly clean draped across my skin. In this place, the soiled little girl with dirty thoughts danced freely among pure, clean, sweet-smelling white linens wearing a clean white billowing dress.

Beaches was an isolate place on the California coastline during summer. I would find myself in the same white dress, only now little white daisies with bright-yellow centers adorned the collar and hemline. At beaches, I would first run fast without stopping. The beach seemed endless and my legs tireless. Splashing through the ceaseless warm waves brought no end of pleasure or excitement. Then I found the best shells, offering the most captivating, soothing sounds. The warm ocean water, a cool westerly breeze, and the hot sun overhead became my companions, urging me to giggle my way across the sand, exploring washed-ashore treasures and playing fun, innocent games.

I loved being in one of my two imaginary worlds. The lurking possibility of waking in the night half dressed and being touched was so overwhelming and nauseating I often visited simply to fall asleep or to escape a stressful feeling. I discovered I could retreat to sheets or beaches even when fully awake to numb the gnawing failure to be good enough or the stark truth of someone hurting me. In sheets or beaches, I was the good girl. I was loved and secure, and I was in complete control. I never wanted to leave!

Some may have grown tired or bored watching *The Wizard of Oz* on TV year after year, but as a child, I never missed it! While the dancing amazed me, the story of a little girl being knocked unconscious and transported to a wonderful, magical world, away from a home where she felt unwanted and misunderstood, was music to my young ears. Dorothy had a kindred soul in me because I was sure if I tried hard enough, I could transport myself out of my painful everyday situation. All I lacked at the time were ruby shoes and a happy ending.

When I was about six years old, I added another equalizer—hitting my nose with my fist. Hide-and-seek is a fun children's game but was a tense one for me during the hiding part. Playing the game with neighborhood friends created stress and anxiety that tasted too familiar! Being highly competitive at any game, I knew I could not come out of my secret spot until the right time, so being alone, waiting to be found or to sprint to safety, stirred identical anxiety to wondering if Shadow Man would come tonight or the stress of hearing a noise in the house and imagining it was him coming. I had to shove down my emotions even under games' circumstances. I would hit my nose extremely hard, making it bleed. The resulting pain and blood flow became a soothing agent, decreasing my stress level.

At first I lied about my nosebleeding incidents. I insisted I did not know why my nose was bleeding. Someone suggested the bleeding was caused by temperature changes between indoors and outdoors. As long as everyone accepted this reasoning, all was well. However, the more I hit myself, the longer it took for my nose to stop bleeding. Before long, my mother took me to the doctor's office to have the blood vessels in my nose cauterized. The smell and pain of having the skin in my nose burned was bad, but it also rose as a glaring sign that I was again out of control. I needed that peace of mind, so I promised myself to stop my hitting ritual and succeeded for a time. It quickly returned. After almost three and a half years of bloody noses and the second round of cauterization, I was done with hitting myself forever.

Simple things, like elementary school friends telling me a little boy liked me, put an incredible amount of fear in me. To think someone was looking at me when I was not looking made me nervous. What if they saw the real me? The dirty little girl. I clearly remember finding some small pebbles on the schoolyard while my friends and I busily played jump rope, and I placed one in my shoe. The small stone did exactly as I thought: it brought pain with every step! The pain instantly relieved the stress about a boy liking me, so I was able to continue playing with the pebble in my shoe. Again, it was about my being in control. The more stones or the sharper points on the stone's edges, the more pain.

There is a scripture that speaks how people can choose something wrong because at that moment it seems so right. I could not see it clearly so many years ago when I was a child, but today I can see how truly deceived I was then. Proverbs 14:12 (NKJV) says, "There is a way that seems right to a man, but its end is the way of death." The many doors that I chose for survival were wrong, but as the scripture above states, they seemed so right at the time. Perfect peace can only come from God, not from invoking my own will, thinking positively, increasing my physical pain to numb my soul pain, or even transferring my thoughts into a fantasy world. Eventually those doors of avoidance, which were only temporary solutions, would each run dry, leaving me in worse shape than when I first started out.

> I think all the little girls in my generation had a pair of shiny black shoes and/or white shoes with a one-strap buckle as standard accessories for church and other fancy events outside of school. One time, I took a red crayon to my white pair so I could have ruby shoes like Dorothy. Of course, that did not go over well with my mother. It didn't go over well with me either because they sure didn't shine like the ones on TV!

4

Dance

What ignites a passion in the recesses of your soul? What one thing seems to embody your reason for being alive? For me, as a young girl and well into my teen years, that experience, that one thing, was dance! I remember going to my first dance class when I think I was about six years old. I felt normal, like a good girl, like all the other girls. I had on the same leotard and ballet shoes as everyone else, and people clapped and cheered every time I did a good job. It was amazing! There was nothing like it for a little girl feeling dirty, terrible, and sinful on the inside. A person can be a terrible sinner, but when they perform, all that people see is what they do at that very moment. Dancing was a way of escape. It was a way, my way, of pretending I was someone else, someone pure, someone wonderful, someone acceptable.

From that time on, I developed a passion for dancing and performing. I practiced the moves at home between lessons.

I found books at the library about great women dancers of the past. I planted myself in front of the television every time a show offered a dance performance of any kind. My dance teachers cooed over my eagerness and discipline, spurring me forward. The dance floor became hallowed ground with dancers serving as gods and goddesses. You know the best part? I was among them!

Performing consumed me. Neighborhood kids were corralled during summer vacations to create talent shows. I urged friends to sing, tell jokes, perform drama, and of course, dance on a makeshift stage, complete with blankets for curtains on my parents' patio, to the delight of family, friends, or anyone who would attend. It was so much fun and very rewarding. One of the best parts was watching others perform the dance routines I taught them. The looks on my friends' faces when an audience clapped for them made me feel good too! I felt accepted and whole. I felt as though I had done something right. For I could see they too felt accepted and whole, and I had no other desire in the world, and I wanted it for others too. Though the applause of acceptance was only for a moment, to me it held great value.

Weaning my thoughts away from inner turmoil took much effort and time. Dance promised solace through the hours of warm-up and practice, the push to achieve, and actual performances. I loved high school for the dance opportunities it offered me, and I grabbed every chance offered. However, academics demand focus, and focus requires sleep. I was not big on sleep during high school days. Dreams seemed to rub against the scabbed wound inside. I often awoke as early as four in the morning, headed to the schoolyard then played my boom box and danced outside the gym, practicing routines and making up other ones, until the janitor officially opened the building at six. Drill team, dance team, and cheerleading consumed any free time. Sleeping and studying took a backseat to the endless, artistic, creative outlets I was afforded through dance. Music and dance drowned out the pain screaming at me when I was alone.

At school I was always full of energy, but at home I was exhausted and moody. I'm sure I was a real teenage pain to my parents as well as other family members. I let my grades slip to the D level during high school. My parents loved me enough to let me know my grades were not acceptable and I could do better. For me, though, school was required, a D was passing and good enough to graduate with, and the sooner I graduated, the sooner I could concentrate more time in dancing. I purposely chose to keep getting lousy grades because grades were something I controlled.

Dancers seldom tell about the pain involved with their art. Poise, rhythm, coordination, and stamina come at a high price. The endless ankle sprains, pulled muscles, blisters, bruises, broken toes, enlarged joints, and spinal injury are constant demons preying on performers. I used these demons to soothe pain in my soul. There wasn't much forethought to it, but pain became my ally, driving me to excellence and self-control.

5

Physical Problems

Stomach problems haunted me from the very first time I was molested. I reasoned at the time that Shadow Man reaching inside me with his fingers somehow messed with my stomach because I always felt a revolting need to vomit immediately after he left my room, and my gut hurt for many days afterward. Even if I wasn't abused on a particular night, my sleep was frequently filled with bad dreams, resulting in a sour stomach the following morning. On these mornings, Mom simply encouraged me to eat some breakfast to calm my insides, and she was usually right. I could spend the day playing without being upset as long as I heard my mother working or cooking or talking nearby.

I was excited to begin school, like most kids, but ran into other challenges in the classroom. School seemed a safe place to hide from Shadow Man since he only came in private at night. However, if class time passed too slowly, I became obsessed with thoughts of Shadow Man, which automatically generated discomfort and stress. I made many new friends of classmates but worried about any of them guessing or uncovering the horrible things that happened in my bedroom. These obsessive thoughts caused my stomach to churn, and I would complain to my teacher of an upset stomach. Teacher sent me to the school nurse, who telephoned my home, and I was frequently sent home for being sick. Just being near my mother brought me a measure of safety and relief.

Mom regularly took me to our family doctor for some answers, but the adults in my life were totally baffled by the cause and frequency of my stomach issues. How well I remember the day, after so many office visits, the doctor looked at my mother and told her that there was absolutely nothing wrong with me. I sat dumbfounded on his examination table as he explained that I was faking the discomfort to get attention and/or just not go to school. I knew I wasn't making up the pain in my stomach, but it was obvious no one was going to believe me. A child knows that the ultimate authority is the adults in their world. I knew I was being called a liar, but how could I prove a stomachache no one could feel except me? My mom drove home that day in silence.

During class a few weeks later, my stomach started to hurt again something awful, and I was sent to the nurse's office again. The school nurse called home, as usual, but Mom didn't offer to pick me up this time. She relayed the doctor's diagnosis to the nurse, who instructed me to just close my eyes and rest until I felt better. As long as my stomach hurt, I lay on the small cot in the nurse's office with the hope of returning to class. I spent a lot of time in the nurse's office during my elementary and junior high school years.

Today, as I minister to others who have been sexually abused, I have found they have suffered stomach issues. For many, the ailments disappeared with time when the abuse ceased. However, the stomach issues seem to come back when a memory resurfaces. This causes the person to desire to avoid dealing with the sexual abuse of their past. To have their stomach pain raging through their body only reminds them of their lack of control, similar to when the abuse took place. To choose to face their past and be open to the healing God can bring to their soul are something they desire desperately, but their self-protection-mode habits can get in the way.

6

Triggers

Who would ever imagine everyday smells carry the power to trigger serious emotions? But it happened to me. From as young as six or seven, the scent of deodorizing air freshener would be enough to make me gag, flooding my mind with fresh waves of pain from Shadow Man's abusive behavior. One of my girlfriends once tried to explain my gag reflex as some kind of allergic reaction, and sadly, I believed her.

I must have been about nine years old when my sister and a neighborhood friend played outside my sister's bedroom window while I pestered them by jumping up and down just inside the open window. This neighbor girl thought it would be funny to return my peskiness, so she grabbed the spray disinfectant from the bathroom and sprayed me in the face the next time I jumped up to tease them. Of course, it stung my eyes something awful! I screamed in pain, and Mom came running to see what was going on. She rushed me into the bathroom and washed my eyes with cool water, trying to calm me.

It was more than just deodorizer in my eyes. The scent reminded me of the pain caused by Shadow Man in my room at night and created panic inside me that everyone else saw what happened. It was more than I could bear, so I shook and gagged involuntarily. Mom did her best to soothe me but thought I was overreacting.

I cannot remember the exact date, but all the horrible night visits finally stopped. My prayer was answered! Nightmares continued, but the instigator at least never returned to my bed. I shoved all those insecure feelings and thoughts of being dirty deep inside. Since my prayer to God to take away Shadow Man had now been answered, I began to pray, "Oh God, please help me forget. Make it as though it never happened."

7

Superglue

Though Shadow Man seemed gone for good, I was restless to manage the pain and frustration that always surfaced inside at the most inconvenient moments. Dad and Mom began mending broken things around the house with a new product, superglue. My brother found out how quickly fingers can be glued together, but my older sister rescued him by dipping his fingers in nail-polish remover to safely release the bond. At that moment, an idea spread across my mind. What if I can remove skin while scratching real hard and put it back on?

I began to experiment and quickly learned to carefully remove one layer of skin with my fingernails before gluing the layer back in place. Sometimes I grabbed any object within reach—like the cap to a ballpoint pen, the metal band holding a pencil eraser, or my all-time favorites, a paper clip or a hair clip—to carefully peel away some skin. The trick was to cut just enough, not too deeply, and then quickly repair the damage. The act of cutting and gluing—well, let's say it developed into a compulsive art form to me. By cutting, I controlled my world and eased my heart pain. By gluing, I became a good healer, in a sense, and learned to do it perfectly with great results.

Superglue not only provided the perfect camouflage to self-abuse; its burning sensation on raw flesh tranquilized my searing soul pain. I purchased my own small bottle and carried it with me as part of my arsenal against inner pain. Putting superglue on my open skin gave me the same feeling as cool water going down my parched throat after a strenuous run on a hot day. My mind could think of nothing but the pure pleasure of that moment, forcing tension to lose its grip on my mind. With just a bit of the overwhelming tension gone, I could then play dead to the rest of my emotions as much as possible until I could figure out how to deal with the internal pressure going forward.

8

Changes at Home

Being raised Catholic from birth, I never missed attending mass each Sunday, even when sick. My parents made catechism class mandatory, as well as participation in the holy sacraments: communion, confirmation, and confession. I knew God and the fact that He loved everyone. My interpretation in my soul when I heard about God's love was that maybe God loved others because they obeyed so much better and had such pure thoughts. God knows everything, and because of this, He obviously knew of my evil thoughts. Yes, He loves everyone, perhaps He didn't love me as much as He did others.

Home began to change around the time I turned ten. My parents were the ones who changed actually, not me. Mom and Dad came home one night telling us kids that they were "born again." It was awful! My parents, who never showed public displays of affection to each other or their children, began showing affection all the time! They started holding each other's hand, kissing each other good-bye, and hugging us kids when we were leaving for the day. To top it all off, my mother began writing little love notes and putting them in my father's lunch sack. The two of them acted like they really loved each other and us.

My family was never the "touching" family, which was fine with me. In fact, the only touching I ever got was getting my hair washed and styled. I avoided any invasion of my space. Mom wasn't a touchy person, and Dad never tried to show affection to his children, so I used to think other parents rather odd when they hugged their kids for no reason. I didn't desire to be held or hugged. I was angered that my parents now, all of a sudden, wanted to touch me

My parents not only bought Bibles for themselves but for everyone in the family. Worse, they expected us all to read and enjoy it. They said this book contained a love letter from God, but all I could think about was how the Catholic Church warned us about people like this. My parents became obsessed lovers of Jesus! They went beyond the Catholic Church to attend other churches in their hunger to feed their newfound faith.

This whole "Christian" thing with my folks really confused me. My parents were staunch, dedicated Catholics, born into Hispanic Catholic families. On one hand, I could not deny that they genuinely changed for the better, and part of me yearned for what they were showing in loving actions and attitudes. On the other hand, I struggled to grasp how good, religious people seemed to switch overnight. Honestly, as a kid, I couldn't understand why anyone, like our Anglo neighbors, would choose to be Catholic and put themselves under all the rules and regulations. For someone burdened with all kinds of guilt, like me, the thought of such a drastic, dramatic change was too good to be true.

A movie called *A Thief in the Night* hit the theater about this time, and my parents took the family week after week. The movie portrayed a girl named Patty who found herself left behind after Jesus' second coming. Each night moviegoers were given a chance to accept Jesus Christ as their personal Savior by leaving their theater seats and walking to the front stage for prayer. I felt I could not turn my back on the Roman Catholic Church's God, whom I loved all my life. I was committed to Him and the Catholic Church.

One night, after about a year of their new life, my parents called my younger brother and me into their bedroom. They explained the gospel and asked us if we wanted to accept Christ as our "personal Lord and Savior." I remember my brother and me both saying no in unison. My parents explained how all my siblings were now "born again," and they wanted all their children to believe in Jesus and go to heaven. They didn't want anyone left behind, like Patty in the movie. Dad talked more about the Bible while my mom cried and begged us, but I stubbornly stood my ground and did not jump ship for this new Jesus. I was happy with the old one!

Finally my father said we were not leaving the room until we prayed the "sinner's prayer." My brother and I relented and repeated the most stubborn, most ungrateful prayer ever heard by heaven. Boy was I angry!

Our family began attending a small community church about forty-five minutes from home. My parents loved the pastor and congregation, Sunday school, and all the services, but I resented the new church. The people in our new church were too nice, too perfect for my liking. I would sit there bitterly listening to the sermon on Sunday so that I could point out to my parents during the week how they failed at being "Christian."

In Sunday-morning church services, I dutifully listened to the sermon to pick up enough ammunition to gun down my parents for their failures. I hounded my siblings, neighbors, classmates, teachers, or anyone over inconsistencies between their words and practice. The dirty little girl began to morph into a teenage monster! Part of me resented my venomous tongue and attitude since God wouldn't approve; but I sensed that my hatred, my attacks, my craving for control, my love to escape represented the dam inside me brimming over and spilling my true ugliness on those around me. The old saying "Hurting people hurt people" was completely true for me. I not only was hurting others, I found myself taking more frequent trips into my fantasy worlds for escape. I danced harder and longer. I sliced into my skin more often, hiding the cuts with superglue. In reality, I wanted it all to stop, but

I needed to unleash my anger on someone, something; and often, even the hardest of dance workouts, to the point of barely having the energy to make it home, could not keep my past from hounding me.

A few years had passed. I'm not sure if the tidbits secured from the Sunday sermons wore down my rough edges, or the internal and external exhaustion depleted my defenses, but the monster within started to dissolve. The reservoir of pain abated mildly. As the pastor used Bible stories and verses to solidify a point in his sermon, I began to open my own Bible to check the words for myself. I became fascinated by this new God I found in the pages on my lap. Yes, He was the same God I had heard about all my life. Jesus was the same Jesus celebrated at Christmas and Easter in the Catholic Church. God's Holy Spirit was still the same Spirit empowering the apostles to perform miracles for the sick, lame, blind, and sorrowful. But something was vastly different!

One night, after watching *A Thief in the Night* for the zillionth time, I ventured into the unknown. I didn't want to give my parents the satisfaction of seeing me walk down the theater aisle to pray with someone near the stage, but I told Jesus in my mind I was sorry for my ugly, hurtful sin. I told Jesus I needed relief from my guilt, that I wanted hope for a better life, and that I desired to know Him better. I pictured myself straining against everything threatening to expose me, everything poised to pollute everything and everyone in sight. However, I cautiously eased away from fears, from

Shadow Man, from pain, from control, and from anxiety. I gave my heart to Jesus in that moment.

After a while, though, I started to open up the Bible I was given and was fascinated by the God I found there. He sounded like the same God from the Catholic Church, and Jesus appeared to be the same Christmas, Good Friday, and Easter Jesus I had heard about all my life. Something was different because this God and Jesus seemed more personal, more real than I ever imagined. This God not only forgave sins but He forgot them too. How amazing is that! I wanted more from life, wanted relief from guilt, wanted hope for healing, and felt I could get all I wanted by getting closer to Jesus. I still harbored bitterness toward them, yet this step was a beginning—a very good beginning!

9

Confiding

An older sister asked about my sullenness during a private girl chat and mentioned my family's concern. I considered talking to her about my inner pain and desire to die but feared she would tell Mom and Dad. Her pleading eyes and words built a measure of trust, and her promise of secrecy prompted me to drop my guard and share my hopelessness. I admitted to wanting to kill myself, but her stunned face prompted promises to ditch future death wishes. Unfortunately my sister told my parents. I again felt completely betrayed!

Counseling resulted as the next humiliating step. Though my parents paved the path to the counselor's door with assurances of their love, I was so bitter and angry toward them! I was also confused at the mixed feelings whirring in my heart. Mom and Dad loved me enough to confront some issues, but not the true, deep-seated source of my pain.

Counseling shouted as an attempt to control me, and I hated being seen without control.

I hated the female counselor more than I hated being counseled. Each week she asked the same mundane, senseless questions. "How are you today?" "How was school?" "Your parents say you are sad and depressed, so what are you thinking right now?" Each week I offered nothing in reply. Her queries made me incredibly angry and seemed a complete waste of my time and my parents' money.

One particular session stands out in my mind above all the rest. Mom picked me up from school on the assigned day and drove toward the counselor's office. I had never been in the mood to entertain a woman grilling me with ridiculous questions, but this day I was in a particularly foul mood. My session began as usual with the sugary-sweet attitude and the repetitive questions. I erupted!

I brazenly told her she was an ugly woman, her mustache kept her from ever attracting a man, and she should consider purchasing some real clothes with the fee my parents were paying her. I mimicked her actions, expressions, and stupid questions to mock her sincerity. I informed her I wanted no more counseling from her or anyone else and the only reason I came at all was because I was forced against my will. I spewed how counseling was a colossal waste of my time.

My remarks were cruel and ugly, but to my frustration, she patiently sat and waited for me to finish. I had never been so disrespectful to an adult in my life and knew I was wrong.

Guilt crept into my throat as I awaited her response. Yet all she did was look at me, tapping her pen on her tablet of notes. I was emotionally exhausted, and surprisingly I told her with great anger about being molested by Shadow Man when I was little. And because I could tell no one, I felt incredibly hopeless and very alone. Immediately I refocused on her and finished with more unkind comments toward her. When I finished, I wished I could take back all I had just spoken. Before I could say a thing, the counselor said, "Okay, we will see you next week." She had a look of satisfaction, which started in her eyes and spread across her whole face. For the first time in all my appointments, I had spoken, and my unflattering rant was a breakthrough moment in her book. I got up and left her office feeling guilty, confused, drained, and alone.

My next appointment found the counselor informing me that she had talked with my mother about the accuracy of my being molested as a child. I could not believe what I was hearing. Betrayed, I attacked her with accusations of breaching counselor-patient confidentiality, to which she assured me discussing a minor's sessions with parents is legal and ethical. Cornered, I grudgingly listened as she explained that I had mentally entertained the act of being molested as a child so often I believed it to be true. She added that I had never actually experienced any molestation but possessed an overactive imagination. She reasoned I was suppressing an innate need for sexual activity, resulting in great frustration and depression. She advised immediate abandonment of my pretend past to focus on a promising future, further suggesting I accept invitations for dates and to "let go" sexually.

Fury caught in an undertow of helplessness. Trust again found no mooring. I refused to cooperate any longer in counseling sessions, forcing my parents to change counselors yet again. When was I going to learn? Who would ever believe a dirty-minded girl? Why should I care if no one believed me? Promising future? Not for me!

10

Amusement Park

The summer before my freshman year in high school, an older sister, who recently obtained her driver's license, offered to treat my younger brother and me to a trip to a nearby amusement park. What a blast! We rode all the rides and even selected the food we wanted for lunch. Choosing rides and food made us feel grown up, and we appreciated the special treat. Deciding to test our nerves in the fun house, our trio entered the mirrored maze. Black lights illuminated the hallways with a glowing aura. We laughed and teased, using hands to feel our way along the spooky path. Not keen of dark places, I comforted myself by the sight of my brother's bright-white shirt glowing ahead of me. The mirrors played tricks on my eyes, and before I knew it, my sister and brother were out of sight. Panicked, I found myself running into one mirror after another to join my siblings.

I heard someone approaching behind me, and I hoped to see my brother or sister. The clothes told me the man was neither. He trapped me against the mirrored wall and began touching my breasts. I struggled frantically to free myself, screaming against the loud music for help. He kept pushing and pulling, rubbing against and groping my body. The whole event was surreal because it was happening while I was awake during daylight hours, and molestation only happened at night after I had fallen asleep. It was happening in an amusement park, and unwanted sexual attention only occurred in my bedroom. And it was happening while I was standing up, and I usually played dead lying down. I screamed louder and flailed wildly until I was able to jerk away and make my escape!

Outdoors felt so freeing! I found my siblings laughing about the scary fun, but I immediately told my sister about the man in the fun house and how he had touched me in bad ways. She checked for signs of an attack on my clothes and skin but announced that I looked fine. The incident wasn't a big deal, and I should forget it ever happened. She warned against telling anyone, especially Mom and Dad, or we would never be allowed to venture out like this again. A wave of nausea hit me!

Head hanging over a toilet, I relived the attack. This wasn't just a bad dream but a terrible reality, and my emotions ran wildly crazy! I was frustrated at my failure to protect myself. I was angered by my inability to control my body's nauseous reaction. I was panicked at having to head out the bathroom door and function normally with my sister and brother. I was smothered by a filthy feeling. I couldn't separate and process all the screaming, conflicting emotions inside, which only added stress. I knew I couldn't cry because crying showed a lack of control in my mind.

My assailant had grabbed my breasts first, so I reasoned my breasts were the problem. And there, in the amusement-park restroom stall, I started clawing at my chest. I hated being female! I hated the man's uninvited touch! I hated male attention! I hated myself! Seeing marks on my breasts made me instantly realize the stupidity of my impulsive action. How could I have been so careless? My thoughtless marks could easily be seen by others when I wore a swimsuit, and I did wear my suit almost daily each summer! A pulsing, stinging sensation spread across my sensitive skin, oddly soothing my nerves, so I was able to take deep breaths to calm myself before pasting a smile on my face to join the others. I promised myself to avoid exposure until the scratches healed and determined to enjoy the rest of the day.

11

Childcare Class

As high school started and life moved forward, everything seemed under control from my point of view until freshman health class included a focus on childcare. The topic of child molestation was introduced in a movie, and every horrible memory that I thought was suppressed forever rose with fury to the surface. My disgusting ordeal was talked about openly by victims and authorities in the movie while I cowered and some classmates chuckled. Did my teacher understand they discussed me? Part of me wanted to hide, yet part of me felt like standing up on my desk and screaming, "I am that child!"

Shadow Man only recurred in dreams, so this topic triggered a new onslaught of fierce night terrors. Night after night, I would wake up startled, sweating, and physically nauseated. I suddenly faced the reality of wanting to know Shadow Man's true identity. I was hurting, and in turn, I hurt myself in order to soothe the pain. I needed help. I needed control. And I needed sleep.

Who better to approach than the one who showed the movie and unashamedly spotlighted my nightmare? I reasoned my health teacher would know what to do with my suffocating feelings but was ashamed to talk face-to-face. I wrote her a letter briefly explaining Shadow Man, the molestation, the stirring from the movie, and the difficulty in ridding myself of the past. I left my letter on her desk, hoping she could help me.

A week or two passed without response, and I started to wonder if she received my letter. Finally, one day as I was ready to leave the classroom, my teacher asked me to stay behind to chat. My heart instantly raced as thoughts whipped to a froth! Should I have written the letter and given it to my health teacher? Can I actually talk aloud about Shadow Man to a stranger? Why did I do something as stupid and embarrassing as desperately confiding in my teacher? Though I yearned for help, at that moment, I wanted to run out of the classroom and vomit!

In the empty room, my teacher explained she found and read my letter. I avoided any eye contact as she politely thanked me for writing the letter then instructed me to talk with my parents about the molestation. The conversation ended. Rejection and relief collided in a violent storm in my soul! How could I talk with my parents about the very thing I tried to tell my mother all those years ago? How could I explain to my father that I shunned his affection because some man repeatedly abused me under his roof?

I truly wanted to die! No one really cared about me, did they? My family would be better without me, wouldn't they? I severely fought depression because death promised a forever end to the pain, didn't it? A dance with death could be from God, couldn't it? Contemplating suicide triggered new waves of uncertainty and failure. Thinking and planning the details of ending my life drove me into depression.

12

Suicide

I don't know about you, but my resolutions to change are usually met with resistance somewhere along my path to improvement. For a kid like me, trying to figure how to handle life in the aftermath of abuse and grasping my new relationship with Jesus Christ, pain dogged my every step. My pain was more mental and emotional than physical, but still memories came back to haunt me at the most unsettling times. And little things, like smells or sounds or even the silence, triggered painful thoughts and emotions without warning. My mind insisted I was not normal like everyone else, though I tried to release everything to God. I admit I struggled with bouts of depression.

Mom and Dad sent me to a Christian weekend retreat shortly after my decision to believe in Jesus, and I must admit I liked the staff and those who attended. I'm not sure I can say why, but one evening, I fell into one of my deep dark pits of despair and chose to make a clean cut from this life—literally. My plan was to slice both wrists with a razor blade I brought from home, but I became too light-headed after the first cut and passed out on the bathroom floor. When I awoke lying on the floor in a puddle of my own blood, I was incredibly afraid of anyone finding out what I had done and even more afraid of myself for doing something so drastic, of losing self-control and going so far. No one ever discovered this first suicide attempt because I was able to doctor and hide my wound with superglue until it healed; plus, my fear drove me to clean the blood from the bathroom floor in spite of my wooziness.

In high school, I just tried to maintain my sanity and move forward in daily activities. Basically I needed to pretend. I wanted to pretend to be a good Christian, a good daughter, and a good girl until I could leave home for some place safe. Since dance was my love and New York City was as far away from my sleepless California nights as I could imagine, studying dance and landing a job as a dancer in New York was my goal. I basically wanted to run away from my problems because home just reminded me of them. If I could get to New York, I could forget my past and keep the old memories away.

I wish I had the perfect words to explain my thoughts, but one day I was in a really low, really depressed state of mind, tired of pretending. Sleep sounded so good. My relationship with God had truly changed me because I understood and believed God—the One who showed love to the woman at the well, the One who seemed to live in a pain-free, love-filled heaven—actually thought I was special. Even though I was soiled, hurting, and broken, my Bible and church sermons all gave me pretty good odds that He loved me. I wanted to be with Him. I wanted to go to heaven. I wanted to be in control, and that included when I should die.

I dodged high school sophomore classes and planned to break free of life using sleeping pills. With Dad at work, Mom busy at some sort of church event, and my siblings absent from home, my plan was simple: ask God to take me home, swallow all the pills, and fall into a fuzzy, sleep-filled eternity. My plan worked flawlessly until my mother returned home for something she'd forgotten. Realizing I was in bed on a school day, she tried rousing me. I groggily recall her asking questions over and over. Sleep claimed me again until I felt someone pulling me up, demanding I walk around the house. Mom splashed cold water on my face and told me how I had to keep moving to avoid going to the hospital. I recognized Mom's pastor as my walking partner, making me feel irritated and humiliated. Both explained a hospital visit spelled trouble, as in reported suicide attempt, psychiatric evaluation, and a stint in the psycho wing. *Eternity must wait,* I reasoned in the fog and willed myself to stay awake.

Dad had been at work through this drama, so the first time I saw him was when he came into my bedroom that evening. I thought for a moment he might pull me to his chest and hug me. I know I longed for his love and protection yet knew inside I couldn't handle that kind of affection from him at that moment. I needn't worry because instead of hugging away any hurt, he was furious. He demanded to know why I wanted to end my own life. He demanded to know who had hurt me so badly. He flatly informed me other people in the world lived under much worse conditions and wanted to survive. He demanded again to know why I wanted to end my own life, but I just couldn't answer any of his questions. He told me that what I did was the most selfish act possible. I was shocked. My father rarely raised his voice, so this was so unlike him. Inside I was screaming, *Because I am in pain!* but outwardly I said nothing. That's when I saw the look of hurt in Dad's eyes. He wanted an answer, and I gave him nothing. Thick silence hung in the room until, with a sigh of great frustration, he turned to leave. At the door, he looked back at me and said, "You better never do something as selfish as that ever again."

My parents sought the help of a psychiatrist. The cold woman voiced concern but did not hesitate to point out how my selfish action harmed my family. Icy questions, statements, and predictions pressed home one crystal-clear fact: if I attempted suicide again, admittance to a sanitarium was certain. Her threat rang true! A book also found its way into my hands, stating suicide grieved God so much He would not allow the person into heaven. Wanting neither the sanitarium nor to lose heaven, I resolved to do better. I fought miserable suicidal thoughts, worked grades higher, hid behind the joy of dance, and pretended to be the happiest girl in the world.

13

Dating

High school usually signals the beginning of dating and boy-girl parings. I turned down every date because I was too scared to be alone with a male and my parents encouraged double-dating and courting-type relationships. These two factors made me feel like a square peg in group setting. I overheard plenty of cafeteria chatter about dating "fun" and saw numerous girls "fried" by mistakes, rumors, and nasty assumptions. Time after time, I made excuses and declined. I made sure word got out that I would not date anyone at our school.

Believe it or not, when I was sixteen years old, I reluctantly agreed to a blind date with a girlfriend's stepbrother. My friend and I grew up across the street from each other, and she had confided her struggle at her mother remarrying. Out of love for my girlfriend and empathy for her plight, I consented to a group outing with my parents' approval.

Several teens converged in the neighborhood street in front of my house on the appointed day and settled to meet at a nearby restaurant. My date, fresh from military boot camp, opened his car door to escort me alone to the rendezvous site, but instead of heading toward the restaurant, he made a speedy detour into the local rural hills. I mildly pointed out his navigational error. He turned up the radio volume. I told him I wanted to go home. He ignored me.

Formulating a plan to jump from the car once it stopped, I stared straight ahead, willing my stomach to calm. Steering into a secluded area and killing the engine, my date moved toward me with lightning speed. He started passionately kissing me before I dared launch my escape plan. I pulled away, but he tightened his grip, assuring me it would not hurt that bad. All I had to do was relax. I pushed against his chest, and he released his seat back, pulling me with him into the backseat. His strong, fast hands were everywhere, and the next thing I knew, my shirt dropped to the floorboard. I needed a different plan and fast; however, running home shirtless sounded unappealing. Playing dead popped as an option, followed quickly by the memory from the amusement park. I refused being a victim again!

As he tried to unbutton my pants, I begged God for help. I then did something that went against every part of my being. I don't know where the idea came from; in fact, there was no prethought to it. I just grabbed my attacker's face tightly with both my hands and kissed him as intensely as he had been kissing me. Immediately he relaxed his grip. My behavior must have shocked him, and I know it did me! I then yelled loudly in his face, "If you touch me again, I will kill myself tonight!"

I got his full attention because he threw my shirt in my face, calling me derogatory names, climbed into the driver's seat, and angrily drove me home without another word. I left his car and did not look back.

I headed for the shower, attempting to wash away yet another painful memory. My stomach churned with the familiar feel of nausea while my mind replayed the episode and wondered how I had failed again. The warm water soothed my skin, but not my soul. Stepping from the shower, I noticed my reflection in the mirror, and my eyes immediately landed on my breasts. The guy had ripped off my shirt first. He wanted to touch my chest first. My breasts, in my thinking, were the part of me that attracted so much unwanted attention, so I insanely ripped the wire from my bra and frantically slashed my chest to cut them off. Only when sheer exhaustion stopped my shaking hands did I see the blood everywhere. I sat on the bathroom floor wanting to cry, but no tears would come. Hate came easily. Yes, I hated my friend's stepbrother, but I hated myself and my body even more!

My girlfriend asked about the date the next day, and I told her what a pig the boy was and how I would never date him again. Her stepbrother, in turn, had told her I was not his type, causing him to drive me home earlier than planned.

Neighborhood life was easier after that day because the young GI never took leave at home again. Sadly, my girlfriend moved to live with her grandmother within that same school year because her stepfather raped her in her bed one night, her mother asleep in the next bedroom. I cringed to hear how the stepfather had assured my neighbor-friend that it would not hurt, all she had to do was relax, just like what the son had said to me. My friend's mother refused to believe the accusation, but her grandmother did and offered her a safe place to live for the rest of the school year. I was disappointed and angered during our tearful farewell because I knew too well the pain of living a life where the ones closest to you refuse to believe the truth about your being sexually abused.

14

The Pastor

Summer before my senior year in high school found me soaring. While attending band camp and drill-team camp, I found hope and focus by being elected as cocaptain of the drill team, placing me in a key role to choreograph routines and dances for the upcoming year. This position gave purpose to my dance energy. To maintain positive momentum in my life, my parents arranged for me to have counseling sessions with our church's new pastor. The deal: I go, I come out of meeting ready for a new school year, happy with no signs of depression. My goal: get this done and over with and pretend I was happy. I had gone to enough counselors over the years, and the one thing I knew, pastors were pushovers. Show a little emotion or sorrow for your mistakes, and it goes a long way.

Though appointment day dawned hot and sunny, the air was chilly between Mom and me on the way to church.

The new pastor and my mother exchanged small talk, and he readily promised to drive me home to save our family the forty-five-minute trip. I casually examined his office while waiting. The shelves of books and cluttered desk spoke of hours of study. Extra chairs inferred regular meetings and counseling sessions. The carpet looked old and worn while the chairs were mismatched, and all the furniture looked too big for such a small office. I chose the softest-looking chair should the session grow unbearably dull or excruciatingly long.

After excusing his secretary for the day and locking his office door, the pastor assured me of privacy. Uncontrollable nausea formed in the pit of my stomach as he started our meeting with prayer. This man of God prayed sincerely while I battled old demons. He didn't say amen but rose to turn off the office lights. Natural light, he explained, aided his communication with the Almighty, but the next hours proved prayer was not on his mind. He tried to rape me!

The pastor stood before me, laid his hands on my head, and prayed earnestly, commanding demons to leave my body. *Okay*, I thought, *This is how it is going to be?* I preferred the pastors who liked to just talk endlessly and fill the forty-five minutes with the sound of their own voices. He then stopped praying and told me he believed my accusations of being molested as a child and asked for details. *What?* Immediately I felt betrayed. I never told this man anything about myself. My mother must have spoken to him about my accusations of someone molesting me as a child. This was embarrassing. The pastor then rested his hands on my shoulders briefly before pulling me from the chair to "hug away the pain." His prayers and commands grew in intensity as he pinned me to the floor, stripped off every piece of my clothing, and struggled to remove his own clothes. Every night of molestation, every fear of not pleasing my parents or God, every means of escape, every cry for help, and every barb of pain assaulted me on that floor!

I desperately fought to get out of that office! If the man touched me, I squirmed. If he tried to kiss me, I thrashed. If he forced intimacy, I bucked. Pain blew at hurricane strength, but my constant writhing and struggling twisted my assailant's exorcism into anger. Frantic clawing to reach the door meant being dragged naked across the carpet. Counseling turned into vulgar brutality. He constantly referred to me as a whore or a witch. His actions were completely confusing to me. One minute he was smothering me in his slobbery passion and the next treating me as though I was a demon-possessed piece of trash over which he had the right and power to rule. I begged God to take my life right then and there! He constantly tried to get my mouth to open, but I kept my mouth shut tightly and kept moving my head. In anger, he pinched my nipple fiercely, causing a cry of pain, and he immediately plunged his tongue deep into my mouth. I bit down hard, forcing him to recoil.

The pastor's frustration and anger only seemed to increase as time went by. I was drenched with sweat, sore from being dragged, pushed, and pulled about the room. I kept thinking he would give up, only to realize there was no end in sight. Young and never being with a man before, I could not understand his rage with me. Though I did not understand male anatomy at that time, I can see that his goal was to rape me, but for some reason, his body was not cooperating, and I believe this was what was fueling his temper.

I moved away, only to be violently grabbed and perpetually jerked from chair to floor and back. The pain inside and out was an incredible incentive to fight for my life. He whipped my body carelessly about until I finally blacked out. I am not sure if I hit my head on the leg of the desk, but I remember waking up with my head leaning up against the leg of the desk. Regaining consciousness, I found myself limp with exhaustion on the floor and my assailant less aggressively touching my body in very inappropriate ways. My mind scrambled for a plan to extract myself from the messy situation, my eyes searching for something heavy or sharp to launch. Freedom meant fleeing naked through an unfamiliar neighborhood, but remaining vulnerable led to an unknown, unwanted ending. I watched for the right moment and made my move toward the door.

I never reached my goal as he dragged me once more across the carpet and knelt recklessly atop my thighs. My muscles bore the full weight of the man while he chided my foolish behavior, knowing he was in full control and there was nothing I could do to stop him. He went back into his "casting out demons from me" plans. I begged again for God to take my life. Exhausted, and with my body screaming out in pain from his knees bearing his full weight on my thighs, I retreated to the only safe place I knew—I played dead. I figured I would let him do what he was going to do. Immediately playing dead made all my physical pain disappear. Somehow I detached from my body, yet there was a part of me that was at war with myself, knowing I had let another person take control over me. Though I felt I could go no lower, this only increased my desire to die. I had failed yet again.

By the fourth hour, he was done. Trying to dress a limp adolescent proved too frustrating for the pastor, because after managing undergarments and shirt, he gave up and left the room. I felt no pain now, no desire to flee, and no desire for anything. I just lay there on the floor numb, listening to my breathing. When I fully comprehended that he had left the room, fear returned, nudging me to find my clothes, dress, and push for the building exit. However, I only made it to an office chair because the pastor reentered the room and turned on the lights. *God, help me!* I breathed.

He immediately asked if I was ready to go home. He proceeded to tell me he had made arrangements with my mother to take me home after we were done. I was in a state of shock, and I could not answer him. I pushed my sweat-soaked, tangled hair out of my face. There was no part of me that wanted to go anywhere with this man, but I was desperate to be outside and have a chance to get away. I got up and went out the door, not knowing what to expect, for it was obvious the pastor was in a completely different state of mind. He spoke calmly and did not act at all like he was angry with me. This made things very confusing for me. Was all I just experienced a dream, my imagination?

We both made it outside, and I immediately started to walk away from him. He calmly directed me to his car, but I hesitated. His strong tone and firm grip on my wrist made me comply and confirmed the gut-wrenching truth of my "session." He maintained a jovial monologue during the drive to my house while I sat as close to the passenger door as possible. My plan: wait till we got on the freeway and let myself fall out of the car. There would be pain, but it would not last long. However, if I was to live, I knew the pain of what just happened in the pastor's office would last forever. The pastor must have realized my plan, for as we entered the freeway, he put on his automatic locks and pulled me close to him on the front seat. He said, "Come on now, we are having such a good time. Let's not ruin it." He then grabbed one of my wrists and did not let go till I arrived home.

It was a long drive home, in which he joked and laughed. He spoke of the joys of being a pastor and the great honor it was for him to be one. I struggled with my raging doubts and emotions. Did that really happen? Am I going crazy? How could a revered minister do such a thing and act like it never happened? I tried to focus on what might happen next because I had been called a liar for so many years, and I knew no one would believe this episode. I was not sure I believed it.

As soon as the car stopped in front of my house, I leaped to the curb and raced inside to my bedroom. I never saw my mother when I entered the house, but I could hear from my bedroom her speaking to the pastor at the front door. He was telling her I still had a lot of growing to do and many habits to break, but he assured my mother things would go better in the future for me. My mother thanked him for everything, and then I heard the front door shut. The sound of his car pulling away from our house was wonderful.

As I sat on my bed exhausted and terrorized, the brunt of trauma knocked me speechless. Mom stuck her head into the room to ask about the counseling session. I wanted scream, "Help me!" However, no words came from me. I could not even look at her. She walked away. Though fully clothed, I felt exposed. My long hair was a mess. I could smell the pastor's cologne on me, and my insides screamed for renewal. I needed a shower! Undressing, I found my undergarments askew and backward, confirming the attack. Steamy water and scrubbing failed to eliminate the flood of ugliness, but there in the shower, I decided to tell my mother of the ordeal and hopefully save others from the pastor's wiles. After I showered, I called Mom to my room then struggled to tell the truth.

"Pastor took my clothes off, Mom," was all I managed before she cut me off as she had when I was a child.

"That is enough, and don't say anything to your father," she scolded and walked away. I wanted to die.

I sat there feeling incredibly alone and lost. I then heard my mother's voice. She was calling someone. Hope leaped in my heart as I thought she was possibly calling my father and they would take care of things. I opened my door to listen closer and heard her asking for prayer from a friend. She told the person on the phone I was confused, and it seemed I had demons inside me that wanted to tear the church apart by telling horrible lies about the pastor. This was the worst day of my life.

I longed for understanding and feared pregnancy (I was young and naïve and did not understand intercourse was necessary for this to happen), humiliation or stigma, being shunned, or exposure. I stared into the mirror on my dresser while sitting on the edge of my bed. I wondered, Was I the whore the pastor referred to when he was assaulting me? I saw a girl who had failed and sinned so badly that she could never be forgiven. I thought of running but knew I couldn't run from the person I could not stand the most—myself. I did the unthinkable. I played dead, and I hated myself. I took a second shower, willing the water to hold me and love me for just a little longer.

I went back to my room and must have fallen asleep out of sheer exhaustion. When I awoke, I could hear my home full of family members moving about, but the thoughts of ever being part of their world seemed so far away. Again I looked into the mirror. I felt so hopeless. I breathed. *I need you, God, but don't touch me.* I knew I could not receive His love, for I knew I was beyond dirty, and I knew God was holy. Shame swallowed up the cool summer breeze that was flowing through my bedroom windows and left me with the putrid poisoning gas of guilt. You would have thought I had been sitting there cursing my attacker, but there I sat, fiercely hating myself and the hell I now found myself in. The last thing I remember doing before falling asleep that night in complete exhaustion was asking God if He believed me. I needed to know. All I got back was the silence of the night. I sighed the word *help* out loud but knew even God would not defend a filthy tramp like me.

The next morning, I awoke with great pain. Even the hardest dance workouts never left my muscles in this kind of torment. Thoughts of the day before engulfed my mind, and I sat there in my room, wondering again if I had lost my mind. I started to sweat and shake uncontrollably. I started to question myself over the facts of the past day's events. Maybe I made all this up. Maybe my mother was right.

I took a quick inventory of myself physically. My thighs had bruises from where the pastor had knelt on me to hold me down. These ugly bruises and other marks on my body where he hurt me were a sick yet incredibly comforting sight to know that I was not suffering from overimagination as I had been told many times as a child. Okay, so now the focus was to keep a tight grip on reality. My mother and the pastor could pretend it did not happen. However, I knew it did, and no one was going to convince me otherwise. It was obvious, since no one believed me about Shadow Man, that there was no way in the world they would believe my word over the pastor's. I had no choice. I was going to have to press on with life and play dead to my soul pain.

Recovering my heart and soul would be next to impossible! Little things would remind me of what happened in the pastor's office. Anger would rise within me as I remembered the feeling of the pastor's betrayal. I thought about how, after praying in his office right at the beginning, he played on my biggest hurt. He told me with great compassion that he had heard that I claimed I was molested as a child. I remember feeling my face flush, for I was incredibly embarrassed that someone had obviously told him. However, he caught me by complete surprise when he said, "I believe you." He was the first person in my life who ever said they believed the molestation ever happened. The hope that rushed forward inside me was inexpressible.

Yet, with his next sentence, as he moved toward me, he started to ask where I was touched and how. He first caressed my shoulder, arm, and then finally, pulled me into a big hug. He told me, as he hugged me way too long, that he wanted to hug all the pain away from my past. From that moment on, I felt betrayed as he stabbed me with words of love and kindness but was doing anything but that. When I cried out in pain from something he was doing, he would remind me of how much I was loved and created for this. How I was to enjoy this moment of freedom from my sins and enjoy the physical love I have always longed for but never received. A part of me died and fell to the filthy floor of the pastor's office that day.

Great confusion set in as the pain of betrayal from one of God's so-called workers, who was to be trusted, crushed into my world. How could this be? I wanted to run into God's healing arms, but Satan reminded me how I had caused the Shadow Man and my grandfather to fall into sin, and now the pastor. I truly must be evil.

I could not trust anyone at the church. Besides, if and when they found out, I would be painted as the wicked, demon-possessed liar. I had no proof, and though I had incredible friends in high school, there was no way I was going to tell them about the pastor incident. It was too humiliating, and the last thing I needed going around the school was a rumor about me and a pastor. I realized this was going to be one breath at a time, one minute of not vomiting, and then starting again the next day. My soul and physical body still hurt, and yet at the same time, I was numb. I took everything personally. I became more obsessed with dance, perfection at practices, and performances meant everything.

Not too many days later, I spotted something glittery while walking to school one morning, making me halt to admire the simple beauty against the dirty ground. Closer examination revealed a broken beer bottle and its glass littering the sidewalk. Instantly, without much thought, I took off my shoes and put small shards of glass inside them.

I saw no difference between the broken glass and my heart. Besides, I thought, the physical pain could possibly block my emotional pain, and it did.

It's funny to think one source of pain would rule another, but I took comfort in the fact that it worked. I realize now it was wrong, and it was the result of sick thinking. The injury from all the sexual abuse and the fact I was shoving it away and ignoring it was only causing great infection to my soul. My normally healthy thinking went out the door as I grabbed the quickest ways to kill my soul pain and move on with life.

Not long afterward, I injured a toenail and found the daily pain somewhat soothing. I mastered a routine of trimming toenails too much, providing a steady, subtle flow of physical pain. The flow offered a sense of control, normalcy, and wholeness, calming the turbulent internal storms. If memories threatened, pressing my foot downward or walking delivered a welcome diversion.

Hurting myself was only a coping mechanism, the same as those who turn to drugs, alcohol, gambling, etc. Like those addictive alternatives, they are only temporary pain relievers and are extremely poor responses to dulling one's inner pain. It was a poor choice. Another poor choice was to play dead to the reality of what happened to me. To me, to face it would just put me in another psychiatrist's office, and I was done with that. My goal: live out high school and then move away to New York to dance.

15

John

While attending band camp before my senior year, I met our school's new young drum-line instructor, John. He seemed nice enough when he asked me to dance with him one evening of camp week. However, the conversation during our dance told me John was definitely more than a Christian like me. He was a Jesus freak. Since there were plenty of dance partners among my peers, I made excuses so I wouldn't have to dance with him again. Next!

School was in session two weeks after the sexual torture in my pastor's office, and I happened to run into John on the very first day of classes. I simply gave him the cold shoulder, but John seemed to be in my path everywhere I turned. The more I ignored him, the more he insisted on saying hello to me. His peskiness got under my skin quickly, and I felt this always-happy, always-smiling, always-thinking-the-world-is-wonderful Jesus freak needed someone to slap reality into him. One morning, shortly after a two-hour first-period band practice, I got that chance.

John greeted me in the midst of all the band and drill team members, leaving the football field with his usual cheery Bible quote: "This is the day that the Lord has made! Let us rejoice and be glad in it."

I was not in the mood to talk to anyone, so I gave him a condescending look to let him know, in no uncertain terms, that I was uninterested in him or anything he wanted to say. Quietly I gathered my things as fast as I could. Inside, though, I could tangibly feel my anger at God mounting. The pesky presence of this cheery instructor was grating against my very raw nerves. Students hurried away to shower and prepare for second-period classes, but John stayed.

"Are you okay?" he asked. "You've changed since band camp."

My first thought centered on my duties as drill-team captain. I imagined someone complaining that I was too aloof or uncaring. Perhaps John, as an instructor, thought I was coming on too hard or slacking off during routines and practices. He insisted I had changed dramatically in a very short time. I had had enough of his joyful attitude, and when I turned to speak to him, all my bitterness, anger, and hurt lashed out at him.

"A pastor took off my clothes and touched me! Okay? No one believes me!" I screamed in his face. In the outdoor solitude, I finished by saying, "Life is not terrific, John! Life is not good!"

John just stood there stunned, trying frantically to respond to the obvious ache in my voice and eyes. Inside, the storm was unleashing, and I was seething with great rage. The fury that flowed through me now was uncontrollable. In an instant, the force of a hurricane-strength wind blew in my being, and everything inside me was being thrown against the walls of my heart:

The pastor was a person you were supposed to trust. *Slam!*

I knew my mother loved me and I her, but she did not believe me. Everything in me wanted to hate her, and yet I couldn't. *Slam!*

If God loved me, then why did He let this happen to me? *Slam!*

I thought I had been playing "dead" extremely well to my emotions during the past couple of weeks, but this moment proved an intensifying storm of seething rage was lying just below the surface. I couldn't stand there waiting in the agonizing silence any longer, so I started to walk away. Then John asked, "What has been done with the pastor?"

"Nothing!" I bitterly spat. "Absolutely nothing!"

I hated his question but hated my answer even more! I loathed the thought of this minister being free to hurt others in the same sick, perverse way. I hated myself much more for losing control and saying so much. John wouldn't let this issue rest and pushed me for an explanation to why nothing had been done with the pastor. *Is this guy stupid or what?* was all I could think at that moment. However, with sharp and angry words, I explained my mother didn't believe me and wanted to keep it private.

My mind reeled as I recalled the past two weeks attending church. The pastor, whom everyone loved, walked up and down the aisles among the congregation as he delivered his Sunday sermon. The man occasionally reached out to touch or pat his listeners as he passed. It seemed that he put his hand on my shoulder at least once during each service if possible. His touch forced me to relive that horrid day in his office only a few yards away, making me sweat profusely and causing me to want to vomit right there in the middle of church service. Surely that kind of physical response would arouse suspicion in the people filling the pews that I truly was possessed by a demon.

I looked at John and said, "I still attend that church with my family." I added, "I have to face him every Sunday." Suicidal thoughts again poked at my conscious mind.

I turned to go, but John called after me a second time, asking if he could speak to my mother about the situation. He added that perhaps, knowing all the facts, my parents would let me attend church with him Sunday morning. John then asked permission to call the accused pastor and confront him about his actions during my counseling session.

Oh my goodness! I could not believe my ears! Was this guy for real? Was he really a naive jerk? I confided details of my pastor attacking me, my mother not believing me, and my inner feelings about the whole thing, and John thought calmly talking to my mother and the pastor about what happened would fix everything! I had earnestly asked God for help, and He sent me a Jesus-freak-type guy who wanted to sit and have a cozy chat with my mother and the pastor. I knew what their answers would be and how everyone would paint me as a liar. I told John, with great disdain, that I did not care what he did. I imagined John making a complete fool of himself and his saintly Christianity. I walked away from that conversation, hoping John and I would never see each other again! I sure didn't want to talk about the subject ever again!

One thought struck me hard as I walked away from this happy Jesus freak: What if the pastor admitted the truth? Could God do that for me? Could He bring about a miracle in a hopeless situation? If God was really into truth, could He bring truth into the open even though it would make lots of people uncomfortable and make life truly ugly for me? At that moment, I opened the door of my heart just a crack to God. I hadn't prayed or spoken to God since I asked for help the night after the attack, but right there, walking briskly down the school hallway toward my next class, I asked for a miracle.

If the truth and love I read about in the Bible were real, I asked that the pastor would confess his crime and my mother would believe the report. As soon as I voiced my request, doubt flooded my mind. I doubted my pastor would ever admit to his actions against me, knowing his confession might result in his arrest, possible jail time, and the threat of ruining his marriage. I reasoned he was not going to give up his freedom, career, and family for me. I also doubted my parents could ever be convinced an abusive attack had ever taken place since my bruises were fading and the sole proof stood on my word.

To my utter surprise, John arrived at my house that afternoon and spoke privately to my mother. Good news came from their conversation because Mom told me I never had to go to our church again. She was willing to let me attend church somewhere else on one condition: I must change the way I spoke and acted around my family. She explained that my words and actions frustrated and worried both her and my father; plus, it made life difficult for my siblings. I agreed to her terms, and needless to say, I was elated! John then asked my mother for permission to use our house phone and requested the phone number of our church office. Mom gave John both permissions and the phone number, and the call was placed immediately.

I can't remember a time when I had so much hope resting on one phone call, but my heart beat rapidly as the desire for a real miracle grew inside me. John talked to the pastor from another room outside my hearing before returning to ask my mother to join the conversation on the telephone extension in a different room. The entire conversation couldn't have lasted more than five minutes, but all of a sudden, I heard Mom crying and hanging up the phone. She walked back into the room where I was sitting and reminded me not to tell Dad about the events in my pastor's office. She said she feared my father might retaliate and hurt our church's pastor. She also asked me never to speak about this chapter of my life to anyone again.

As Mom walked out of the room, John walked in. He sat on the other end of the couch from me and told me that the pastor admitted to what he had done. I could hardly believe it! The news was so incredible, so overwhelming, I asked John to repeat what he had just said. I felt that God, the awesome God of the universe, heard my simple plea, cared about me, and possibly, just possibly, still loved me.

We sat there in silence. I had so much to process mentally and spiritually besides the fact that I had to keep willing my body to calm down from the high stress of the moment. My stomach was killing me that whole time—cramps, nausea, and diarrhea. John was okay not talking. He allowed me some space and time to process the result of the phone conversation. Somehow I thought he knew I liked having him there, not needing to play host. Mom must have been processing this revelation alone in another part of the house because I never saw her for quite a while. The three of us, all approaching the pastor's admission from very different angles, must have communicated separately with God that afternoon.

On that late September afternoon, as the leaves were beginning to change into beautiful autumn colors, I walked John out to his truck. He asked how I was feeling and what I was thinking after such a breakthrough. I admitted I wasn't sure how to feel since so many emotions welled up inside. I told him that, more than anything, I finally felt God truly loved me. John stood and listened while I explained that, in some way, God recognized me today. John shook his head and smiled. He recalled my story from band camp when I accepted Jesus Christ as my personal Savior when I was twelve years old. He asked if I would be interested in what he called recommitting my life to Christ. At that moment, I was so flooded with love for God and Jesus I said yes. He gently took my hand, and we stood there on the grassy curb outside my house to pray together. My prayer was not fancy or profound. I simply said, "Let's do this, God, and thank you, God, for showing me you love me in a way I can see and remember forever. Amen."

My prayer was brief but heartfelt. I said good-bye to John and walked back into the house and dove into God's Word, something I had not done since being sexually assaulted by the pastor. There was a freedom in my heart from knowing God loved me. The truth released the invisible chains forged when family, friends, counselors, and teachers refused to believe my tales as a victim of sexual abuse. Now I no longer questioned my own sanity. Truth had truly set me free! Recommitting my life back to Christ was like getting a new start. Second Corinthians (NKJV), 5:17 says, "Therefore, if anyone is in Christ he is a new creation; old things have passed away; behold, all things have become new." There is nothing sweeter than a new start.

16

Deliverance

It was not too long afterward that I realized I could sleep at night, and within three or four months, I forgot all about the nauseous feelings in my stomach. Both of these items I had learned to live with over time, and my new freedom brought joy and hope to my world. I grew by leaps and bounds in my Christian faith. I was still wounded, but now I allowed God to pull the knife out and clean my wounds from the sexual abuse, which had become incredibly infected. Without my being fully aware, God was daily pouring His cleansing water and comfort over my raw emotional injuries. The more I got into reading the Bible and taking God at His Word, the more peace started to flood my soul. It was a slow and steady process, not something that happened overnight. God also brought me a great friend in John to walk the journey with, and he became a great prayer partner.

I started attending Sunday church services with John, but the rest of my family continued attending the church where I was attacked by the pastor. Of course, my family members knew nothing about the attack because of Mom's request for secrecy. However, when I heard my sister and her husband had scheduled a counseling session with the same minister, I knew I could no longer be quiet. There was no way I would allow others to experience the same abuse, so I warned them against counseling with the pastor. My brother-in-law, still considering me the same little liar, told John about my wild imagination and attempt to kill myself during my younger years. When John told him of his phone conversation and the pastor's admission, my brother-in-law was shocked.

Mom's team of prayer warriors thought I was spreading malicious rumors about our pastor because of an unforgiving heart. To be honest, I had not even considered forgiveness, and the concept was beyond anything I was prepared to do. No one ever asked me what really happened during my counseling session, so no one knew the pain and humiliation I experienced and carried with me daily. It was more than inappropriate touching in my mind, yet it seemed like everyone brushed off my report. I did not want to shame myself any more than I already felt, so I let people believe what they wanted.

Upon arriving home one day after school, I found my mother and two other couples sitting in our living room. I immediately sensed that this was not a normal, friendly visit among friends, especially when they asked me to have a seat on the chair at the center of the room, surrounded by all the others. I hate being the focus of attention except when performing, and what disturbed me even more was that I recognized one of the couples as having recently begun a "deliverance" ministry. This couple and some of their closest friends seemed to think anyone having life issues was suffering from some form of demon possession. The "deliverance" approach to handling troubles was all new to my parents and family. I saw them as nice people, but discomfort mounted as I complied.

I hesitantly sat on the chair placed in the middle of the room and listened as they began by asking about my day at school. I answered by asking what they really wanted with me. One of them said, "We heard what happened to you at the pastor's office. It was an unfortunate event, but we are really concerned for your spiritual health."

I looked at Mom with embarrassment because her friends could only have heard about this event from her lips. The thought of others knowing the pastor took off my clothes and touched me inappropriately created an overwhelming sense of shame, so I willed myself not to bolt from the room and silently stared at the carpet in front of me. Nausea began to build in my stomach.

One person in the group explained how God loves us unconditionally and how we are to love others like Him. He told me that when a person offends us, we are to forgive them immediately. Others read Bible verses about forgiveness. My ears heard their words of truth, but my mind screamed louder of the injustice of the pastor's actions. When someone asked if I understood all they were saying, I said I did then thanked them for sharing and started to get up off the chair. I needed to get out of that room! One offered for the group to pray with me before leaving, so I settled back on my seat. I figured praying was the proper way of ending any meeting, right?

During their prayers, they commanded me to forgive the pastor plus confess my own sins committed in his office. Again I looked at my mother sitting on the far couch. She never once looked up at me, so I knew I had failed and was still her dirty little girl. My shame gave way to anger and bitterness, a breath of fresh air to my soul that I thought I could control. None of these people truly knew what happened in that office, and I resented their insistence to forgive, so I told them no. I said maybe one day I would be able to forgive the pastor, but not right then. They informed me I was letting demons cloud my thinking about forgiving.

There was nothing more for me to say, so I stood, smoothed out my shorts, and started to walk away. Immediately the couples stood to their feet and laid their hands on my head and shoulders, praying up a storm while pushing me back into my seat. I was trapped, and the stress of being under someone's control caused me to start digging my fingernails into the skin on my thighs. I wanted so badly to just let them pray while I disappeared into one of my fantasy worlds, but they kept badgering me with questions about forgiving the pastor. I explained that I wasn't ready right now but might feel like forgiving the pastor sometime in the future. That wasn't good enough for the couples, and they urged me to make amends immediately.

They told me to say specific words of confession, like—"I forgive the pastor," "I forgive all those whom I have felt hurt from in the past," "I ask for forgiveness for myself and how I have caused others to stumble." I just shook my head and fought to get up. The harder I fought, the harder they pressed their hands on me. The more stubbornly I refused, the louder they screamed and shouted at me. I was panicked! I remembered all too well what the pastor did to me to try to rid me of demons, and I did not want to go through that again! The fact that I was being held down by four adults, two being men, and not sure what they might do was freaking me out.

That was when they started speaking to the demons they thought were inside me, whom they reasoned were blocking my free will to forgive or ask for forgiveness. I instantly remembered the abusive pastor saying he was "clearing me of demons" as he sexually tortured me over and over in his office. I could not believe I had allowed myself to be trapped and physically overpowered again! Feeling ambushed, I began sweating, and my mind scrambled for some way to escape. I again tried to interrupt their prayers and leave my seat, only to be ignored. The group made it plain that I was not leaving the room until I said I forgave the pastor. My fighting only fueled their fervor, so after almost two hours of this torment, I finally, mustering all my inner strength, stopped fighting and started agreeing with their requests.

I knew I was faking my confession and forgiveness, but I wanted to get away from these people as quickly as possible. When someone told me to ask for forgiveness for my sins, I did it. When someone told me to say, "I forgive the pastor," I said it. When someone said I had to cough to get rid of the demons inside me, I coughed. I lied to make them believe I was delivered completely! As soon as I complied, they finished praying and let me go. I was allowed to stand up, and everyone hugged me and praised me.

Inwardly I was angry and screaming at Mom's friends. I hated faking any confession to God and faking any forgiveness for the pastor who hurt me! I hated all this loving and hugging because it was all a farce to me. I beat myself inside with each hug for being such a wimp and a coward to give in to their demands. Needing to be free of all that just happened, I politely thanked them for their time and for praying for me, announced I was tired, and said good-bye to everyone. Mom, still not making eye contact with me and tears streaming down her face, rejoiced with her friends for the victory. However, I thought she was sucked into something wrong but knew I couldn't tell her.

17

The Proposal

In the few months following the incident in the pastor's office and the pastor's admission of guilt on the telephone, I experienced both good and trying days. My relationship with God continued to grow, which gave me real strength on days that I just wanted to quit.

John was becoming a regular friend of the family at my house by stopping by often. Since he attended high school with my older twin sisters, he found familiar faces among my siblings. His love for music matched that of my father's, so the two would jam for hours whenever possible. He quit his position as my high school's drum instructor shortly after the phone-call episode but continued working with a local engineering firm and attending college classes. He gave me and my youngest sister a ride to his church each week, and the three of us often grabbed a bite to eat on our way to or from services. John always encouraged my Bible reading and treated me with respect, and his genuine smile told me he cared a lot about me.

At first I was surprised he even pursued any kind of friendship with me since I had yelled at him after band practice and involved him in my messy past; however, nothing deterred his interest in me. I tried several times to explain how my school and activity schedule wouldn't allow much free time for him, but that did not stop him from trying. He invited me to a Christian concert on a day when I was in a rather sour mood, so I immediately came up with this grand plan to get him to back off his interest. I agreed to go to the concert if I could invite some girlfriends to go along; plus, he had to pay for a sit-down dinner and the concert—for all of us. His smile never wavered, and he said, "Great!" Then I dropped another bomb on John by telling him he had to call my father at work to get permission. John just said, "Give me the phone number."

I was literally going to make John pay financially for wanting to get close to me. My girlfriends were not believers in Jesus, and John knew it. I figured I had the situation under control by attaching so many conditions. Sure, I would be walking into unfamiliar turf by attending this concert, but I figured one date would be enough for John, and there wouldn't be a repeat performance.

On concert day, my doorbell rang right on time. Mom talked to John in the living room while I called my friends to find out why they were so late. The first girl said she was not feeling well, and as I hung up the phone, the second girl called to apologize for not being able to attend. Her parents changed their minds about her going. My plan was slowly falling apart, but I went to the living room to tell my mother and John the bad news and explained that the last girl usually showed up late for everything. It wasn't long before the third friend called to make her regrets.

I apologized to John for my friends. Mom shocked me by approving for me to continue going on the date with John. I was speechless because house rules only permitted double dating or group activities. Mom was breaking the rules to let me go with John alone! I made sure the look that passed between mother and daughter expressed my displeasure enough to be understood. She immediately replied, "John is a good young Christian man. You'll be fine." John completely missed the angry look I was shooting at my mother and excitedly said, "Let's go!" Angrily I left with John, who could not have been happier.

So much time was wasted awaiting my friends at my house that John suggested we opt for a drive-through meal in place of the planned restaurant meal. He told me during our drive that seating for the concert was on a first-come-first-served basis. I agreed to his suggestion, so burgers, fries, and drinks were eaten in John's pickup truck on the way to the concert. Eating kept talk to a minimum and allowed me time to formulate an escape plan should the "date" turn out badly. The arena parking lot was packed with vehicles and people waiting to get inside. Good seats meant finding the quickest, most direct route, and John must have seen a prime opportunity because he suddenly grabbed my hand, said, "Stay with me," and headed for a side door.

His touch immediately triggered emotional warnings to flee, but he successfully dragged me into the building, up some stairs, and into seats with a good view of the stage. John was so focused on keeping me close to him while searching for good seating that he never turned back to see I was unhappy to be clutching his hand. I was frustrated by the raw emotions stirred by his touch, he found the "perfect" place to sit. As John motioned for me to enter the seating row first, he finally released my hand. I thought I did a great job displaying my anger and displeasure, but he totally missed it. This guy was incredibly satisfied having me next to him and couldn't wait for the music to begin. The crowd was on its feet from the first chords and sang along with each worship song throughout the evening. John even bought an album following the concert so he could always remember it. I had a hard time admitting that I enjoyed the whole experience since I didn't want to be there in the first place.

I stayed close to the passenger-side door throughout the ride home that night, having learned from past experiences. John's passion for music kept him talking up a storm from the moment we left the stadium. I knew from band camp that he played several different instruments and was not surprised to learn he was part of a contemporary Christian band. I was totally surprised when John walked me from his truck toward my house, shook my hand, and wished me good-night at my front door. Later I found out my girlfriends all planned ahead of time to ditch me so I would end up going on the date with John alone. They liked John a lot and were tired of me not going out on dates.

John seemed to show up all the time after that first concert "date." Though he was a friend who had come to my rescue and consistently offered encouragement, I wanted nothing more from the relationship. He shared his love for music with Dad, and the two of them loved to play jam sessions for hours at my house. He had already won my mother's trust but proceeded to build good relationships with my brothers and sisters too. It was pretty common to see him seated among my family during meals.

After one particular dinner, John quietly asked me to walk with him to his truck. I agreed but noticed his mood was different from other evenings. He started talking about his future while I politely listened. His question, "So what do you think?" caught me without any idea of what had been said.

"Think about what?" I asked.

"What do you think about us getting married?" he replied.

Oh boy rang inside my head. Never in my wildest dreams could I think John might want to marry me! He continued by telling me how much he had grown to love me and now wanted to spend the rest of his life together with me. He told me he had been praying about this choice for a long time and finally felt God was saying I was the one for him. My mind raced wildly as he declared his affection and intention! I felt horribly bad because God was confirming something to him that I really felt was all wrong for me. I did not want to hurt him and just stood there staring into his longing eyes that waited for an answer. I needed to buy some time, so I told him he would have to ask my father. His strange expression said he was trying to figure out if I was saying yes or no, but I went on to explain a family tradition. John listened intently as I explained how any young man interested in courting one of the daughters in my family were required to treat my parents and the daughter to a nice meal at a nice restaurant, and then, during the course of the meal, ask for the daughter's hand in marriage.

I wasn't at all surprised to hear John say that he would call my father to arrange the dinner. He asked with pleading, longing eyes if he were wasting his time and wanted to know if I would at least give him a hint of my answer. I told him I was not allowed to answer him until he asked my father. With that, I said good-night and went inside. I felt horribly bad because marriage hadn't figured into my plan of graduating and beginning a career as a dancer.

I could not believe the mess I'd gotten myself into. I thought of John as just a really good friend, yet somehow along the way, he fell in love. I certainly didn't feel the same way about him, which made me feel terrible. I went to bed that night thanking God for the friendship I found with John but asking what I should do next. It was then that an idea formed in my mind, and the more I thought about it, the better it seemed.

I promised God right then and there that if my father agreed to the marriage at this special dinner, I would go ahead and marry John. I was certain I knew how it would turn out because I had just turned seventeen, and all my siblings did not marry till they reached their twenties. I felt safe knowing there was no way my father would say yes to John's proposal. Besides, I still had an unmarried older sister, so how in the world would Dad approve my marriage ahead of her? It was so easy to make such a promise to God, for I already reasoned how guaranteed success would turn out in my favor.

When the night of the dinner finally arrived, John was a nervous wreck. He normally brought calm to a room, situation, or conversation, but his steady assurance and even temperament were gone. Everyone seemed to be enjoying the meal and table discussion, though the dinner seemed endless because John was stalling to ask for my hand in marriage. I think Mom had figured out what was going on since her face shone with extreme happiness. Whether Dad was suspicious or not about John's intention, I couldn't tell, but I knew I could count on him to shoot down any idea of marriage for his seventeen-year-old daughter. The restaurant staff was beginning closing preparations when John finally worked up the nerve to pop the question.

Dad just sat back and laughed. "You surprised me," he said. "I thought you were just going to ask if you could take her out again!" He then started telling stories of how my sisters' husbands had asked for permission to marry. I had heard all these tales before, so I was getting antsy for my father to tell John the bad news. When Dad informed John that I still had an older sister who was not married, I knew the he was about to tell John to wait, but John said he was well aware of the fact. I think I must have been holding my breath because when Dad tilted his head and looked across the table at me, asking if I was only seventeen years old, I had to force myself to take a breath before answering.

For the first time in my teenage life, I wanted to look younger than I was. I confirmed my age with a timid whisper then made sure to point out the six-year age difference between me and John. My father sat silently for a brief time, and it was my turn to be a nervous wreck. In my mind, there was nothing to consider. I was willing Dad to just say no. After eyeing me and John some more, he tilted his head again, looked directly at John, and said, "Yes, you can marry her. Meet me tomorrow after work at my house. Bring your tax returns, check stubs, and financial statements."

I couldn't believe what Dad just said! He was supposed to say no! My dinner companions celebrated while I sat there, growing more upset by the minute from the craziness and disappointment mounting inside.

The drive home was absolutely miserable since John beamed as he chatted happily with my parents. My mind was racing to find a way out of the promise I made God. When we got to my house, Mom urged me to walk John out to his truck, mentioning that we were now engaged. Oh, the word *engaged* sounded horrible in my ears and so permanent or binding. What was I going to do? John's feet probably never touched the ground since leaving the table at the restaurant, and his nonstop monologue centered on our future and how happy we would be together. It wasn't until we reached his truck did he realize I was not as giddy with joy as he was. I was ready to explode with anger, wanting out of this mess. My tone was ugly when I looked at him and asked why he was so happy. He gave me a strange look but calmly reminded me that he had just received permission to marry me. I curtly informed him that Dad might have agreed to the marriage, but I had still not given my answer. The surprise on John's face couldn't have been more real had I slapped him soundly, but slowly he asked the question, "So will you marry me?"

John had no idea of the struggle I was waging inside. I made a promise to God. God, the One who had been comforting me after so much hurt had come into my world. God, who gave me a hope and future. Was John supposed to be part of that future? I really only wanted to be friends with John. Emotions collided with facts, and I wasn't absolutely sure what to say or do. Though it was my time to apologize and turn him down, I quieted my internal battle as I exhaled slowly and lifted my gaze to meet John's eyes. Softly I said, "Yes." He must have wakened more than a few neighbors as he whooped excitedly, leaned in to kiss me, and started jumping around. He told me he couldn't wait to get home to tell his parents the good news.

I felt horrible as I crawled into bed that night. John was obviously in love with me, but I still felt only a good friendship toward him. I went back to God lying there under the covers and asked why He let my dad agree. I went down a long list of reasons why marriage was such a horrible idea and cited several rational arguments of the unfairness to John. After exhausting all my logic and emotions, I finished by asking God to help me fall in love with John.

18

The Engagement

Sure enough, the following evening, John showed up at the door wearing a shirt and tie, holding his briefcase. The family ate dinner together, and then Dad and John closed themselves in the living room. When I questioned Mom, she told me not to worry about a thing, assuring me that John was a good man. I did worry though and did what I hadn't done in years: stand next to the heating vent in the hallway outside the living room, straining to hear the discussion inside.

The two men were going over John's financial situation. It was when my father mentioned how expensive it would be to keep me clothed, sheltered, fed, and happy that I wished I had not snooped at all. How incredibly embarrassing to have Dad talk so bluntly about me and my needs! I could not wait for this whole thing to be over, but it only got worse.

Dad and John left the living room and walked toward my bedroom. I quickly ran to another vent to hear my father open the closet and point out all the shoes and clothes I owned. He asked John if he was prepared to support me in like manner. My heart sank because I feared my father was just getting warmed up. Leaving my bedroom, the pair returned to the living room where Dad showed John the medical and dental costs of having a wife and starting a family. I was amazed at how John kept up with my father, listening and respecting all he had to say. Their meeting concluded after John showed my father the budget he had worked out based on his income.

Mom and I were called in. I entered the room with incredible anger toward my father and mother. My mother went to sit next to Dad, and I was instructed to sit near John. My father smiled widely as he gave his final permission for us to be married. John's excitement fizzled when my father asked, "Now, what year would you like to do this?"

John looked first at me and then back at my dad. His face was puzzled, and his voice was tentative, but he replied, "Six months from now, after your daughter turns eighteen and has graduated from high school."

Dad acted like he didn't hear John, but it was obvious to me that he did. Dad laughed lightly as he suggested waiting a few years, but John quickly restated his intention to marry me in six months. I cringed inside, watching the two stare at each other, and though I was sure my father would ask John to leave, he just sat quietly. I sure wasn't going to say anything after overhearing the whole conversation through the air vent and feeling embarrassed to be the focus of so much attention. My father came back with another time frame and then another, but John stuck with the same answer each time, six months from now. Then there was silence. Finally, after waiting forever, Dad agreed to a wedding in six months on one condition: John would have to get our family home whipped into complete readiness before the wedding day. Dad went on to explain the entire house had to be painted, the patio covering had to be rebuilt, some household plumbing was in need of repair, all the trees and shrubs required trimming, new flower beds needed to be planted, and bases for music speakers had to be built in many of the trees to provide music during the reception. Dad agreed to pay for all supplies while John would be supplying all the labor. John happily consented, and the deal was done.

As John and I walked to his truck after the meeting, he laughed and said he felt like he was bartering for a horse from the way my father had treated him. John's only concern at the moment was that my father would trick him on the wedding night the way Jacob's father-in-law, Laban, had tricked Jacob by substituting the older sister for the actual bride (see Genesis 29). I assured my fiancé that would never happen, even though I felt extremely irritated at the moment.

I was angry with my mother for not warning me ahead of time about what to expect at this meeting between Dad and John, but I was even angrier at my father for embarrassing me by taking John into my room, opening drawers and closets, without notice. I felt as if my space was been invaded. Then he revealed my dental records and all the expensive work that may one day become necessary. Boy, all this hit my pride in a very big way!

For the next six months, after he got off his engineering job, John came over to my house every day and worked on the tasks my father assigned. At dinnertime, he joined my family for our meal and often nodded his head sleepily at the table from sheer exhaustion. I imagined that John might eventually refuse to work for free, but he didn't. He was never bitter as he tackled each job with determination. He was happy to have the chance to get acquainted with everyone in my family, plus being with me each evening. Though John was exhausted, he tells me today that my father knew exactly what he was doing.

One day, during the months leading up to the wedding, John volunteered to take my younger sister and me to the local market for some groceries. As we parked in the grocery-store lot, a man dressed in filthy clothes walked up to the driver-side window and knocked, asking John for money to buy food. John gave us the truck keys and asked us to go ahead with our shopping. I found the whole ordeal rather odd and was extremely curious how John was going to respond to the beggar, but he assured us that he wouldn't be too long.

My sister and I watched as my fiancé walked the shabbily dressed man toward a nearby McDonald's. Returning to the truck loaded with the necessary groceries, I could see John and the man in the distance sitting on a curb in the parking lot. The beggar was eating and talking with John. I had never in my life witnessed anyone reach out to a stranger in such a personal way, and at that very moment, something incredible happened in my heart. I saw John with new eyes. Here before me was a handsome man with a huge, truly loving, truly giving heart. I watched John say good-bye to the street-man and walked across the parking lot to rejoin us. I asked him what had just happened, but he just brushed it off and said, "Oh, everything is good. Let's go."

From that moment, I knew I could love this man. Coming from a person who was determined to walk life alone, this was more than just a major decision. This was God doing a supernatural makeover in my heart! My love for John grew daily as I recognized his God-given character, his heart for the Lord, and the true blessing he was in my life. My desperate prayer prayed months earlier came back to mind a few days before the actual wedding day. I then took time to thank God for providing more than just a good friend; John was to be my lifelong partner.

I reasoned marriage to be a very good thing from most of my observations growing up but was naïve about the intimacy factor in being married. Mom never discussed the birds and the bees with me, but I knew after the wedding a woman would get pregnant. During a premarital counseling session, the topic of sex surfaced, but I chose not to dwell on the thought much beyond that meeting. It was a big step for me to hold hands and kiss! In my best imaginings, married lovemaking was little more than the couple lying together naked and enjoying the soft skin and gentle caresses of the other. John and I happily enjoyed each other's companionship, and any additional sexual contact, in my mind, would only wreck or complicate everything.

Unfortunately, continually stopping my feelings midflow was like cutting me off at the knees, which had crippling effects. There was a realization that when John and I married, we would be intimate, but I shoved those thoughts as far out of my mind as possible. I truly battled how I could love John and have a physical relationship with him in many of the ways I associated with bad-girl thoughts. Somehow I was hoping all guilt and thoughts of contempt would magically disappear once we were married, but I was wrong.

19

The Wedding

On July 12, I walked the aisle of our flower-filled outdoor wedding with both my parents by my side. I felt beautiful in my wedding gown, something I had not felt in a very long time. Incredible joy filled my heart as I anticipated the life John and I would begin that day. John beamed at me from his position while family and friends smiled from both sides of the aisle. My folks and I were about halfway down the aisle when I saw standing, smiling, off to my right—the pastor who attacked me in his office. How I longed to be completely rid and healed of the man, the memories, and the pain of that day!

I hadn't seen the pastor during the ten months since I stopped attending his church. I was totally unprepared for this moment, seeing him among the well-wishers in my marriage ceremony, knowing some present knew about the sexual attack. I was instantly flooded with shame. I needed to vomit. I'm not sure how he was invited. I thought it very unkind and thoughtless to include him on the guest list. Though I continued to walk forward, picture-perfect in my wedding gown, dark thoughts aimed at myself—*Who was I to be married to this incredible man?* and *What right do I have to be wearing a white dress?*—ripped my soul. My eyes were already filling with tears when I found myself facing John. I felt it was time to walk away, but before doing something drastic that would embarrass everyone, I looked down and whispered the word *God*.

Though it was only a one-word prayer, it held all my hurt and hope. It was my cry for help. In an instant, everyone else disappeared from view, leaving only John, the pastor marrying us, and me standing before God Almighty. I felt God's smile of love covering me and His eternal plan unfolding before my very eyes. I got a glimpse of God's perspective of me: not filthy, damaged goods but a radiant, beautiful bride. I focused on the covenant vows exchanged in that holy moment, and I took that as a gift from God alone. Once the wedding ceremony was finished, the thought of possibly running into the pastor at all really concerned me, but thankfully, John never left my side.

20

Marriage

To say my marriage started out "rough" would be an understatement. I carried so much emotional and psychological baggage into my new life it wasn't even funny. Just the time when I should be celebrating freedom and joy and love, I was continuing the battle I had hoped would magically disappear.

John and I met with a Christian counselor during our first year together and saw a good amount of growth. However, once I became pregnant with our first child, my raging hormones, coupled with unresolved emotions, made life totally miserable. The counselor felt it was vital to discuss the details of what happened in the pastor's office.

Two thoughts started to consume me. First, John and I truly loved each other, and our love had created a baby through the beautiful intimacy of the marriage bed. I knew this fact was good in God's eyes and our own eyes. Second, our child was conceived using the same sexual contact as the abuse and torture I had experienced most of my life. I was really confused and upset. There was no question I wanted this baby growing inside me, but somehow I didn't want new life to happen through the act of "making love." Two worlds were colliding inside my brain, and at times, intimate moments crossed over a mental line into fear, especially if my memory flashed scenes from the pastor's office. I always felt loved in John's arms but felt nothing except pure terror and fear at the thought of abusive acts done to me. Regardless, this conflict became too much for me, and I totally shut down.

I have very little memory of those days, but I was told I got out of bed each morning, dressed myself, and ate enough to keep my baby healthy. John tells me how I just sat all day without focusing on anything or anyone and not saying or doing anything. He was so concerned for both me and our baby that he stayed home from work for almost a week just to be with me. He made sure I kept appointments with the counselor and the doctor so they could monitor my well-being.

A few visitors came to sit with me, giving John a much-needed break. Many talked to me, and I heard their voices but could not comprehend enough to really understand what they said. Their soft tones conveyed love, but I was in another place devoid of thoughts and emotions. I was numb to everything, including hunger and sleep. Others prepared food, but I would eat very little. When directed to bed to sleep, I obeyed but often lie there staring off into the distance until sleep eventually came. Nothing bothered me, and nothing mattered. All my emotions were gone.

John had the love and support of both our families, plus everyone we knew were praying for us both. He really leaned on God like never before since he wasn't sure if I would ever snap out of this shutdown state. He actually wondered if he was going to have to raise our child alone. His faith was stretched, but he remained faithful.

One day, without notice, I started to respond to little things. I began to look in John's direction if he spoke. I heard and acknowledged a knock on the door. This small improvement gave John hope that I might be coming out of my emotional shell. Finally John entered the kitchen to find me standing near the cabinet on one side of the room, throwing drinking glasses against the cabinets on the other side of the room. I was extremely angry. As one glass after another shot across the kitchen, breaking into tiny pieces and falling to the floor, I vented all the frustration and anger that had been shoved down deep inside, which I didn't know how to deal with. I hated the ugliness of the world and all that had happened to me as a child right through the events inside the pastor's office. For the first time in a long time, I expressed the fullness of the hurt harbored in my soul.

I don't know how long John had been standing by my side while I was lost in my silent anger, but I soon sensed his presence and, not knowing what else to do, turned my tear-soaked face to him. He grabbed my hand, placed another drinking glass in it, and said, "It's okay." I angrily clutched the glass he offered, but before I could launch it against the opposite cabinets, I put it down on the counter beside me. John held me as I slumped to the kitchen floor and started to cry. John was just so thrilled to see a display of emotion, even if it was anger one moment and tears the next, as opposed to the total shutdown he had lived through the previous week. Those tears released years of sorrow and frustration and began the process of great healing inside my soul.

John made the conscious decision at this particular moment in our married life to surrender his needs to the Lord, embrace the ravaged heart of his beloved, and move forward with the healing God gave us. To be honest, I shed more than merely tears that day. I was conquering all the ugly beasts attached by my abuse-riddled past. I felt then that I was done fighting with my painful monsters forever!

21

Reporting the Abuse

It was not long before I realized I needed to go to the denominational office that was in charge of the pastor who sexually abused me in his office. I feared that he would hurt others, and he needed to be stopped, as well as receive help himself. John went with me to the denomination's main offices in Los Angeles.

The supervisor John and I met, whom I was going to make the report with, had a kind face. He seemed genuinely concerned with the knowledge I had some sort of issue with a pastor in his district. When I made the appointment, I let the secretary know we wanted to meet with him due to inappropriate things that happened during a counseling session with the pastor. The supervisor made it clear he was glad we came to him with this matter.

John was great. He was able to the start the conversation. I was so nervous I could hardly stand the thought of revealing what we had to share with this man. John stated that the pastor had taken my clothes off and inappropriately touched me. It was now time for me to say something, and I struggled. No words would come. I sat there getting sicker by the moment.

In the silence, which was probably less than thirty seconds, I beat myself up for coming here and embarrassing myself in such a way. The supervisor started to ask me a few questions, and though I knew the answers, none would come. Inside, I asked God for help. It was then I realized I was not comfortable answering the questions with John next to me. We had not been married more than a few months, and I had never told him any details of what happened in the pastor's office. As I tried to figure out what to do, all of a sudden, John looked at me and suggested that I might feel more comfortable if he waited right outside the door. Oh, what a relief to my heart! Though I did not want to hurt John, I said, "Yes, please." John got up, kissed me on the cheek, and left the room to sit right outside the door.

The supervisor continued with his questions, but his tone changed, and it seemed like he thought I had some sort of vendetta against the pastor. I told him I was concerned for others, and I did not want the same thing to happen to them. He then folded his hands upon his desk and then said I would have to explain in detail the events that happened in the pastor's office in order for him to make a report. It was incredibly humiliating to tell about the pastor taking my clothes off and how he was incredibly angry with me.

He asked if I had gone to the police. I told him no. He then asked why I did not go. I had no good reason except that I figured no one would believe me over the pastor's word. Besides, I was ashamed and incredibly embarrassed. He then asked why he should believe me, for this allegation I was bringing forward was serious. I sat there thinking that I had no proof. Then it came to me. I told him that the pastor did admit to doing it to John and my mother. He then thanked me for coming in and that he and his associates would look into this matter.

A month went by, and nothing seemed to change at the church, except that I heard of another family member going in for some marriage counseling. It was then John and I made an appointment and went to the police station. I met alone with a nice woman officer who was going to take my statement. She was kind and patient, but she wanted everything from the moment I walked into the church to when the pastor delivered me back home to my mother. I had not told anyone in detail what happened in the pastor's office. She explained she needed it for the report.

I sat there ill to my stomach and with great need to vomit. It was there in that moment I realized if I could separate myself from the pain of the abuse and to do it with the pain of remembering what happened in the pastor's office. There I sat, starting from the beginning, giving facts with no emotions. It was like playing dead, but it made it possible for me to survive the ordeal of communicating to her the hell

I went through that afternoon in the pastor's office. When I finished, keeping my emotions separated was not possible any longer. Shame gripped me tightly, though I knew I had finally done the right thing. I went directly into the restroom and vomited.

22

Placing the Blame

It had been at least a year since the attack in the pastor's office when it seemed many of those who attended his church, including his wife, found out something happened sexually between him and myself. I was blamed for trying to seduce the pastor. Though it was not true, I was incredibly embarrassed and felt great shame over the whole incident, so I said nothing. Not long afterward, I was blamed for the death of the pastor's child. Cruelly some said it was because the pastor fell into sin and this was his punishment. Of course, he would not have fallen into sin if I had not led him there in the first place. His wife left him. The church was falling apart, and because of the continual horrible looks I got from others, horrible guilt festered inside my wounded heart. The people at the church were hurting, and in their hurt, they lashed out, saying some pretty ugly things to me. I had no words to reply.

The stress at times was more than I could bear, and I would go off into one of my fantasy worlds of beaches and sheets, which had become commonplace. John would catch me at times just staring off into space and ask if I was okay. I would respond with *of course* and refocus on whatever we were doing at the time.

23

Forgiveness

I thank God for bringing John into my life. He never focused on my forgiving the pastor. He figured—as I grew in relationship with God, and He kept healing my soul—I would walk the journey of forgiveness in due time. Meanwhile, John encouraged me as he showed me truth in the Bible, how I needed to live by the Word of God and not by the lies of people who were being deceived by the enemy. His unconditional love toward me, even when he knew I was wrong for holding hate toward these men in my life who had abused me, actually made a way for God to enter into my hating heart. This was not something John could see happening. It was one of pure faith in God, trusting in Him to work in me, not John's trying to force a change in me. This was huge.

One day, while reading my Bible, I came upon a scripture I felt was staring me straight in the face and was requiring a response. Though I had read it and heard in many messages, today it seemed I heard it differently.

> For if you forgive men their trespasses, your heavenly Father will also forgive you. But if you do not forgive men their trespasses, neither will your Father forgive your trespasses. (Matthew 6:14–15, NKJV)

I did not need anyone to explain this scripture; this one was obvious. I knew I had hard feelings toward the pastor. I also knew I had no forgiveness for the Shadow Man or my grandfather. They hurt me. It seemed to me that if I was to forgive them, I would be letting them off the hook from taking responsibility of what they did to me. These men were guilty, and I was not going to let them go free in my heart, mind, or the jail cell of my soul, to which I held the only key. To hold them tightly in my anger, bitterness, and resentment meant I controlled them. Nowhere in the verse did it ask if I understood the command to forgive. It just asked me to do it! I was not sure God had the big picture.

It took several days of studying the Word and what it had to say about forgiveness. The more I read, the more convicted I became. I desired to do the right thing. I wanted to be more like Christ. I came across Romans (NKJV), 5:8: "But God demonstrates his own love toward us, in that while we were still sinners, Christ died for us." I knew the story of Jesus going to the cross and dying for my sins. However, it was as if the verse spoke to me in a whole new way. I realized for the first time that Christ died for me knowing all the sins I would commit, and still He died for me. I can't imagine the pain and sorrow my sin had brought my Savior. He not only took on my sin but that of the whole world. Was God asking too much of me?

The next day, I came upon Matthew (nkjv), 18:21–22. It tells of Peter's coming to Jesus and asking, "Lord, how often shall my brother sin against me, and I forgive him?" Wow, now that was a great question. Then Jesus answered Peter, "I do not say to you, up to seven times, but up to seventy times seven." I did not like Jesus' answer.

Jesus immediately told the parable of the servants and the talents, Matthew 18:25: Here was a story of a servant who owed so much money there was absolutely no way he could ever pay the debt. He was now going to be sold, along with his whole family, and this was his plot in life because he could not pay his debt. Immediately I saw myself and knew my sin was too great. It was a debt I was never going to be able to pay. I needed Jesus to pay for my sin, and that is why I accepted Him as my Savior. He saved me from going to hell. I sat there after reading this story, thanking God for the salvation He gave me, for freeing me of the debt I owed. As I did this, something happened to my heart, mind, and soul.

I knew my grandfather, the Shadow Man, and the pastor were never going to be able to pay the debt they owed me, an emotional one, so severe it was never going to be paid in this lifetime. Their debt was unpayable like my sins. Jesus freely forgave me, and now I knew I needed to trust God in His directions and forgive them. Not just a little bit but completely, just like He did for me.

In reality, these men had no idea what I had gone through. My, holding back the keys of forgiveness for them had actually held me in the bondage of hate and kept me chained to my past. As I thought about what they had done, my anger grew from within. Immediately hate filled my heart, and I was reminded of how these men deserved absolutely nothing from me. Was God expecting way too much? Experiencing and living through these wounds and just freely forgiving, without their paying anything, just seemed so unfair.

The next day, my anger had subsided some. As I got into the Word, I asked God to please make things clear for me, to help me understand what I thought I must be missing. I read John (NKJV), 20:23: "If you forgive the sins of any, they are forgiven them; if you retain the sins of any, they are retained." Holding on to the unforgiveness was torturing me, and somehow, in the beginning, I thought holding on to it was my way of getting back at them.

My anger still burned within me. I knew I needed a change in my heart but was just not ready to let go. As I studied more, I saw that God wanted me not just to forgive the men who abused me but to make forgiveness a normal part of my everyday life, from the big things to the littlest offenses that came my way during the day. I'll be the first to admit the forgiveness came slow. It was giving up my will daily and desiring God's. Had I forgiven those who abused me? No, I started and was making it a habit of letting God have one situation after another.

Just walking those baby steps of learning about forgiveness and implementing them in my daily life helped me understand the principles God was trying to show me. For as I read God's Word, I could see that when He forgives, He wipes the slate clean. He does not go back and rehash for the zillionth time how that person keeps doing wrong. In 1 Corinthians 13, it states that love takes no account of evil done. *Love*, that pretty much sums up God. Every time I fall short and sin, God never shoves those wrongs in my face. I am sure I have disappointed Him, but each time, He has patiently waited for me to come back to Him and repent and seek forgiveness, which He always hands out freely.

One day, after some time, I came across the scripture that mentions we are to pray for our enemies (Matthew 5:44), and not only pray for them but also bless them. I really felt this was truly pushing the love thing to the edge. Pray for them? When I really thought about it, I realized I had only been thinking badly of these three men who had abused me. I never, for one moment, wanted good for them. Bless them? Oh no. How could I? Instantly I wanted to go and find the pastor, kick and punch him till he begged for mercy, and then absolutely give him none. I wanted him to hurt like I did. I wanted him to suffer, walk around sore for weeks, and cringe wondering if there was another attack just waiting for him around the corner. My thoughts were ugly and horribly hateful. It shocked me how my thinking could change so quickly.

I sat there and breathed the words, "Oh, God." It was in that moment I realized God was not with me. Though He is always present, He was not with me as I had those awful thoughts about the pastor. It left me with a longing to have God join me in my thinking, but I knew I was wrong. In the silence between God and myself, I heard Him speak to my spirit, "Pray for them." For me to pray for them just seemed useless. I did not love these men the way God did. Even thinking of having any love toward the pastor at that moment seemed impossible. The more I thought about it, the more frustrated I became. "Help, God," was all I could say.

It was then a question formed in my mind. Does God love the pastor, the Shadow Man, and my grandfather like He loves me? Instantly I knew the answer to that question, for the Bible says that God loves us all. It was then in that moment that I was able to see for the first time that what I hated was the wrong these men did to me, but not them. Just for an instant, I was able to separate the men from their sin. These men gave into the temptation of perverse thinking and used another human being to fulfill their lustful desires.

My desire to obey God because of how He loves me moved me forward. I admit my prayer was plain cold words, not anything of compassion from my heart. "God, I forgive them, and I ask that you bless them." That was one of the hardest prayers that ever left my lips. Ninety-nine percent of me did not desire the words that came from me, but at least there was 1 percent that did, the 1 percent that was willing to take God on in faith that this was what He desired for me to do.

Week after week, month after month, whenever any of these men came to mind, I would stop and pray for them. I was not happy to do it, but I did it. I figured if God knew everything, then He knew I was only doing it because He asked me to.

After some time, probably about six months into praying for these men, I started to actually begin to hurt for them. The first time it was clear to me, I was shocked. I could not figure why I should be praying for them, and now for their hurting heart? After seeking God, I realized these men too were in a prison, a place they allowed themselves to be in. A sin so secretive and unacceptable for others finding out would ruin their lives. In turn, when I prayed for them, I found the prison doors of hate toward them was starting to disappear. My anger, when speaking to God about them, was greatly softened, and an unconditional love was replacing the fierce hate I had harbored for so long in my heart. This increased my vision for these men, and I started to include praying for their family members as well.

Forgiving for me did not happen overnight. It was a process: one of my forgiving when I did not feel like it, of praying for them when they came to mind (which was not all the time), and of following Jesus and His example, even though I was not sure of the end results.

In the Easter story of Jesus on the cross, where He started praying, He said in Luke (NKJV), 23:34, "Father, forgive them, for they do not know what they do." The bottom line was the solders knew they were killing; this was their job. What Jesus meant was they did not know the full extent of what they were doing, and He forgave them right there on the spot. I believe to this day that the men who abused me did not know the the full effect of their actions on me afterward. They did not see me years later trying to kill myself. What they focused on was fulfilling the lust inside them, looking at their own immediate needs and putting mine aside. This reality kept me moving forward with forgiveness for these men.

At times, seeds of hate toward those who hurt me come to mind, but I do not let them take root. I still do hate their sinful actions, but not them. I am not saying in the beginning it will be easy. However, done consistently, forgiveness will become natural to you. Whenever my pride starts to fight forgiving someone easily, I am reminded of what Bob and Sherry Reeve, good friends of our family, say: "Start by just forgiving for this moment." This is so wise. By forgiving for just one moment, it will lead to the possibility of another and another. It is important I forgive quickly, give them over to God, and pray blessings for them. In the end, I am set free.

24

Facing the Shadow Man

Unfortunately I would startle my husband from his sleep by waking up suddenly, gasping for air, and usually wet with sweat. This was normal for me, and I would, after waking up so violently, just turn over and go back to sleep. However, for John, it would startle him awake to the point where he could not easily go back to sleep. In fact, he would start asking me questions, as in what I was dreaming about. The last thing I wanted to do was start a conversation in the middle of the night. I really just wanted to forget the dream and go back to sleep. At one of these times, he asked me what I was dreaming about. I think I told him, "Oh, it was just the Shadow Man." He then started to ask me questions about the Shadow Man. He tried to convince me that if I knew who the person was and not this shadow figure of a man, I would not be so fearful, and maybe I would have fewer nightmares.

So there in the wee hours of the night, we tied down two possibilities. The Shadow Man could possibly be my dad or one other person. John felt the only way to know was to go and ask these men. To me, though we went through the list of possible persons, it just seemed impossible. These two persons loved me, and I could never imagine asking them such a question: one, because I would be implying I was thinking they did molest me; and two, because why in the world would they admit it if they did? Immediately I remembered how ridiculous I thought it was for John to make the phone call and ask the pastor if he abused me and admit his guilt, and the pastor did just that. With much prayer and since I did not want to ask my dad first, John and I went to see the other person.

When we got to this person's home, the stress level became too much for me. I told John I was sorry, but I could not go through with it. I told John I was just fine. I really did not need to know. John could see that the fear of the Shadow Man, even after so many years, still had a grip on me. Lovingly he told me he did not want to see me living like this anymore. He then asked if he could go inside the person's home and ask the person himself. After much talking back and forth, I gave him the permission. John got out of the car and went into the person's home while I stayed in the car. All I could do was pray and wait. My prayer went something like this, "Oh God, oh God, oh God." I knew I wanted answers, to know who the Shadow Man was, but to ask this person if he was the Shadow Man was so unthinkable. I wanted to know, but then, at this point, I did not want to know. For I loved the man inside that home. I also knew the man inside that home loved me. I hated we came to the conclusion that he might be the Shadow Man, and my heart ached.

There was also the possibility that John and I guessed wrong, and this person was not the Shadow Man. I could imagine this person shaking his head and telling John, like everyone else, "Your wife has always had an over active imagination. There was never a Shadow Man. Annette has never been molested. She just thinks she was when she was a child."

The anxiety level inside me was becoming too much as I sat in the car. I started to get nauseous. Before I knew it, I had taken away all the skin underneath one of my armpits without leaving any skin to glue back on. I think it started with a need to itch, and from there, I was out of control. I felt no pain, but I knew eventually I would. I wanted to leave, but John had the keys to the car. I also was in an unfamiliar neighborhood and did not want to walk around outside the car.

John, who seemed like he was in the house for an eternity, finally came out the front door of the house. He sat next to me in the car and told me the person in the house wanted to talk to me. This was too much for me! I wanted to leave right then and there. John proceeded to tell me the person in the house admitted it was him. He was the Shadow Man. I immediately went numb. I did not know how to react. It was one thing to think it could have possibly been the person in the house, but for this one moment of realization, to be confirmed it was him shook my world. I was not sure how to take it all in.

As I sat there in shock and unbelief, John explained how this person was very sorry and wanted to ask for my forgiveness. Somehow it seemed easier to say I forgave the person, to bless him and his family from miles away, than to actually have to talk to him face-to-face and hear him say he was sorry. I was scared. I was beyond being comforted. I wanted again to turn back right then and there and go home. I could not grasp, no matter what I tried to tell myself, that this person was the Shadow Man. A great confusion set in. How could this be? I thought this person loved me. Why would he do such a thing? My anxiety level went way off the chart. I knew I needed to make a decision to speak with the person right now, and all I could think of was how I was going to relieve this inner pain stabbing at my heart. John wanted an answer, yet I had no answer. I said absolutely nothing. No words would come.

John reached over and took my hand in the front seat of the car. He started to pray for peace to come over me. I prayed as well, "Help, God." It was a short prayer, but I was glad at least those words were able to come forth. It was immediately after my short prayer that a realization came to me. If I knew I had hurt someone, I would want the chance to tell them I was sorry and ask for forgiveness. Oh man! This was not fair.

I knew God put that thought in my head. I knew it because it was truth. I would want that opportunity to apologize to the other person. Here I had someone who wanted to say he was sorry to me, and I was not willing to give them the time of day. This was frustrating. I had come all this way; and when I was told by John this man was the Shadow Man, instead of being relieved that I finally knew the truth, I felt betrayed.

I loved the person inside that house with my whole heart. This person knew how my family always talked about me as just an emotional, moody teenager with plenty of issues. At least once a year, we would go and visit him and his family, or he us. Never in my life did I think he was or could be the Shadow Man. I felt stupid because I was so blind, and my hurt turned to anger. I wanted to leave!

John let me sit in silence as I processed all the new information. He then, in a tender voice, softly spoke, "Annette, he is truly sorry. He desires to ask your forgiveness. He has had no idea how you have been tormented all these years by what he did when you were so young. Annette, please give him a chance to talk to you." My thoughts, which were traveling at incredible speed just trying to catch up to the present moment, slowed when John spoke those words. Hesitantly I agreed.

John went inside the man's home, and the man came out to our car. He got in the car with me with tears streaming down his face. All I can say is a miracle happened that afternoon in the front seat of that car. To hear the person admit his wrongs brought such peace to my mind. All my doubts for so many years were cleared up as once and for all it was confirmed there was a Shadow Man. I did not make up the events that tortured me in the middle of the night. I was not a liar just trying to make trouble in our family. I was not crazy! To hear the person say he was so sorry was like a healing salve put over a painful ache that was in my soul. I actually was able, at the end, to hug this man with all the love I had within me. A healing happened that day. Praise God!

Another thing happened that day. My trust in my dad grew because I knew without a doubt he was not the Shadow Man. It was a huge blessing to be able to hug my dad from then on with no more questioning feelings. It took many years to develop a closer relationship with my mother, but I was thankful it finally came. I believe becoming a mother myself helped me see what a tough job parenting can be. My mother is an energetic grandma and an incredible prayer warrior.

25

All in All

About twenty years later, God shed more light on some dark corners of my life. Because I was uncomfortable, I pulled back, and darkness started to creep back in.

There is a worship song that speaks of giving God our all. Many years ago, I was on our church's worship team, and we sang this song quite often at Saturday night's services. After the worship team finished that particular song, our associate pastor Gerald challenged everyone to see if we really were giving God our complete *all*. I sat there quietly asking God. I knew the answer, for I thought I had given everything to Him and was holding nothing. Yet, as I continued to be silent, I sensed the Holy Spirit's speaking to me about not giving God my all. It was then He revealed to me that I did not trust Him.

Though the service continued with Gerald preaching, my conversation with God was in high gear as I sat in that pew.

With all my righteousness, I mentioned to God how I had given Him so much! He then showed me what it would mean to give Him everything. A total and complete 24-7 control of my life. In turn, I immediately thought that if I did this, He would probably send me to a country without running water, with snakes and spiders, and make me sleep on a dirt floor. God knew I did not want to go to those places or be around those creepy-crawly-type things. I was afraid He would ask me to do just that.

As quickly as that thought came into my mind, another started with God showing me thirteen years in the past. He had moved my family and me to the High Desert in Southern California. I had been apprehensive of the move at first, for I knew there might be snakes and black widows there. Growing up in the city, I never had to experience any of those things. Yet I remember that the day we agreed to purchase the property, there was only peace. Strange, I never realized it then, but I sure did now.

I can remember asking for God to keep the creatures away. In the thirteen years we lived there, He did. We only had one snake in the beginning, and that was when we were in the midst of clearing our property. My daughter found our dog barking endlessly in the back of the yard, and saw the snake. My husband killed it, and that was that. Yes, the snake scared me, but I did not live in terror of going back outside. God was in control, and He never gave me a situation that was beyond what I could handle.

After I pondered these things in my heart while sitting on the pew, God showed me that wherever I go, He will be there with me. In fact, I had been living with snakes and spiders all around our property, and because it was the desert, we mainly lived on dirt! This realization was a wow moment for me. I loved the little farm we lived on, and I was happy there. God showed me I could be happy anywhere as long as I was where He wanted me to be. Bottom line, I needed to release my control and let God be truly my all in all.

No one could see the 180-degree turn that happened in my heart that night. It was a slow and persistent walk of going God's way day by day and not choosing to go on my own. Each time I did choose God, my relationship with Him grew, it seemed, three times faster than ever before. Now I was really going into places in this Christian journey. I had my eyes on the I AM, and it was finally all or nothing in my mind. My goal: keep my focus on God and follow Him.

26

Baptism of Healing

I now lived my daily life feeling completely healed of my past and with much hope for the future. This was great! Sure, I had scars from the wounds of my past because those things did happen to me. However, the past was all done with. At least, I thought it was. God still, it seemed, had plans to do more work in me, more light to shine on areas that still were held in the dark, which I did not even realize existed. I truly felt I was seeing everything so clearly. Nevertheless, God wanted me to stay focused, keep walking with Him, and keep learning what giving Him my all really meant. Even at times when it seemed impossible to accomplish what He was asking me to do, all I had to do was simply obey. This might sound like easy faith, but to go back to a place where I was hurt in the past was anything but simple.

Sometimes scars will cause us to walk unknowingly around certain things so we do not hurt again. They can be like ugly reminders. In my case, it happened in September 2002. My youngest son, Louis, noticed one afternoon that our church had a hidden baptismal behind the stage area. Making this discovery, he asked questions about why and how a person gets baptized. In fact, with great curiosity, he walked around the house asking everyone when they had been baptized. When he spoke to his older brother and found out he had not yet been baptized, they got really excited. This was something they could do together!

Louis had not come and asked me yet, but I could hear him coming toward my room as he continued to ask others in our home. Something inside me dreaded his question, which I knew would be coming. When he finally made it to my bedroom, where I was working on the computer, he asked if I was baptized. I told him I was and kept on working on the computer. He then asked how old I was when I was baptized. I told him it was when I was a baby, as most Catholics were. He pressed on with more questions and wanted to know what was the actual age, and I told him, "Maybe a few weeks old." He just looked at me for a few seconds and then said, "I guess that really does not count then, does it?" Then he just skipped out of the room to ask others the same question. I could not believe such a simple question could leave me with so much conviction.

Somewhere deep inside me, I knew infant baptism "didn't count," yet no one had ever pointed this out to me. I had been a Christian for over fifteen years, and when the subject would come up, I basically just ignored it. To be honest, I was not sure it was something I had to do. I chalked baptism up as another ritual like many others of the Catholic Church, which had nothing to do with salvation. This baptism thing at the Christian churches seemed just like something done as a tradition. Or was it? It was time for me to actually look into the matter of baptism. Yet it seemed there was something in me that struggled with the whole concept, and I could not put my finger on it.

Each time I started looking into the Bible about baptism, I would just want to quit. I prayed constantly for God to show me why it seemed I wanted to avoid the subject. I also was praying that He would show me with great certainty if this was something I needed to do. If I really believed I gave God my all, then I would do whatever He asked. I wondered if it was pride that was holding me back. Was it too humbling to be baptized, not only as an adult but as one who had been a Christian for so long?

The more I studied, the more I realized the need to be baptized. Matthew 28:19 stared me down, and I was losing this battle. Bottom line, Jesus was the one who said in that verse to be baptized. If I truly believed Jesus is God, then I would obey. Being baptized as a baby is not what the Bible speaks about. I was not making a statement of faith at a few weeks old but taking part of a church's tradition. My final conclusion was, this was a command from God. When I finally got this reality and all was clear to me, immediately a fear rose inside me. I questioned myself repeatedly why I felt fear.

The next day, I went into our church building. No one was inside. I walked up to the front of the church and stood above the baptismal, which was now uncovered. Staring into it, I noticed my body started to shake. This made no sense at all. I knew how to swim, and I was not afraid of water. Yet fear gripped me tightly. Taking a step back, I sat up by the baptismal and tried to think things through. More than anything, I was feeling trapped. I longed to be obedient to God, and yet I knew I was too fearful of going into the baptismal. I just knew there was no way I was going to be able to do it. Right there on the stage, I began to pray and ask God to please show me what I was missing.

I knew this fear was familiar, but I could not really place it. Somehow right there, looking into the baptismal, this fear from long ago stared back at me. Yet the picture was too fuzzy, and I was lost. I walked off the staging area, asking God to please help me.

That evening, I went to bed and dreamed some of the incidents that happened in the pastor's office. It had been many years since I had a nightmare about the pastor. I awoke abruptly and was sweating profusely. Of course, waking up with such a start, I also woke up John. He was used to my having these kinds of dreams earlier in our marriage, but it had been such a long time that he was surprised. He asked if I could remember the dream. I told him I did. It took me a few minutes, but then I explained it. I could see myself sitting in the front of my bedroom mirror after being dropped off by the pastor back at home after being abused. I remember telling myself this would never happen again, *ever*! No matter what it took, I would never allow myself to be taken advantage of by any man, especially a pastor. Never! John prayed with me, and I fell back to sleep.

Later that day, as I was cleaning around the house, I remembered the dream I had the night before. I then asked God what it had to do with anything. Slowly, as I went back in my thoughts about the dream, God showed me I had built a wall around myself on that day while sitting front of the mirror. A wall to protect me from ever being hurt and a prejudice toward pastors, even our Pastor Jim, whom we had known for over eleven years and who had been a great family friend. This was incredibly hard to digest. This could not be true. As I spoke to God honestly, the more I saw it was true.

I knew God was saying it was time for the wall to come down, for me to trust Him and let more healing take place. I remember telling God, "I am healed. You have healed me!" I shared my testimony so many times with individuals and groups about God's being able to heal the deepest wounds of your heart. I felt I was done with needing any healing from the sexual abuse.

What I did not understand was that the healing of my soul was not a one-shot deal. Healing sometimes can only be done in areas where a person is willing to let God in and, of course, in God's perfect timing. Growing in a relationship with God built a trust level between us, and this allowed for another healing to be made possible. All I had to do was be obedient, trust Him, and He would be faithful. Sounded simple, seemed extremely hard.

This was an eye-opening moment for me. Again, I was blind to this so-called wall with so little trust of pastors. In fact, my husband was starting his schooling to become a pastor. Little did I realize if I had let this wall remain, it would cause a huge rift in our marriage. It was so many years ago since I swore never to let a pastor get close to me that I had completely forgotten all about it until I had that dream.

I knew I needed to get baptized. However, I was extremely afraid I might not be able to do it because of the fear inside me. I did not want to possibly scare or embarrass myself and family by going up to be baptized and just walk off the stage if I could not do it at the last minute. All of a sudden, an idea came to me. I asked my husband, John, to ask if Pastor Jim would do a dress-rehearsal baptism. He agreed. John explained to Pastor Jim about the pastor incident when I was a teenager and that I was afraid. Pastor Jim said he had never heard of a rehearsal baptism. Yet John explained that wedding rehearsals are done all the time, why not a rehearsal for a baptism? Pastor Jim agreed. We set the day for Thursday at 5:00 p.m.

By 2:00 p.m. on Thursday afternoon, I was ready to call the whole thing off. I felt completely stressed. Yet I still could not figure out why I was so fearful and anxious. I called Pastor Jim on the phone and asked if we could talk. As I spoke to him on the phone, I explained I had never, to my knowledge, been fearful of him—cautious, yes, but not fearful. I went on to tell him I had no desire to be baptized at all by him or anyone else. At that, he laughed, knowing I was just being honest with him. I explained it was something I needed to do to be obedient to God. After studying the Bible, there was no doubt in my mind that I was to be baptized. Just actually going through with it was the issue.

Pastor Jim was very gentle and kind with his words and told me it would be okay for my husband to do the baptism if that would make me feel more comfortable. Besides, since he was going to school and interning at the church, it would be part of schooling. At that moment, I couldn't remember feeling so bad. Here I was on the phone with a good friend of our family's, and I was acting like I did not trust him. Not only did I know it, Pastor Jim knew it as well. Yet he, in no way, sounded upset with me. He just wanted to help me achieve my goal of following God's command to be baptized.

I thought about Pastor Jim's offer to have John baptize me. It sounded really great! I was ready to tell him, "Let's go that route!" when a thought came to mind: what if I was to freak out at the last minute and decide no to the baptism with John's doing it? I would not want him to feel like I did not trust him. I explained this to Pastor Jim, who agreed. He said he would not be hurt if I walked away from him, but he felt

God was in this, and I would be perfectly fine. Inside, I knew God was in this, and He would not ask the impossible from me. However, the stress level inside was at an all-time high! We said our good-byes over the phone, and he said he would see me at 5:00 p.m.

I spent the rest of the afternoon alone with God. I felt like He was telling me this Christian life was not something mastered in a one-time event. It is a race of endurance, not a fifty-yard dash. This is a marathon, the starting line being Matthew (KJV), 6:33[a]: "Seek ye first the Kingdom of God." That means in everything in life. Start, be consistent, maintain your breathing, and keep your eyes on the finish line.

God reminded me that I was a lot stronger and wiser than when I started on this race. He began to show me the muscles I had developed in my training of seeking Him first. I was surprised because I did not realize I had been changing and growing all along. Little did I know that when I took off at the start, God was making me, Annette Eastis, a marathon runner. Bottom line for me to remember is, never start off fast when you are running a marathon.

Time for a dip! Five o'clock arrived quickly. John and I showed up at the church. Pastor Jim was there, ready to go with his swim trunks on. He was with his precious wife, Marcia. I had on a pair of jeans, a T-shirt, and tennis shoes. They asked if I was going to change. I brought a pair of shorts and a shirt with me to change into, so I excused myself and said I would be right back. While in the bathroom, I kept taking deep breaths, for there was no greater desire for me at that moment but to walk out the side door and head home. Without thinking, I started to claw at my head, and in a matter of moments, there were small touches of blood on my fingertips. I did not even realize what I was doing until it was too late. When I saw the blood, there was a part of me that felt some sort of relief from stress, but I knew I needed to stop it. I washed my hands and walked out of the bathroom.

With extremely shaky nerves, I came out and just wanted to get it all done and over with. I had not changed my clothes. I was too stressed to even think of doing that while in the bathroom, and to be honest, I was comfortable the way I was dressed. This included leaving my shoes and socks on as well. John looked at me and asked if I was going to change. I replied more sharply than I should have, "No!" I guess John figured at that moment not to push for me to change. Good friends as they were, Pastor Jim and Marcia went along with the clothes I was wearing and said nothing. They could tell I was really stressing out. Pastor Jim and Marcia asked John and I to pray with them before heading up to the baptismal, and we did.

After we prayed, we headed up to the front of the church-stage area. Pastor Jim went right up the stairs to the baptismal like there was nothing to it. I started to go up the stairs, following behind him, and then I stopped. My heart was beating so fast, and I was starting to feel sick. All of a sudden, in my mind, I started to question myself about all

I knew about Pastor Jim. Doubt crept in, and I could go no further. I asked for a moment alone with Marcia outside the church building. We stepped out the side door, and though I was embarrassed to ask the question that was on my mind, I was desperate to know the answer. I asked her if there was ever a report filed on her husband or if someone had ever mentioned that he hurt them. Marcia just looked at me with tears in her eyes and replied, "No, Annette. Don't worry. It is going to be okay." I was sorry I asked.

With no more words spoken between us, I turned and went back in the building with Marcia following behind. I now started back up the stairs to the baptismal. It was time to get this over with and get in the water. Pastor Jim was still waiting for me. "Oh God," I prayed, "where is that peace that passes all understanding? I need it right now." Immediately I felt like I got my answer. Not that I liked it, but I knew it was Him speaking to me. I felt like God was telling me to get in the water, "I am there." My response was, "Yeah, right!" The scariest place to be at that very moment was in the water. I did not know why, and I was in no mood to find out.

It took everything in me to push myself down the first few steps and into the water. As I headed down the stairs, Pastor Jim reached for my hand to help me down the steps into baptismal. Immediately I instinctively jerked my hand away, and I was instantly sorry. Here was a man and his wife, with whom we had been friends for over eleven years, and in that moment, I treated him as though he was my enemy. He then stepped back and said, "Whenever you are ready, I will be waiting. Take your time." I did not dare look up to see my husband's or Marcia's faces. I had no excuse for my horrible behavior, or did I?

It was at this moment I realized, more than ever, that I was not completely healed of my fears, especially towards pastors. Before me was not the friend I had known for years. Pastor Jim actually represented a person I no longer hated, no longer had unforgiveness for, but still would not trust and was not going to ever trust. The promise I made to myself years ago in my bedroom in front of the mirror was for my protection. I needed it.

I finally got to the bottom of the stairs and let out a gasp, which shook everyone up, even me. I was so frightened with the whole ordeal and stressed that I had forgotten to breathe. We all laughed a little, which helped reduce the stress of the moment.

I was now in the water, and Pastor Jim started to show me how things were going to proceed. He explained how to pinch my nose. I was paying close attention so I would not miss anything. He then moved his hand toward my face to show me how to do it. That was it! I headed right out of the baptismal and out on to the outer stairs. I was sopping wet with my jeans, T-shirt, and shoes, which flooded the carpet, but all I could see was his huge hand coming at my face! I was not going to stick around for him to hurt me.

This had become so frustrating. Why did this have to be so hard? I wanted so badly to be obedient, to be baptized, but this seemed far beyond the call of duty; at least this was my excuse. I turned and repeated the words that God would not give me something to accomplish if I could not do it. Immediately Isaiah (NKJV), 43:2–3 came to mind:

> When you pass through the waters, I will be with you; And through the rivers, they shall not overflow you. When you walk through the fire, you shall not be burned nor shall the flame scorch you. For I am the Lord your God, The Holy one of Israel, your Savior; I gave Egypt for your ransom, Ethiopia and Seba in your place.

I had read that passage during the past week, and it was replaying in my heart and mind. It was, the confirmation I was looking for. It was like God was saying again, "I am in the water. Go!"

Meanwhile, John and Marcia tried to tell me from the sidelines how small Pastor Jim's hands were for a man. Pastor Jim said he had been told many times about how he had small hands. I felt so bad. Finally, as I was getting ready to go in the water again, Pastor Jim said if his touch was the issue, he did not even have to touch me to get baptized. Now he was talking the words I wanted to hear! I liked the sound of that idea. However, a voice inside me told me not to be afraid and to let him touch me. God wanted me to trust. I sensed this greatly. I finally just asked Pastor Jim if it was okay for me to go straight down on my own and he could just put his hand on my shoulder. He and everyone else loved the idea. I think at this point they could not wait for this stressful situation to be over as well.

I started to go down into the water, and Pastor Jim placed his hand lightly on my shoulder. His hand signaled great fear, which enveloped me completely. I hated his touch, and I wanted to strike out on him before he would strike out on me. Inside, I asked God, *What is going on here?* I knew my thinking was wrong. I then remembered I had promised I would never put myself in the position of being hurt again, especially by a pastor. Again, it was the silly wall I had put up, which by now had become a strong fortress in my imagination and a stronghold in my life. I was in the middle of a spiritual battle, and the fight was on full force. I was given instruction from God, and I knew all I had to do was to be obedient and go down into the water.

I knew it was irrational thinking, but the thought that ran through my mind continually at about one hundred miles per hour was at the moment I would come out of the water, Pastor Jim would have the advantage. He could strike me across the face and up against the baptismal wall. Yes, John would probably do him in and stop him, but John, like Marcia, would be unable to stop the first strike. In the end, it would be my fault again for putting myself in the position of being vulnerable. I swore so many years beforehand I would never put up with this. God knew this. How could God ask me to go through with this?

Finally I held my breath and went under in faith. While under the water, I saw a vision as plain as day. John and I were at some kind of meeting with couples, listening to a speaker. We were all happy, very joyful. I was in a room full of pastors and their wives, which normally would have been extremely uncomfortable. Yet there I was in the vision, as comfortable as could be. It could not have been for more than two seconds, but the vision was as if I was there for at least five minutes.

The next thing I knew, I was up and out of the water. I went right into my husband's arms. I do not know what happened with Pastor Jim and Marcia. I think they just quietly disappeared while John and I cried and thanked God it was over. It was a pretty emotional experience for us all. God really was in the water! I could not wait to tell John about the vision I had seen!

Later, Pastor Jim came by the room where I was putting on my shoes. He seemed a little hesitant but asked from the doorway if I was doing okay. I said I was great and gave him a big smile. Then a sensation came over me. It is hard to explain, but I just knew I had to reach out and touch Pastor Jim. It was the strangest thing, but I knew I needed to do it quickly before I lost my courage to even ask. I looked at him and asked if I could touch his hand. Here was a guy whom I just gave the hardest time—to whom I showed the most unloving way of pulling away from in the baptismal, even grimacing when he put his hand on my shoulder, which I myself asked him to do—and yet he just smiled and walked toward me with his hand out to me.

When Pastor Jim put his hand on my shoulder to baptize me, I could remember how I hated his touch, but I now vaguely remembered thinking the number 9 but let it go, for I had so many other thoughts filling my mind. This, of course, all happened within mere seconds of him placing his hand on my shoulder. However, now, when I reached out and touched his hand, which he held out to me, there was nothing, no number. I even said out loud, "Oh my gosh, you don't count anymore!" This, of course, sounded really bad at the moment if taken out of context. Still Pastor Jim just smiled like he always does and laughed a bit.

Realizing what I had just said out loud, I was embarrassed. I then told Pastor Jim that for the first time in my life, I just discovered I had been counting all the times he had touched me over the last eleven years. I was shocked, for I did not even realize I had been counting all this time. I guess I had been counting subconsciously. Pastor Jim was now curious and asked in amazement, "When was the eighth time I touched you?" Instantly I knew the answer, as if somewhere inside my brain, I was keeping track. I was shocked. I replied, "It was last Thursday, a little before 7:30 p.m. I was taking some kneepads off after painting a design on the church basketball court, and my knees hurt." I told him that he walked over and asked how I was doing and said my knees looked sore and one was bleeding. "You then reached out and touched one of my knees with your finger." Mind you, it was just the tip of his finger, just for an instant, but somehow I counted it without even realizing it. I did not have any bad feelings toward Pastor Jim then, but because he was a pastor, I counted it.

Wow! It was as if my eyes had been opened. I never realized I was so cautious and prejudiced against pastors. Here was my husband, in school and interning to become a pastor. I am so glad I was obedient to be baptized. It tore down walls that scraped fear against my old wounds, which I had no idea existed. God knew what I needed in life, even when I felt I was perfectly fine.

Pastor Jim and I talked more about what just transpired over the last hour. He said I did not have to go through the baptism again, that this was a lot for me emotionally, it counted, and not to worry. I was obedient to what God asked, and he was sure God was pleased with me. This gave me a sense of relief. However, by Saturday evening, I knew what God desired of me. He wanted me to go and be baptized on Sunday with everyone else, including my sons. My fear of Pastor Jim was gone, so it was a nonissue there, but I still had my pride. Here was my husband, working as an associate pastor at the church, and his own wife, who had been a Christian since she was twelve years old, had never been baptized. This was going to be humbling.

Without telling my husband or children ahead of time, just in case I chickened out, I went to church with it in my mind: I would be baptized. I spoke to Pastor Jim before the services started, and he told me it was up to me. He did not want to pressure me. My job was to prepare those who were in the restroom changing for the baptism. As I was handing out gowns, I noticed Pastor Jim had his wife stick one extragown in there for me if I decided to go through with it. To my husband's and sons' surprise, I showed up on stage that Sunday morning. Nervous, but no fear of the pastor. I was nervous because Pastor Jim was asking each person one by one what this baptism meant to them. In my case, I told them it was an act of obedience. I explained how I thought it was more of a church tradition, but as I searched the Bible and did a study on it, I realized it was a command by Jesus Himself.

My husband was up on stage, finishing up some baptisms, and was stepping out of the water on the far side. As he was doing so, his eyes caught me standing there, ready to be baptized. I walked into the water with no fear, and it went smoothly. My husband, John, stood by with eyes filled with tears, for he knew God had brought us to this incredible moment.

There was a special brunch being held at the church to celebrate the baptisms. When everyone had changed out of their wet clothes, I asked John to please just quickly take me home. We lived close by the church, and I knew he could return without anyone knowing he had left for a few minutes. Though I was filled with inexpressible joy and peace, I was exhausted from a week that was extremely emotional and spiritually challenging. I told him I was just going to lie down in bed and that he should return to the church to celebrate with the rest of our family. I slept for six straight hours in a place of such contentment with what felt like a complete restoration for my soul.

Later that evening, I thought about all the things that happened over the past week. I was still incredibly surprised by not being aware of the counting I did when pastors touched me. When I thought about it, I could immediately name the pastor and how many times I felt his touch. It could have been a hug or a simple shake of the hand at the door. Praise God for leading me to a place of healing and restoration. My sons and I shared a special day together—Sunday, September 15, 2002, the day we all got baptized. A memory I hope always to remember.

It was not long after that day when I shared about being baptized with others who had received Christ as their Savior. I remember this one young man who just looked at me and said, "You have been a Christian all that time for so many years, and you were never baptized?" He was really surprised. I explained that I really did not understand at the time that it was not a ritual. However, when I knew the truth, I went forward in obedience. I had no idea what was going on in this young man's mind. However, he proceeded to ask again why I should be baptized. I repeated that it was an act of just obeying what God asks of us and proceeded to show him the scripture.

All of a sudden, I could see the look of hopelessness and fear come upon him. Then he said, "Mrs. Eastis, the church's baptismal is deep. It is a complete body dunk!" I reached across the table and touched his arm. He then told me he could not swim. It was then I was able to read that verse from Isaiah, which God had given me, the verse that fed my soul on the day I went for my rehearsal baptism. He thought it was the coolest scripture, and so did I.

We talked for a while, and I found out he too came from a rough church background and did not trust pastors. I explained how patient and kind Pastor Jim was and he had nothing to worry about. The young man was soon baptized, and God was glorified! It seemed as though God was healing wounds everywhere.

I continued working with my family's ministry, reaching the youth of our community. That is right—me, reaching out to others. God showed me early on that reaching out to others and not dwelling in the pit of stinky thoughts was where I would find a fulfilling life. Reaping a harvest for the kingdom is ten times better than planting seeds of lies in my heart from Satan, who only wants to tear me down.

One day, I felt God's call to go back to school like my husband did and get my pastoral license. Yes, I realize this might be hard for one to believe. Here I was, a person who held such hard feelings and prejudice against any pastor who would come into my life. However, I found in the ministry my husband and I do, I needed to have access into juvenile hall, ICUs at hospitals, mental wards and help with funeral services—to which I had no quick access without a pastoral license. When God presented the idea to me about going back to school, I was not crazy about it at all. I thought my husband, John, would think I was nuts! However, he was my greatest encourager during the years it took me to go through the process.

In 2007, I received my pastoral license, which was a huge day for me. It represented to everyone who knew me that Satan had no power over me any longer in this area. God had complete victory! On that special day of my graduation, this verse burned within my heart: "But Jesus looked at them and said to them, with men this impossible, but with God all things are possible" (Matthew (NIV), 19:26).

27

The Dream

The days of feeling controlled by all those experiences seemed so far away. There were still days where a familiar lie would be introduced to my mind, but I had gotten into the habit of challenging the lie with the truth of what God had done for me, and immediately the lie would be squashed. This may sound really great on paper, but in the beginning, it was something that had to be practiced daily in order for it to become a habit. It was a choice of my will, and it still is to this day.

To be open to God and not reach for a quick small-*g* god by leaning on all my fleshly defenses to save me from some sort of pain I might have to face is not always easy. This is basically a complete opposite of being in control, yet God has proven to be safer over the years and much more comforting than any of those small-*g* gods that are always mixed with lies. The truth provides a solid foundation no matter how painful something might be in the beginning. My human instinct is to avoid pain if at all possible, but it is not always beneficial.

Lies mixed with truth would never provide a solid foundation. Sure, the lies provide temporary foundations that will sometimes last for years, but when the tsunamis of life hit there is nothing left. My foundation lasted me twenty years or more until one day it started to fall apart, leaving me hopeless and distraught beyond anything I could imagine. This could have all been avoidable if I would have had a foundation made only of truth. I could have withstood life's storms. We all come to God with some sort of foundation already in place, some in much better condition than others.

I thought I had faced all my past with the abuse, but what I discovered was that as I matured in Christ, so did my ability to handle more truth that God wanted to show, things I needed to get right with Him in order to be close in a relationship with Him. I am beyond grateful that God has been patient waiting for me to be able to drink in the truth then catching me as I fall from the false foundation that gives way beneath me, faithfully replacing it with the truth. The following verse states,

> Therefore everyone who hears these words of mine and puts them into practice is like a wise man who built his house on the rock. The rain came down, the streams rose, and the winds blew and beat against that house; yet it did not fall, because it has its foundation on the rock. But everyone who hears these words of

mine and does not put them into practice is like a foolish man who built his house on sand. The winds blew and beat against that house, and it fell with a great crash. (Matthew (NKJV), 7:24–27)

Over the years, I have spoken at many events and conferences about this incredible freedom God has given me, the blessing in the midst of feeling so lost and the hope one can only find in Christ. If you were to ask me if I had been healed completely from the abuse of my past, I would smile at you and tell you, "Absolutely yes!" I was done with my past ever influencing my life ever again! All I had were praises for my God, who is the Healer of my soul.

What I failed to understand was that with past abuses like the ones I had experienced, the healing is a continual process. We all behave in certain ways due to our life experiences, which include good and bad. Our past has an impact on our daily decisions. Though I had grown stronger in my relationship with God over the years, it would be about six more years before I faced my biggest challenge yet.

An opportunity presented itself to go to an online class with some friends of mine. The class was going to use the book *The Wounded Heart* by Dr. Dan B. Allender. This book discusses sexual abuse, its effects, and how God's Word speaks life back into a wounded heart. I had already read this book many times and felt I got all I could out of it, but I was willing to take the class in order to help counsel others who had been abused.

The class started well. I got through my reading quickly since I was familiar with the book. However, it was the first time I used the workbook. There were many questions. They were good, but more time-consuming than just reading the book.

The class was taught by a Christian couple, John and Linda Oelze. I was familiar with John O., for he taught one course I had taken a couple of years beforehand when I was in school for my pastoral license. Linda, his wife, worked with the women in the class, and John O. worked with the husbands. All seemed to be going fine until I started to get into some uncomfortable questions in the workbook. I was not sure why I was feeling so uneasy, so I sought God on it. In turn, I had a dream that evening.

Dream

I was going to drive the car for a long distance, and because of this, I knew I needed to get a drink in order to stay awake. Anything past thirty minutes of driving for me is long, and I always want to stay alert. I saw myself in the dream stopping at a fast-food restaurant to quickly purchase a large drink. When I noticed the drive-through had a long line, I decided to park my car and walk inside. As I walked in, I noticed they just opened a register close to where I entered, and there was only one person ahead of me. This was perfect!

While standing in line, I started to notice a distinct, smelly body odor of sweat, fish, and wet sand. That was when I realized the smell was coming from the man standing in line in front of me. I now noticed he had obviously gone to the beach but had not washed all the sand, sweat, and gunk off his body before walking into the restaurant. I casually took a small step back to give more space between us, only to notice he was starting to play with the cups at the counter right next to the register as he waited for his order.

These were the cups everyone behind him would be drinking out of, including me. This man's hands were filthy brown with sand, and it seemed obvious to me he was not even aware of it. He casually then started to play with the straw container. I could not stand it any longer. I mentioned to him that the sand and dirt from his hands were starting to stick on all the straws, and it would be best if he stopped playing with them. He looked at me quizzically, as if I was being too picky, and picked up about ten straws and wiped them off on his shirt, which looked worse than his hands!

It was now my turn at the counter, and I stepped forward to order my drink, only to see the girl behind the counter grab one of the disgusting, dirty cups! I asked her to please get a cup from a different location, for these cups close to her were obviously dirty. She looked at me as though I were being the pickiest person in the world. With great frustration, she picked up one of the cups by the register and started to wipe it off on her sleeve and put ice in it. I could not believe what

I was seeing. This was ridiculous. She turned to put the drink on the counter and asked how I was going to pay. I told her I was not going to purchase the drink after all as I was not that thirsty and started to walk away.

The man who smelled and was covered in dirty sand asked what was my problem. I told him I needed a cleaner cup, and it seemed this place could not provide it for me. He mentioned to me he thought he had seen me many times in this restaurant, and the girl behind the counter agreed with him. I told them I actually had only come in the building twice before, but all the other times, probably over a hundred or more, I had just gone through the drive-through because it was so close to the freeway entrance.

The girl behind the counter looked at me and said with a bad attitude, "What then is the problem?" I explained again that today the cups were not clean. She said that there was no difference from today's cups and the cups from all the other days I had visited. She was obviously irritated with me, thinking she wasting her time trying to serve such a picky customer as myself. She then picked up the dirty cup she prepared for me with soda, stuck a horridly filthy straw in it, and drank deeply. She then looked at me and the long line of people that had now formed behind me and proclaimed, "It tastes great! There is nothing wrong with it!" I walked out frustrated and yet still in need of getting something to drink in order to make my long drive. In fact, for some reason, I could tell I was now a whole lot thirstier than when I first entered the restaurant.

As I walked to my car, I could see another restaurant across the street. I left my car and walked over to that place and ordered a large drink to go. I noticed right away that the cups were held in a clean silver container, away from customers' hands. Their straws were individually wrapped, so no matter what or who touched them, the insides stayed perfectly clean and sanitary. I looked around waiting for my order, and I noticed the place was not as crowded as the one I left, which now had a full drive-through and whose walk-in line was almost around the building.

I was then given my drink, which was cold to the touch, clean, and when tasted, was completely refreshing. I then asked the clerk what was going on with the place across the street. "Did they get a new manager?" She asked why I mentioned it, and I explained to her what had just transpired. She replied that their service has always been like that and nothing had changed. I looked at the young lady and said, "I can't believe that place has not been shut down long ago. It is disgusting!" She then told me it would be shut down one day, but not just yet. I said, "You have got to be kidding me! That place is a health hazard. There are obviously many health violations being broken. You're even losing business to those guys. You should do something!" The clerk smiled and said, "Yes, we are serving the best, but people do have a choice. Some have just become blind to the dirtiness of the cups and straws they are served." She continued to explain to me that the customers over there get quick service, and that was what mattered to them. "They must not feel it is bad, or maybe they don't think they deserve better. The list is long as to why people drink from a restaurant like that." She ended with, "The good news is we are here to serve clean cups of cool refreshing drinks available twenty-four hours a day."

I paid and then walked back to my car across the street, which was still parked in the restaurant with dirty cups and straws. I was almost to my car when I saw a young family walking up to the front doors of the restaurant with the dirty cups. I could hear them talking about how this was their first time eating there. I cringed at the thought and walked over to them. I stopped them and explained that the cleanliness of this place was pretty bad and they should consider eating at another place. They turned and looked at me and asked how I knew it was bad. I told them about my encounter earlier. The father looked at me and replied, "So you mean to tell me you have eaten and bought drinks from this place over a hundred times before? It could not have been that bad!" They then turned away from me and walked right into the dirty restaurant.

I walked away stunned and sat down in my car. I put my clean cup down in the cup holder only to notice a cup from the day before. It was from the dirty restaurant. I picked it up to inspect it, and sure enough, it was filthy. The straw was dirty, and so was the cup. There was no drink left, for I had finished it the day before. I was sick to my stomach. Why would I have ever done something like that? I thought back to the day before and remembered I was in a rush and had to get on the road quickly. The drive-through line was short, and I just buzzed on in and out with my drink, popped in the straw, and never really looked at it or the cup. I was just thankful for a drink that would keep me awake on the road and drank away.

That is where my dream ended, and I woke up. Wow, my mind was reeling from the dream. I felt really frustrated with the restaurant that used such dirty straws and cups. It was just a dream, and this was really silly. However, I could not shake my frustration. I immediately shot God a quick prayer, asking if this was supposed to mean something, to please show me; otherwise, to please help me let it go. Just like that, a revelation came to me. My frustration vanished, and I was left with the truth trying to come forth. Here I asked God. He was obviously answering, but I was not prepared for this moment of revelation. I then mumbled, "Oh God."

It was as if my vision of how I looked at things had been blocked. Now full light was coming in, and I was able to see things coming into focus. I sat there reflecting on the past abuse. As I sifted through my thoughts, I still could not place how the dream had anything to do with my past. I felt a nudge to go back further in my thinking to when I was first abused by Shadow Man, and I needed something fast. It was then that my world felt as though it was spinning completely out of control. In order to get past the horror of being touched, the rejection of my mother and her not doing anything, and the pain of the shame crushing me, I had to do something. I needed to survive. I wanted protection, yet I could not find it. I was, in a sense, thirsty, desperately thirsty, and I took a dirty cup and straw that was offered me, and I drank. Slowly at first and then in large gulps until my world was in control again. From that point on, it was all about satisfying my thirst. I don't remember questioning for one minute the cleanliness of the cup or the straw.

I continued to drink in this revelation. It had been so many years since that night. It was as if someone turned on a bright light, and I could see the same dirty, disgusting, stupid cup in my hand today. I wanted to drop the cup instantly. Yet I knew somewhere inside me, I was still metaphorically holding on to it. The question came to me, Why would I purposefully drink from a dirty cup? I shook my head, trying to make sense out of all this. I felt so uneasy, and I started to regret asking God what this was all about. Yet I felt Him prodding my spirit, showing me it was true. He showed me that I still drank from a dirty cup and straw just like I did when I was a child. Not as often as I did then, but the fact that I did was a horrible thought. Frustration and a stress rose as my shoulders tightened. I was done with all the abuse junk! I thought I was healed from it all. Yet it was also obvious at that very moment that God was leading me to face something. I was not looking forward to facing it.

I became agitated and spoke to God with much pride and attitude. Fine, I got a dirty cup? I wanted answers, but it was as though I was not to ask the questions. I was to respond to the question He wanted answered, which kept bouncing off the walls of my heart, *How much light will you let Me shine on this?* You would have thought I called out to God and asked Him to help me, saying, "Bring it on! Shine all you have on it, God!" However, my flesh wanted to get the light turned down a bit lower. With the amount of light He had begun to shine on me, I realized where God was going. I knew He was going to take away something from me or take control of something I felt I needed.

In my dream, the dirty and clean cups were available for me to freely choose. This seemed simple. It was common sense not to drink out of a dirty cup! I played over the scene from the dream in my mind many times. I knew dirty cups were wrong, and clean cups were right! Pretty basic stuff. What God was showing me was that *sin* equaled the dirty cup, and the clean ones represented living life His way. God wanted me to choose the clean cup He was offering. I wanted His will, His way of doing things, the clean cup, but I was not sure if what I thought God was pointing to was something I even wanted to mess with or touch—as in what sin was He speaking about?

I sat there and tried to piece together what God was showing me. It was then I realized that the dirty cup represented how I coped with the abuse, as in playing dead. I never thought it was wrong then, and I did not now. Or did I? This was a thousand times more serious than I had thought.

God, with great patience, was trying to show me something; and I, in panic mode, decided to just shut it down—as in I stopped talking to God. Of course, this meant I wouldn't be able to talk to God at all comfortably, knowing He was waiting to discuss this subject. My conclusion was to just take a break from talking with Him.

This was a horrible idea. Talking to God all day long has been part of my life; it was like breathing air, not something I really consciously did. To starve myself from conversation with Him was like not eating any food all day long. I had to stop reading the Bible because I could hear Him speak to me, as well as listening to music or many other things. I was starving myself. I missed God so much, but then an idea came to me. I could play dead to my hunger, and so I did.

All day long, every time I reached for a cup, I thought about the dream and God. When something good, bad, or sad would happen, I wanted to share it with God, but I couldn't. I had to start going back to the beaches and sheets of my thoughts so I did not have to feel the starvation from not having such a close relationship with God.

One day, I realized my playing dead to my need to communicate with God also meant playing dead to many emotions. I was in each day but not truly living in each day. I could see it in my husband's eyes and in my kids'. I could see this was hurting my family, and it had been less than forty-eight hours. To some, it would have looked like my mind was preoccupied, or I was depressed about something. I needed this fixed.

Instead of turning to God, whom I felt would expect perfection all at once, I turned to my own devices. The next day, I worked extra hard on looking like I was happy. I would make sure not to let my mind wander off into beaches or sheets. This seemed to help at home greatly, but inside, all this pretending was making me sick physically and spiritually. My self-fix methods were all failing, and I needed help.

I tentatively—out of great starvation and, well, just desperation to have a relationship back with God—asked Him what He wanted to talk to me about. I had a good idea. Immediately I said, "What is so wrong with playing dead?" Nothing. There was silence from both of us. About five minutes later, my mind began to ponder things I passed over quickly in *The Wounded Heart* workbook. I pulled it out and started to reread the chapter called "Secondary Symptoms."

As I read, I could see it was speaking about symptoms as producing bad fruit because some parts of the tree's root system had become diseased. It explained that when a fruit tree produces good fruit, nothing is questioned. However, when it produces good fruit and then in some portions starts producing bad fruit, the farmer starts to check out the tree much more closely. In this case, the diseased portion is from its roots. Sure, the farmer could pick off the bad fruit as quickly as it appears so that it does not affect the tree any further, but to ignore something is wrong will affect the tree as a whole in the long run. This was not hard to understand, and it made sense to me.

The book also directed the reader to make sure they had faced the abuse, as in not being in denial of the abuse that had taken place. This and other explanations are given on why symptoms happen for some, because they remain kind of like a silent witness to the truth. Identifying the symptoms will help point to the specific struggling area in the root of the tree and lead the reader to seek God on getting spiritually healthy in that area. I felt I had faced my past and grown immensely with God in all the areas of my past abuse. I was not in denial that it occurred. God had healed and cut my bad roots out so that there was nothing more to deal with. I was left very puzzled as to what God desired me to do.

I proceeded to go down the questions in the workbook. Most were just simple, straight-line questions, nothing really difficult to answer. I was to simply put a check mark for yes by the answer and move on. This seemed simple enough, so I proceeded. The next set of questions were about how a person comforts themselves rather than going to the Comforter, who is God. I am a Christian, and I would like to think I go to God directly in any situation I face. However, my spirit pulled to a stop after quickly finishing up my check marks in this section. As in, I should reread my answers. This was frustrating because I wanted to get my homework done quickly, and I pushed it aside and went on.

I proceeded through the next section having to do with, "Have you ever done any of the following?" The list was long, and most of my answers were no. Only one really stood out to me, which seemed like the weirdest question I have ever read, "Have you ever scratched?" Immediately I thought this was so stupid. What kind of question was this? Everyone in the world scratches themselves when they have an itch. Immediately I remembered scratching the back of my head uncontrollably as a child till it bled. I never really thought of it being bad; it was just a tic. And this was a ridiculous question! I was ready to move on.

However, the question just would not leave my mind clear to move on. The book was trying to show the reader that it was more than a bad habit but one that had roots. It explained that the itching soothed the pain of the memory of the abuse. This helped me survive the moment and the days that followed.

I started to reason with myself. I knew I did not play dead or scratch myself anymore like I did as a child. I could tell that, as I pondered these things, I was becoming defensive and pretty irritated by the whole subject. Immediately flashes of the times not so far off came to mind, where I chose to play dead or scratch to soothe my soul. I was startled by this realization and quickly shut the door to those thoughts. I was done. I did not want to know more. I wanted a change of subject right away. I reminded God how far we had come since I was child. I spoke to Him about how He had totally healed me of all my past abuse, and we were completely done. I let Him know the subject was closed. There was nothing more to discuss. Of course, this was my immature way of taking control instead of letting God be in charge. I felt a panic rise within me, and I needed a break. I shut the book, shut down my communication on the subject with God—as if saying, "Hands off"—and got up, went away, and did something else.

Choosing not to continue in conversation with God was working on was a huge mistake, and confusion started to seep in. The Bible states in 1 Corinthians (NKJV), 14:33, "For God is not a God of confusion but of peace, as in all the churches of the saints."

With my thoughts getting jumbled and confusion settling in, a wave of great stress joined in. I knew I needed to grab on to God's peace, grip His shield of truth, and basically seek what God wanted.

Yet all that happened was anger growing inside me, as well as a great frustration, in realizing that God was showing me how the dirty cups and straws have been a part of my life. I felt as thought I was in a battlefield with two great desires. My flesh wanted more than anything to have the light of God's revelation of my past turned off. However, my soul ached for the light to stay on so I would not, as God was showing me, keep picking up dirty cups and straws and drinking out of them.

At different times, when the subject came to mind, I would console myself by reminding God why I needed a drink from the dirty cup every now and then! I needed it under my terms. I felt I had to explain to Him, for He obviously did not understand that I was extremely thirsty and needed the quick fix to survive the pain of my parched throat (the pain of the abuse). The dirty cup was the first available thing to me. Surely if God really knew me, he would just have to understand. I remember telling Him, "We are done dealing with the past, can't we just please move on? Can't you just help my soul settle down and go on with life?" Funny how we can have conversations with God and ask Him to fix things when already in our hearts we have decided not to listen to God's response.

Each day my anger grew as I could see God was not giving in to my request to leave things alone. The darn dream of the filthy cups and straws continually floated in and out of my mind. The thought of drinking out of such a filthy cup over a hundred times made me nauseous. However, I consoled myself that in my dream I did cross the street and went in search of a clean cup!

A thought came to me: *I should be sorry for choosing the dirty cups and straws.* As quickly as this thought came to me, another followed just as fast, which was God obviously was not understanding the situation at all! I was desperate. I needed something fast to soothe my soul when I was a little girl. It was something I needed to survive. Was it pretty? No! Was I blind to it? I did not know, and I surely was not looking to find out. However, it was clear I was not blind to it any longer. Maybe I could not see it for over thirty years, but it was never out of God's sight. He had always known. I knew He wanted me to walk this part of the journey with Him, but I had no desire to join Him. I was fine.

28

Wake up Call

Three days later, I was at work; and a young man, who was a fellow employee, came up to my desk and asked for help on one of the computer systems in my office area When I first met him a year before, I felt great concern for his heart and had been praying for him. However, he worked in a different department from me, and I rarely saw him I cared about his well-being. When he asked for help, I jumped at the chance and came up right beside the computer station where he was located.

As I was helping the young man, I started to notice an unpleasant odor coming from him. I continued to coach him on what keys to press next while taking a quick look at his outward appearance, which seemed clean. However, the longer I stood by him, the more nauseous his odor became. I tried to wait for the smell to pass, for I really wanted to have this chance to help him. Still I was not sure how much longer I would be able to stand next to him.

My phone in the same office rang at my desk, and I excused myself and promised to return to him. Taking this quick break was great, for I was able to get some fresh air. I took the call, meanwhile asking God what was with the horrible smell. It was at that moment when I remembered what the smell reminded me of. I have smelled it when I was working with those who were seriously ill or in the process of dying. Odd. I shook off my thoughts and went back to helping the young man. However, when I returned to him, the smell was even worse. It was then, while helping him, that I became sure I was next to the smell of death.

As he continued to work on the computer, I thought back to the first time I met the young man a year ago. He had walked into my office, and I introduced myself. At the same time, I noticed he had an odd bandage on his finger. Obviously something had happened, and I asked out of concern if he was okay. He replied with no hesitation that he was fine. He just cut off his finger over the weekend, and it was just healing. What?

I was not sure he was being serious with me, so I asked how he did it. He openly shared with me that for the past two years it had been something he desired to do. I asked if he had spoken to anyone else about it before actually cutting it off. He said he spoke to his parents and even went to a counselor of some sort to make sure he was not going nuts. I asked what they said, and he said his parents were not cool with it but told him if it was really something he felt he needed to do, then it was okay with them. I asked about the counselor, and he said he was told it was his body and he had the right to decide for himself. Wow! He made it sound so simple as getting your ears pierced, nothing more. Our conversation then got interrupted, and the subject was never brought up again.

A year later, there I was standing next to this young man at the computers. As I stood there, I noticed he had a six-inch nail, the kind used to build a house, sticking straight through his earlobe. His whole ear was red, swollen, and looked incredibly sore. I asked him, "When did you get your ear pierced?" He told me he got it pierced the night before. It was obvious it was not a normal ear piercing, so I inquired how it was done. He explained that a friend hammered the nail right through his ear. I asked why he did not at least use a smaller nail or just go to an ear-piercing facility and get it done by a professional. He told me he really liked the style of a large hole. I asked him if he numbed the ear first with ice or anything. His response was, "No, I'm okay." All sorts of thoughts formed in my head as to what to say to him, yet each time I was going to speak, a conviction I could not explain swept over me, and I said nothing. Stunned and still smelling the awful stench of death, I was anxious for me to be done helping him on the computer.

We finished up on the computer a few minutes later, and he went back to work. I walked over to some nearby desks and asked some coworkers if they smelled anything out of the ordinary. They replied they smelled nothing unusual. It was time for my break, so I went outside to get some fresh air. I immediately asked God, "What was that all about?" He confirmed to me that what I did smell was death. I waited for more information, and nothing came. I could feel my spiritual thirst increasing, and a pain deep within started to well up. I shook it off and tried to clear my mind.

During the next few hours, the young man came to my mind often. I tried to put the pieces of the puzzle together: He was probably about twenty-two years old and looked healthy overall, definitely not sick. He did have the wild, youthful appearance of most skaters and BMX riders my husband, John, and I work with regularly, but the young man surely did not look like he was dying. I finally asked God, "Is he going to die?" No response.

Later that day, I started to pray for him. Though I did not speak to God about *The Wounded Heart* workbook, I freely spoke to Him about other things. As I was talking to God about the young man, a great feeling of unrest started to form in me. I hated seeing this young man hurt himself, but more than that, I was concerned for the state of his soul and his relationship with God. All of a sudden, the light went on; I understood the smell. It was as clear as it could be. The smell that came from him was sin. The sin of self-mutilation. And all sins bring death. It was an aha moment.

Now the hard questions started to come. Obviously God was trying to speak to me about the sin in my life. This caught me so off guard, and at the same time, I was not sure I wanted to address it. I never looked at the ways I physically hurt myself at all like how I saw it in this young man's life. It was as if God was showing me that this young man and I were dealing with the same type of sin. When this thought came to mind, my pride and self-righteousness pushed forward with much denial. There was no way I was like the young man. What he did seemed definitely worse compared to anything I had ever done (interesting how one can justify their own sin by saying another person was worse than them). I remember wanting to help the young man, but the feeling of condemnation came over me, and I knew I was in no place to offer help. Now it was clear where the condemnation was coming from. I felt stuck. Then a thought came to me, which I could barely let flow through my mind. I wondered how bad I smelled of death to God? I knew then that denial would be useless.

When I was being shown the sin, my eyes, which were once blind, now were completely open to the ugliness presented before me. My heart hurt. I was instantly thirsty for God yet so desperate to hide from Him all at the same time. I knew God desired for me to seek Him, and He was just there waiting for me. I knew that to do this meant I would have to repent. Excuses that seemed completely logical filled my heart and mind. Maybe I just needed a bit more time. I felt I was building a good case to take to God so He could better understand *why* I needed to do what I did in order to function. So I started a list:

1. I had been doing some of these survival habits since I was a small child.

2. These habits were a way of life.

3. I was not hurting anyone else.

4. No one knew. It was completely hidden, and I functioned just fine in life with it.

5. I did not do it very often, nothing like my younger days, maybe only twice a year.

6. Most often, I just did it. There was no thought to it. It was like breathing. I would not even know if I could catch myself before doing it.

7. I did not do drastic things like the young man cutting off a finger.

This was getting out of control, and I was completely frustrated. I wanted God and His will in my life, but this was going to be uncharted territory, and I just was not sure I wanted to go there. Guilt gushed through my soul. I knew this was something I was going to have to unpack and not shove away. I kept trying to sort out my emotions from the facts, but it was not going too well. My fortress of pride, built up of my self-will to overcome without God's touching too much of it, was becoming incredibly stressful. This definitely was not a moment of my giving God my all. It was more a time of pulling back.

My relationship with God became stressful. My biggest issue was that I was not sure I really wanted the sin out of my life. It is not that I did not understand it was not good keeping it. God made it real clear, when my blinders were removed, that it existed. God used the dream and then the realization from the guy at work to show me what was in my life. This seemed so obvious. I felt so stupid, and it was humiliating for me to just now recognize it in my life.

There were things I wanted to know ahead of time, such as what would replace those automatic actions I had been doing for years. To give them up without a plan would mean trusting God in an area I had never gone before. This was not an easy thing. Fear flowed through me, for my desire to keep the sin in my life was greater than that of giving it up completely. I knew this was wrong. Guilt became a heavy weight I started to carry.

I knew repentance had to do with fully being sorry, fully giving up my will and wanting God's perfect will in my life. I knew this meant not doing anymore those acts I had been doing for over thirty years. I wish I could say I immediately repented and ran to God. I knew Psalm 7:1: "O Lord my God, in You I put my trust, save me from all those who persecute me, and deliver me."

Could God deliver me from myself? The deal was God had proven to me over and over again in my life that He is my refuge and strength, as in Psalm 46:1: "God is our refuge and strength, and ever-present help in trouble." Still I did not choose to trust God in the struggle before me. In turn, I felt maybe it was something I could control and manipulate on my own. It was not something I did every day of my life. Maybe just once or twice a year; not that often.

My biggest enemy was my pride and the shame that started to consume me. If I was to confess my sin to God, I would be admitting the following:

1. I was doing this as a bad habit.

2. I was doing this as a Christian.

3. I was doing this as a wife and mother.

4. I was doing this while I was a licensed pastor.

5. I was doing this obviously because of my lack of trust in God.

6. I was doing this without God.

7. I was doing this because I chose to play god.

I would be honestly saying I was sorry, and I knew I could not do that. I was not sorry.

This spiritual battle was complex. Truth, lies, and pride mixed heavily with one another. I had kept it hidden for so long from everyone including myself. From experience, I knew better. I knew I had to make a choice. Taking my sin, having a good look at it, and leaving it at the feet of my Savior Jesus was the right thing to do. I had done it so many times before it was not like this was a new concept for me. Not once have I gone before God and He ever turned me away. In fact, when I went in brokenness and humility, I have always been engulfed in pure love. My thinking was wrapped around, How does a person who is not broken or does not feel humble go to God? All I felt was guilt, shame from my sin being shown to me, disappointment, and anger toward myself for knowing I was failing God.

I had already judged myself and had found myself guilty. It is amazing how heartless and cruel we can be to ourselves, yet we would never act or treat another human being in such a way. Luke 6:37 states, "Do not judge and you will not be judged. Do not condemn, and you will not be condemned. Forgive, and you will be forgiven."

This verse holds so much truth. God's Word states that He is the only judge, and yet I judged myself and condemned my failures to a sentence of more pain. Truth like this verse is the best weapon to use against the lies of the enemy, but shutting down to God kept me from seeing the truth. To not condemn oneself is a discipline that has to be practiced daily. This was a part of what God wanted to teach me. In my anger, I ignored the verse and continued to judge myself harshly.

I knew I needed God desperately, but communicating with Him about how I felt without really being sorry or repentant was unchartered territory. I was beginning to feel the crushing pressure of fear. It was not like fear was a new enemy, but this was a new arena for God and me to walk through together and be honest. I really did not want God to go with me, for I knew I was not ready to shut the door on my sinful behavior.

29

A Week Later

I was still in *The Wounded Heart* class, but as far as participating in the class online, I knew my heart was not right. I wanted to quit. However, each time I considered not continuing with the class, I felt God pressing me to make a wise decision. I knew He desired for me to continue. I knew I was failing by not repenting, but to quit would only be moving further out of His will. If I stayed in the class, at least I was meeting God partway.

Linda, the one leading the women's portion of the class, noticed my struggle. I would be questioned in class and give pretty basic short answers. She pressed to know if something was wrong. I gave her an honest answer. I said I was struggling with some of the questions in the book but was not willing to discuss any of them at this time. I was honest but closed off.

In her kind yet persuasive manner, Linda pressed in and would, in great wisdom, listen to my basic answers. She then would find just one word and hold on to it. With that one word, she would then try to get me to walk with her to discover the root of my struggle. I think I mentioned to her that I had a disturbing dream. She wanted to hear about it. I was in no mood to share anything, but in order to get her off my back, I told her I would e-mail her what the dream was about. This was the ticket, because for the rest of the evening in class, she did not pepper me with questions any longer.

I did send her the story of my dream about the dirty cups and straws. She wrote me back with the following:

> Annette, what an incredible story/illustration of where you are in your journey. That was so revealing. Thanks for sharing. In your dream, you had to get so frustrated with the dirty cups that it was not worth even tasting the drink to temporarily satisfy your thirst and perhaps cause you illness. In your dream, it was worth the risk (once you were so disgusted). You chose to leave and go across the street for something different. The great irony was there weren't many in line for the clean cups.
>
> In real life, this is so true for you as well. I believe you are disgusted with the way you have tried to temporarily cover up the pain and provide temporary satisfaction for your thirst. I believe you see this as sin and shame.
>
> As you are now "stuck," you are in the crossroads of choosing what to do. I guess it comes down to what do you want to do? Is repentance an option, or does it

feel like one? As a redeemed person who understands your sin up to this point, whose heart is beating for Christ, what do you really want to do? What is your heart telling you? What would it mean to risk and move toward others in love? Choosing when and who to trust is control—not faith.

Answering these questions and acting on them will help you move forward from here, Annette. Be assured we are praying for you and John.

Linda

Those were tough questions Linda had for me. What did I really want to do? I wanted to pretend I never ran across any of these truths God was bringing my way. That was what I really wanted! Yet I knew if the doctor (God) said I had cancer, I would want it removed immediately. Though after the surgery there would be pain with the recovery, my brain knows well enough that if I do not get rid of the cancer, it will continue to grow. God was not forcing me to let go of the sin He revealed to me; it was as if He was asking me to trust Him and, out of my free will, to climb up onto the operating table.

My heart, in fear, was telling me to run and go the other way. Play it safe, ignore, shut out, and eventually this stress will go away. Jeremiah (NASB), 17:9, it says, "The heart is deceitful than all else and desperately sick; Who can understand it?"

God knows the human heart. In all truth, I did not want to face my past actions, stop my responses to life, or repent.

I believed I needed those actions, though I barely did them as often compared to when I was younger. Just knowing they were there as an option mattered greatly to me.

The last question Linda asked was, What would it mean to risk and move toward others in love? I guess it means not to hide my pain, admit I had been a fool for years, humble myself, and ask for prayer, wisdom, and worse, possibly accountability—which means surrendering my control to others. It would also mean repenting, which I was struggling with more than any other component. I knew I was not sorry one bit. My lack of unwillingness to go to God, my Savior, left me bitterly ashamed.

It felt like a hopeless situation, and I started to get angry toward Linda. I sat there after reading what she wrote and decided her questions were ridiculous. I then sat and complained to God about her. I guess because I was not willing to look at myself, she was a safe person to get angry with. In the middle of my rant to God about Linda and how she just did not understand and was being a pain to me, I was drawn back to one of her statements: "I believe you are disgusted with the way you have tried to temporarily cover up the pain and provide temporary satisfaction for your thirst. I believe you see this as a sin and shame." She was right. I was more than disgusted. I was mortified and did not want to look at it at all with God or anyone else. When thoughts of how I did things came up, I would shove them away and go do something else. I wouldn't face the gruesome, haunting past that seemed to want to come out of the shadows. Linda O. was right. The relief those actions provided was only temporary, and the pain would come creeping in when I was unprepared.

I felt shame had control, and I was being swallowed up in its power. I had seen pictures on some sort of science channel of a tsunami (an earthquake at the bottom of the ocean floor) taking place and, seconds later, creating a tidal wave that moved to the shore. It flowed past the rows of beachfront properties and in the mainland. In one moment, the people on the mainland were at peace, enjoying life; and the next, they were involuntarily dragged into the ocean, crushed by cars and wood and consumed by the ocean water backing into the ravaging sea. At first, when the water was flowing rapidly down the main street, people started to run away. Then when they were consumed in the current, they swam with all their might away from the water in panic. Most would die in vain, and a few survived the waves' path, but I will remember forever the look of fear on their faces, which engulfed them as they swam for their lives.

I felt like shame was trying to drag me where I had no desire to go. I fought the current dragging me out to the sea. To regain control, I regularly bashed myself with vicious words of contempt. I guess I hoped my disgrace would disappear if I beat myself up enough. It was not great; it was wrong. Again, this only seemed to prolong the inevitable—making the decision whether to face what God was trying to show me or shove its crud down an area where I would not have to face it. Playing dead to all this mess and feeling no more emotional pain seemed like a good option and the easier path to choose. Unfortunately I had not played dead for so long, I found I was not really good at it. I had given so much over to God through the years He had become my foundation in so many instances. He was whom I ran to in times of trouble. Not being able to play dead was incredibly frustrating beyond words.

I went to class the following week. No one knew what I was working through; they only knew that I said I was struggling and did not want to discuss it. I avoided any communication and distractions by listening intently to others. Every now and then, Linda would ask a general question she wanted answered by everyone, but I was pretty good at distracting her. My goal: make it to the end of class each week till it was done. It was now an obligation to complete.

Again, I was very much out of practice playing dead to my emotions for such a long time that when needed, it took a lot of focus. I felt as though my body physically was failing me. Right before entering class each week, I would get incredibly anxious, and my stomach would start to feel nauseous. Many times during class, I had to step out to vomit. I kept asking God to help me just get through the darn class and to have it go by quickly. Funny how I wanted God's help physically not to vomit but not with the sin in my life. The class was two hours long, and by the second hour, my body would usually go into a mode of cramping, and then the diarrhea would set in. This only made me angrier over the situation and at myself. I knew my body was out of control, and no matter what I wanted, it was not going to cooperate.

One day I sat to do my reading for the class and realized the sick feeling starting to rise in my stomach. I thought, *No more! This is ridiculous.* I reminded God I was done with all the healing from my past. We had traveled down that road many times together, and He was to be praised for all I had been able to walk through. I was grateful truly, and this other area was something we just did not need to look at.

While talking to God, a calm did come to my stomach, which was incredibly wonderful. It was then I looked down and saw where I had scratched myself uncontrollably, and I had drawn a little blood. At first I felt shame and tried to hide what I just did. Immediately it reminded me of Adam and Eve. Once their sin was found out, they too hid from the One who wanted to do whatever it took to get them back in His arms again. God did not want to leave them in their sinful state. Instead, they hid from God, hoping He would not see what they had done.

In my shame, I refused to let my soul be touched by sorrow. I was angry, angry at myself, at God, and at my past. Couldn't God see these little tics like scratching were soothing to me? It just proved itself! My stomach did not ache anymore; it was in control. I obviously needed these habits to provide what God could not. I knew that thought sounded awful, but though it was bad, it was comfortably true.

There I sat with even more truth in front of me. I realized I did not trust God completely, even though I called Him Savior and Friend. The One I said I gave all my life to! Yet all this time, I had been living in a world of my own design when it came to relieving great pressure or stress. Yes, I was generalizing in big ways, but I wasn't going to judge myself fairly anyway. I closed my workbook in disgust.

That night I went to bed, but I could not sleep. My thoughts raced to the little moments along the way of life where I soothed my pain. So many acts that I considered part of my life, just like breathing, were now looking wrong. It started out with the pain from the abuse, but somehow it found its way into other areas of my life. It was a weed that had roots ensnarling themselves tightly by thin threads, and I never saw them wrapping themselves around me over and over again until I was now bound.

Lying there in bed, I continued to reflect. I could see the positivity of the coping skills of my bad habits over time less and less. As I got closer to God and opened up my life more to Him, more healing came. Because my relationship with God was closer, I had no need for soothing measures in my life. It was then I started to welcome the idea of turning away from this sin, which I had used for survival as a child but now had actually become a cruel enemy, and I had been walking with it for over forty years.

I started to talk to God about what He would replace my sin with. What would I do now? What would be my soother if I needed one? I figured I was here, and I was willing to finally listen, and I received no answer from God. Nothing. God's silence became deafening in the quiet of the night. If I was going to even consider giving up this way of life, I needed to know what would take its place. This seemed completely reasonable.

After some time the thought of just trusting Him and His providing for me came. I blew it off as the stupidest idea ever suggested. I became angry. Here I was, starting to be open about stopping this behavior, and "trust Him" is what I am supposed to do? I felt God just did not understand. If this was about control, then I was willing to give it up to God. But again, I needed to know the good options waiting in the wings to replace my old behaviors. In reality, I still wanted to be in control, and it seemed God knew it. He wanted me to trust Him and to be honest. My soul wanted to trust Him as well. However, I wrestled with the shame and embarrassment of the small-*g* god who had for years been there for me—myself.

30

Bad Decision

Hours of sleeplessness went by, and it was about 3:00 a.m. when I got up in complete hopelessness. I had verbally beaten myself up over the last sleepless hours, and a great pain from bad decisions haunted me. If only I could take it all back. My heart was heavy with great regret. Though the house was quiet, for everyone was asleep, the shouts of accusations, which all had a piece of truth in them, consumed my mind. I should have awakened John, and asked him for prayer. I knew I was in a spiritual battle, but I would not be able to explain to him what I was going through without revealing my shame.

My thoughts swam with how what I thought brought so much relief was now considered wrong. I felt betrayed. These actions in the past were comforting and soothing; in fact, they were inviting me back to them at that very moment. When I would say to myself, "I can't, it is wrong," contempt would stab back at me. I was reminded of how I thought I was walking in God's strength when, at times, it had been my own strength after all, and this left me even more hopeless.

In the end, I could see I was the betrayer. I was the betrayer of God and everything He represented. Crushed glass sounded more soothing than warm lotion placed upon my skin. The next thing I knew, I was in the dark, out of bed, at my office-desk area. By the moonlight, I could see my penholder, and that was when I reached for my X-ACTO knife and held it tightly. Just holding it gave me a sliver of relief. I walked calmly to the bathroom, consoling myself that I was only holding the blade and I was not going to actually use it.

Again, my soul cried out to seek God, but I knew He would not be in any part of this. As I sat there on the side of the bathtub trying to think clearly, I went down a long list of incredible family and friends I could call; but with each name, I shut the door. This temptation was too wicked to try to explain to any of them. None of them would understand, and I could not blame them. All I had was myself, the sinful person I knew I was—the me whom I called a Christian yet would not trust God to soothe my pain in order for me to function normally in the world.

My mind raced to when it all started. At five years of age—or was it back to when I was three years old?—escaping my grandfather's grasp was not enough to bring me peace. Though I got free from his grip, all trust was broken; and his once-loving hands, which used to rock me, and his lovely singing voice now only brought back horrible memories. In a swarm of thought, I remembered it was then that I found chewing the insides of my cheeks comforting. The habit hurt in the beginning, but like most things, within seconds, it felt much better than the pain and the fear of grandfather catching me. Chewing on the inside of my mouth took away the anxiety of having to be around him.

From there, my mind raced through the pain of the moments I never wanted to replay in my life. This was becoming too much. I stood up with the blade tightly in my hand. I knew I just needed to get rid of it and walk away.

I reminded myself that I was not a cutter. I never once took a knife or blade and purposefully cut myself for relief. My husband and I work a lot at the local skate park in ministry and have come across many who had cutting issues. I always wondered what brought a person to that state of mind, where they would willingly harm themselves. The answer pounded in my head—*pain*! The pain inside them was so great that it took a counteraction with some force on the outside to relieve it.

I consoled myself, knowing I was not like them. Immediately thoughts of how I had soothed myself over the years came flowing in. This was obviously Satan accusing me, and I was coming up guilty as charged. It was as if he had saved up for this moment all the stupid, irresponsible things I had done in my past, hurting myself on the outside to soothe my inner pain. There was no question in my mind I was guilty. My shame grew more intensely by the second.

A question formed in my mind, *What if you use the blade? What difference would it make? You have already failed miserably, and you need to get relief. It would put you back into being in control.* "My emotional pain had gone to the point where I felt I was suffocating.

Out of desperation, though I knew I was clearly doing wrong, I did the unthinkable and sinfully used the blade on the backside of my knee. I pulled it up across my skin in anger and complete frustration, not with myself but with God. He became the focus of my blame game. I did not immediately reach for something to wipe up the blood, for a release came to me, which soothed the ache in my heart. Oh, had I been waiting for this moment. This, of course, was sick thinking and should never be done by anyone. Yes, I did these actions. They were wrong, and I regret I did them.

This use of a blade was nothing like I did in my past. Besides, it was done in a more violent manner. I then reached for some toilet paper and applied pressure to stop the bleeding. A fearful thought raced through my mind: I had just opened a door that I should have never even considered walking through.

Fear gripped me. I immediately reached into my bathroom drawer and pulled out the superglue. Familiar with how to work a wound with good pressure, glue, patience, and more glue I had the perfect seal in no time. The chemical-burning, stinging sensation helped soothe the great fear climbing its way into my heart. This chemical sting also gave me the temporary peace to relax and not stress over what had just taken place. Sure, there was a part of me that felt like I failed again, but this time, only worse. However, the stinging of the glue was incredibly soothing and felt like an old friend. If I could only go on living with this type of relief all the time, how wonderful and easy life would be.

I was so relaxed I started to dose off, sitting there on the bathroom floor with my back against the wall. Moments before, I was tormented with terrible anxiety, and now I was to the point of dosing off to sleep? Sleep came. I must have been asleep for about twenty minutes. However, just like that, my head jerked forward, and all peace was gone. What I had done twenty minutes earlier replayed in my mind. I shook my head in disbelief. I wanted to get out of the bathroom. I quickly cleaned up and made sure there was no evidence left behind, telling myself over and over I could do this and that everything was under complete control. You would have thought I threw the blade away at least out of disgust; but the thought, as tiny as a sliver, that just in case I would need it again I should just keep it handy in the bathroom infected my being. I left the bathroom, content, knowing the blade was readily available anytime I needed it. I went back to bed and fell fast asleep.

The next day, I arose and felt great. I did check the back of my leg, and it was healing just fine. I went about my day and even did my homework for *The Wounded Heart* class without a care in the world, until I went to Renee's home. She and her husband were interning with us in the ministry. I was going over to help her answer some questions in her studies. As we talked, she asked if I was okay. I said I was fine and brushed her concern aside quickly. We finished the paperwork we were working on, and she again checked on how I was doing. I got busy pulling my things together off her coffee table and acted like I did not hear her question. She then asked how the class was going for me. I told her I was working on some stuff, even struggling with some issues, but overall I doing as well as could be expected. All those words were true, but they hardly spoke the real truth she was looking for.

The more we talked, the harder it was to hide. I started to feel anxious and stressed. A thought came to ask her to pray for me, but I shot that down immediately. There was no way I was going to explain to her the struggle I was going through. Here she was with her husband being our interns, and I was in an ugly mess of sin. I knew at that point that I was going to talk to John that night and let him know I wanted to step down from working with interns in our ministry work.

Renee interrupted my thoughts with her eyes all puddled up with real concern. She said she had been praying for me, and whatever my struggle was, God was bigger. Yeah, yeah, I had heard that before. I knew from experience God was bigger, but He also does not force Himself. I was not sorry for what I did in the bathroom. To be honest, Renee was now really getting irritating to me. I told her I needed to get home; I had things to do. She then started to accuse me of being involved with something that was not good for me. My defenses were at an all-time high, and she was now getting me angry. It was time to leave.

I told her good-bye, and then she blew me away by asking if I was taking drugs. I could not believe she was asking such a stupid question. I practically bit her head off for making such a ridiculous suggestion. I felt like I was sharing my life with the woman, being honest with her (Well, not telling her about the cutting or how I soothed myself, but that was none of her business. Heck I had only been made aware of it!), and now she crosses the line with our friendship. She then asked questions about me having bulimic or anorexic issues. Frustrated with her questioning, I told her no and took my things and walked toward the door. It was then she asked the question, "Annette, are you hurting yourself in some other way?" With all that was in me, I wanted to say no. I had to say no. If I did not say no, then the wave from the tsunami I had been trying to desperately swim away from would pull me away, and my world as I knew it would be destroyed.

I seriously took my responsibility of working with the interns God sent us. I felt that John and I were to always give them our best. Here I was, ready to save myself and my pride by lying and saying no. I was desperate. I opened my mouth to respond, and to my surprise, I answered yes. Shocked and ashamed, I could only look down and away from her. Relief swept over me, for only a split second, that I did not lie to her, but I knew now nothing would ever be the same.

She then asked softly and calmly how I was hurting myself. I thought as quickly as I could for an answer that would not sound too bad. She then began to press me with more questions, not giving my swimming mind a chance to think. Oh, I was so angry at myself for slipping up like this. Stupidly searching for more time, I asked her exactly what she meant. She then asked if I was involved with cutting. The word *cutting* brushed up against me with such force I did not want to answer. She waited and said nothing more.

I then said, "It depends on what exactly you mean by cutting." She looked at me, knowing I knew what she meant. I sat back down on the couch where she was sitting and started to explain how I might have—kinda of, sort of, might have—at times relieved stress by displacing it with pain. I was awfully pitiful on coming clean. I so desperately wanted to fight this moment. She looked at me, puzzled, but pressed for an explanation. I proceeded to tell her that at times it could be something as simply taking off a layer of skin so that the air burns it, slicing my skin with an object—nothing big, it was things like that. She still did not seem to understand and pressed for more. Now she was just making me angrier. I wanted to go home. I did not want this to be a point for any discussion. However, I knew I had to contain this fire before it got out of control. She looked extremely concerned, and I did not need her to make something big out of something that really was so small, almost a nothing.

I explained to her that on our bodies there are natural creases where you bend at the joints. I perhaps had sliced, sort of, only a temporary opening on my skin and then carefully used superglue to create a perfect seam. This way, no real scar would show, and no harm really took place. She sat there and stared at me in silence. It seemed as though she may have understood, but I was not sure. She then asked, "Annette, are you cutting yourself?" Darn, this girl could be so ruthless! I answered, "Yes, but only once, and it will never happen again."

I then explained quickly so she would not think I was a person who did this all the time. I was superstressed two nights before. I explained I did the stupidest thing I could have ever done, and I was sorry I did it. She asked if I had told John. All I could think of was, *Is this girl crazy?* She obviously did not seem to understand. I told her I would never do it again. It was a one-time stupid act. I was done with it.

She sat there with a stance that demanded I tell John, that this was serious. I got up to leave. I was done with her and her so-called concern. I left her apartment and started down the hall. She followed me and shouted from her door, "I will give you twenty-four hours, and if you have not told him, I will." I looked at this woman, who has never, in all the time I had known her, ever acted in this manner. Furiously I turned and walked back to her. I said in great anger, "This is what I get for trusting you!" I so desired to frighten her into backing off. I needed her to back off. I could not have people thinking I was a cutter! Though she pulled back physically from her doorway, she did not budge from her decision. She told me she would be calling me the following day. I walked away. I left, knowing I would have to tell John. How does one explain what I did? I knew he would not understand, for I myself could barely grasp it. No matter what, though, I had to tell him before Renee did, for she would definitely make it sound much more serious than it actually was.

That night, I went to bed with John, but of course, I could not sleep. I knew I had to tell him in a way he would understand and to make sure he comprehended that it really was no big deal. Obviously I did not want him to react like Renee. About 3:30 a.m., I woke up John, telling him we needed to talk. He, of course, was groggy from being awakened. I began with telling him I did something wrong, and I was sorry for it. He was not completely awake at the time and told me, "Honey, don't worry. I forgive you." Boy, did I want to leave our conversation at that! However, I still had to deal with the Renee factor.

I explained to my groggy husband what happened at Renee's apartment. Then I went on to explain what happened a couple of nights before in the bathroom. I did not have to wait long for his response. He then said, "What?" I explained again, but this time, I could tell he was finally starting to wake up, enough to understand what I was talking about.

He then immediately sat up in bed and flipped on the bedside lamp. Now he was definitely awake. He said, "Are you saying you cut yourself on purpose?" He was obviously upset, and he let me know it right away by the tone of his voice. His words were not what I expected at all, and I was not sure how to respond. John is a calm guy. He rarely gets upset, and only once in our marriage has he ever raised his voice. For over thirty years being married, I would say this a pretty good record, except for this moment. He told me, with great frustration in his tone, that he was not going to stick around and watch me kill myself.

What? What was this guy thinking? I jumped in and explained I had no intention of killing myself. He then shot back, "Where do you think you will eventually end up if you keep going in that direction?" I told him he did not understand, and he was making this out to be something more than what it was. He walked away and went into the bathroom.

The pain inside me flushed to the surface. John and I, in all our years of marriage, have never have spoken the word *divorce*. However, in his anger, the words that stung my heart were, "I will not stay with you." I was crushed and prayed for God to hurry up and help with this situation. I was honest about hurting myself, but I never meant to hurt anyone else. This was so stressful, and without even realizing it, I had already been digging into my skin. I stopped instantly when I realized it, but I had already done the damage. This situation was getting extremely out of hand, and I had no way of controlling it.

John was gone for less than five minutes. When he returned, he apologized for his words. He then told me I had scared him, and in his fear and frustration of feeling completely helpless, he said what he said. We held each other, and then he climbed back into bed.

John then began to start asking me questions. He wanted to understand what I did and why. He asked when I started doing this type of cutting, to which I shot back immediately, "I have not been cutting all this time! However, I had discovered over the past week that I have been doing other things since I was a little girl." I tried to explain to him that it was part of my life. It was normal, and it was like putting on your shoes or brushing your teeth. He could not understand. He then said, "But I have never seen any scars on you!" I told him sadly, "I know."

This confused him even more. I then tried to explain to him that cuts and scars can be questioned. People just naturally care and ask how you got hurt. The best way to avoid questions was not to scratch, slice, or hurt myself where others would see. I really did not want to go into the explanation of how I accomplished this. More than anything, I wanted out of this nightmare. I was ashamed of my mutilating/cutting actions. This was difficult for John to process, and he was quiet for a long time. My hope was that he would soon just fall asleep.

He then started to speak to me again. He said we needed to pray and ask God into this situation. I agreed. We started to pray, and then in what seemed like forever, John asked if I had repented. I told him I had not. I told him I wish I was sorry, but I was not. He sat up in bed with a face that looked completely lost. I told him I understood what real repentance was. I was not stupid, but I also knew I was not truly sorry for my actions. In fact, this was the struggle I had been fighting this past week with God. He said, "This is not like you. You love God. You are always seeking His ways." I agreed, but in this case, I told him I was just being honest.

I explained I wanted to stop "scratching." I honestly did not want it to be part of my life. However, giving it up would mean living life with nothing to relieve me from pain. I told him that the worst part for me was to see how I had been playing the small-*g* god in my life, and I hated myself for it. I admitted I was in a terrible cycle, and I was not sure how to break it. He asked if he could talk to his instructor from *The Wounded Heart* class, who was more of an expert in dealing with people with past abuse. I told him it was fine. I also told him he could speak with Eddie, Renee's husband, since this way, he would have someone close by to pray and confide in. The last thing I wanted was for anyone to find out, but I figured by now Renee would have told her husband.

A trust was broken that night between John and me, which I never saw coming in our marriage. Here was John feeling he knew his wife at least well enough to know if she was doing something like this. He was hurt, and I could see it in his eyes. His care for me and his desire to get past this moment in time drove him to stay committed and to walk through this with God giving us both the strength we needed.

The following day, my husband spoke with his teacher from *The Wounded Heart* class, John O., after which, my husband seemed to have a direction in which to go. John O. reassured John that most cutters are not suicidal, though most people assume they are that way. He encouraged my husband to support me during this time and advised us to get professional Christian help. He gave John some names and numbers in the area we lived in so he could call them right away.

Unfortunately it seemed like every person we tried to contact, for one reason or another, was not working out, and this created a lot of extra work for John. I was glad he was tied up in the mess of searching for a Christian counselor with the special experience of dealing with a person involved in cutting and sexual abuse. I love my husband to pieces, but he became a person who seemed to start hovering over me. It was like he did not want to leave me alone and was always wondering how I was doing or where I was. If I were he and things were in reverse, I would probably have reacted in the same manner. I understood what he was doing was out of love, but I felt as though he was smothering me.

Now, my intern Renee and her husband, Eddie, both new about what John and I were walking through. Linda and her husband, John O., were also in the know. This was good for John because he really needed others' support overcoming this dark valley in our marriage. We had a few friends to whom we wrote a generic e-mail, letting them know, without giving specifics, that we needed prayer as a couple. We were in the midst of no small spiritual battle, and we needed all the prayer we could get.

I think a week had gone by, and I was running an errand in town. I went to a store that had what I needed, but the only one left was on one of the highest shelves. This required a large ladder and store-personnel assistance. The employee got up on the ladder, went up, grabbed the box I needed, and handed it down to me. Immediately, when I grabbed the box, pain stabbed the palm of my hand. The employee had an open box knife in her hand, and when she handed me the box, it accidently went into my hand. The employee felt bad, but I told her I was fine. The cut was deep, and the skin was not going back together.

I left the store with my head spinning. No one was going to believe me that I did not cut my hand on purpose. A panic rose in my throat, and I was not sure what to do. I wanted to use superglue, for it would fix it ASAP! This was getting complicated. Stress rose within me, and then the thought of just enjoying the pain of the wound right now to relieve my stress came to me. Immediately I called out and said, "God!" My mind slowed, and I walked into our apartment. I told John what happened and thought if I wrapped the wound tight with Band-Aids, it should be fine. He asked me why; I told him about the incident. I told him I was trying to be accountable. John was wonderful, not at all what I expected; and bit by bit, trust started to build itself back up in our relationship.

Three days later, my hand now became infected, and there was an obvious gap where there should have been smooth skin. I asked God in prayer if it was okay to use the superglue. It was not like I got any kind of audible answer, but it was like I got an okay in my spirit to do it. I cleaned my hand the best I could and used the glue. It burned, but it glued well. By the sixth day, the infection was all gone, and now there was just a small scar.

Meanwhile, I went to my first counselor's visit, and though I was not looking forward to it, I knew it was going to make everyone else extremely happy. The woman asked why I was there, and I tried to explain. When I explained the situation to her, it was coming out the same way as when I tried to explain it to Renee—"I kinda do this type of thing, which is really nothing, and I kind of—rather, sort of—got a blade one night and cut myself, but it was really nothing. It was a mistake, and I am not going to do it again. I realized it was pretty stupid. However, my family and friends are concerned, and well, that is why I am here. Oh, and I would like to stop doing this kind of behavior, but I am not sure how."

The counselor filled the session time with much talk. I knew, after the first ten minutes, that I was never going to come back to this woman ever again. When she said the words, "This is not something that can just be stopped, and it will be a long process," I was done. My goal was to go to the counselor, she tells me how to stop the cycle of behavior, and I stop—done. I was warned by Linda that it would not be a quick fix, but I pushed her thoughts from my mind because I liked my plan much better. This was frustrating.

When I returned home from my counseling appointment, John could tell things did not go well. He, being his bright and cheery self, said there were many more counselors out there we could try. I was not interested in any more counselors. I hated that a few people already knew about the situation, and I was embarrassed. However, I tried another one, which turned out not to be a good fit as well.

It was then that God opened a door of opportunity, which seemed much less stressful and with at least someone I had known for the past six weeks. We agreed to try having me do sessions with Linda, the teacher from *The Wounded Heart* class. We would meet once a week, go over things, and also keep not only her but John, Eddie, and Renee as accountability partners. John O., Linda's husband, was also in the loop for advice and prayer. Tough request, but I felt it was something I could do. This was done with the agreement that if things got worse, I needed to look into the possibility of an inpatient therapy. The concern was because I had been involved in this mutilating behavior for over forty years, and they knew stopping it would be difficult. Going to an inpatient facility as my option kept me more than willing to put up with Linda O. and her prying questions. I knew brushing her off and not being honest would not be wise.

In the beginning, I had my good days and my bad ones. I replaced bad soothing actions with walks. This meant that at all hours of the night or day, you could find me walking off some sort of strife, stress, etc., and fight the urge to physically hurt myself. Though I had not been very active, maybe mutilating/cutting myself twice a year, things changed when I purposefully took that blade in the bathroom during those early morning hours and chose to sin. I opened up a door to allow temptation to hound me day and night.

One night, when I was walking outside, angry at myself for not being willing to repent and surrender to God, I came across Eddie, Renee's husband, in the parking lot. He asked how I was doing, and I told him I was fine and kept on walking. He then asked me to wait up, but I was in no mood and kept on going. Poor Eddie had to hustle to catch up. He tried to communicate that he and Renee had been praying for us and that it was all going to be okay. I turned around, so angry at this guy, and bit his head off with my unkind words. I told him I did not know if *it* was going to be "okay," and from there, our conversation started to go downhill. I kept walking while he followed beside me.

When we came to his family's car, he stopped and motioned for me to stop. I thought, *Here it comes. He is going to say some sort of line that is supposed to make me feel better about the whole mess.* True to my thoughts, he said something to the effect of everyone has trials and valleys to go through. That was it—I had had enough! I was not going to hang around for his next line of lame wisdom! I told him, "Sure, they do have trials, but you don't, do you! You are always Mr. Kickback, Mr. Happy, when you walk in the door. However, it is not real. You hide and never tell people how you're really doing. You smile all the time, but do you struggle? No one would think you do! You hurt. You hurt just like the rest of us but say nothing. I hate that you don't share what is really going on inside you yet expect others to open up to you!"

We both stood there in silence for quite a bit. I immediately was sorry for acting so cruel toward such a good friend, yet I did not apologize. I was still seething with anger, and it was not going to be quenched easily. I had never spoken to Eddie in this manner, and obviously I had caught him off guard because he just stood there. I was so frustrated, knowing I was wrong but so incredibly angry. I walked away. I knew I was going to have to ask Eddie for forgiveness. I was not really angry with him; I was angry with myself. I walked away from him in order not to be any more hurtful than I had already been.

When I came around the building, continuing my walk to get rid of all the anxiety and anger flowing through me, there stood Eddie just where I had left him. To my complete surprise, Eddie, in a soft voice, asked me to wait. I could tell he was speaking from his heart, and his countenance changed.

As I stood before him, he started to tell me about a time in his life when he had a problem with sin. I had never heard him speak to me like this before, and it was what my soul was longing for. He revealed the ugliness he struggled with long ago. He then told me when he realized he needed help to get out of the sin he was in. He explained that he and some men met together. Each one stood over him, and they prayed as Eddie confessed his sin. He let those men in his life so they could keep him lifted in prayer and be a good accountability for him. Eddie said that from that moment on, he no longer struggled with the sin in his life. This sounded awesome; I wanted that! I said nothing, but inside, I started to soften.

He then turned to me and told me his wife, Renee, and John, could just gather together and do the same thing. We could gather, I could confess, and they would pray for me. I truly felt love from this man, who had every right to yell right back into my face after I had been so cruel to him, yet he did not. I told him I appreciated his offer, but I was not sorry, and I was not ready for any repentance. The hollowness from the lack of hope that hung in the air between us was heavy. I wanted what Eddie spoke of, *freedom* from sin. However, I knew the price was to give up in a one-shot, all-or-nothing deal this sin I was so entrenched in.

We finished our walk back to our homes in silence. The hopelessness of the situation seemed to engulf me even more. Eddie said, "Turn to God, Annette." I knew from experience I could turn to God, but just not in this one area. It was like

I had a loss in my life. It grieved me. I did not allow God in a space where I needed Him so badly, and I ached for Him. Worse, I knew I was the one who was keeping Him and His love out. For the first time, I cried. I cried hard. I fully mourned for the love of God in my life. This sin issue was painfully separating me from Him.

The next day, I could see things in my home were not going well. Not being able to use the crutches of my soothers, no matter how small or insignificant they were, put me on edge, which of course only made me want them more. I was thirsty. I was getting to the point of being willing to drink out of a rotten, disgustingly dirty cup, and I knew better. I did not want to hurt the people in my life, but it was obvious I did. I could not promise perfection, and this was what I felt they would expect if I were to repent.

Two days went by, and the more I thought about Eddie's offer with his wife and John, praying together and my repenting, the more it started to sound like a real option. I was desperate. I knew something had to give, or I was going to give in and mutilate/cut myself soon. I was mentally exhausted. Physically, it was hard to eat or sleep, and all I could think about was the darn blade in my bathroom drawer.

I asked God for help to walk across the street where the clean cups were available. I wanted what was right, but I knew I needed help. I was not going to be able to do this on my own. This baby step of talking to God about the sin in my life took a big edge off my stress level. I talked to God about repenting and how I did not want to go back to my old ways of dealing with life. I told Him I was not sorry, though I wish He would give me what I needed now before I gave up my old ways. I then walked into my bathroom, took the blade I had carefully hidden, and walked it all the way to the Dumpster outside where it would not be an option any longer. I went to John and asked him if he would contact Eddie and Renee to see if we could meet, and he made arrangements for the same evening.

When Eddie and Renee showed up for that evening, we went to my husband's office and sat around the large business table. John sat across from me, Eddie beside me, and Renee on the end nearest Eddie. At first it was uncomfortable even to look at one another. Though we were good friends—I think everyone was just trying to be sensitive—I made it clear that I had a bad experience with a group of people praying over me when I was younger. Not that I did not trust everyone in the room, but because of the subject matter and because I needed to maintain some sort of control, I felt everything could be accomplished with all of us just remaining in our seats. No one seemed to have a problem with it, which was great.

I think I said something to the effect of, "Let's do it." John started off praying. Renee prayed a bit, and from that moment on, Eddie led the way with the guidance of the Holy Spirit. It was an open conversation with God and all of us in the room. I believe Eddie asked me what I was repenting of. I started to do the *kinda* and *sort of* in my mind but knew

God saw through all that, and so did all the others in the room. I then stopped and went with the sin that I clearly knew was in my heart. I went with the sin of using a blade to cut myself to relieve the stressful pressures in my life. I apologized for playing a small-*g* god and not going straight to God first. I then confessed to the scratching and the other things that came to mind. I did the best I could, for I had been mutilating/cutting my body for over forty years.

After I was done, the room became sweetly silent. No one spoke, though I knew they were all silently praying. As for myself, I was enjoying the first few moments of finally letting go of something I had held so tightly for protection and comfort and giving it over to God, letting Him be my ultimate protection and comfort in times of need. My soul felt as though it was finally in a restful place. No, I did not know how I was going to live life victoriously without ever mutilating or cutting myself again. It is hard to explain in words, but I knew I could not trust myself; and in the end, God was the only trustworthy, faithful, reliable source in my life.

After a brief period of time, Eddie asked a question about pain and how I handled physical pain in my life. This seemed like such an odd question. I answered that I displaced it as far as I knew, as well as with most emotional pains. He said he just remembered a conversation he had with many of the men in our group at a barbecue a while back. Eddie said they were talking about childbirth and how their wives were during the process. They all were looking forward to hearing John share his story, for they figured it would be pretty funny. However, Eddie told us John's story was the most boring. John said I was quiet during the birthing process, mostly did the breathing exercises without saying a word, and stared off into space. None of the guys believed it, for I can be a very animated person to get my point across, but John stuck with his story. He said he could tell the first three children were easier than the last two. Yet I still just did the breathing and stared off into space. When Eddie finished telling us what happened at the barbeque, he said, "Annette, it just does not seem right. You should have been in excruciating pain. Childbirth is painful. No one gets out of it unless they are under medication." Eddie asked, "How could it be that you lay there quietly?"

It took a moment to think back on the situation. It had been so long ago. However, as I thought about it, especially when Eddie brought up the part of how the pain level was more uncomfortable when I had the last two children, things started to make so much sense to me. I told Eddie that the closer I got to God over the years, the less I used my own methods to block out pain. This was probably why I felt more pain during the childbirth with my last two.

Eddie asked how I blocked out the pain. I told him I would go to a place where there was no pain. This confused him, and he pressed for a better explanation. I told him that when I was in intense pain—whether from childbirth, migraine, or emotional stress—I would to go sheets or beaches.

John sat there with a surprised look on his face, for this information was new to him. I looked at him and said, "It is not a secret. I never mentioned the places because they were not something I really even thought of as out of the ordinary since they had always been part of my life." The others all looked at one another as if they were hearing something strange. For me, everyone had a place they went to so they could escape the pain of life when needed. My places were just so different from theirs.

The room fell silent, and I waited to see if we were done. Eddie then stated he did not think sheets or beaches were from God. I immediately got defensive because I felt he was going to ask me to give them up. These two places were part of my life. They were my safe harbor when life turned upside down; they actually prevented me from mutilating/cutting myself more than I did. These were good places. All this was rapidly going through my mind when, all of a sudden, I heard Eddie say, in a very soft voice, to stop and ask God quietly if I should be closing the door to these avenues of relieving the emotional and physical pain in my life.

The room now fell silent, and in my spirit, I asked God if there really was a problem with going to those places. Immediately I opened my eyes, and I knew the answer was yes. I grieved for a moment. I really enjoyed going to those places. I had such great memories of being there. I was not completely against the idea of giving them up if they were not what God wanted in my life. It just seemed like those in the room had no idea what I was saying good-bye to. These places were mine. They were safe, and they kept me from feeling any pain. John, Eddie, and Renee never had the pure pleasure of leaving reality and going to one of these places. To walk away and shut the door to them as an option of not feeling life's pain was tough.

I decided I needed to be sure. I told Eddie, "Just a minute." I again checked with God before speaking my answer out loud to Eddie. Thankfully everyone remained silent, heads down and praying quietly, as I figured out with God what my next move would be. It was then, speaking to God, that I felt for just an instant being in the place called beaches; and in that moment, it was wonderful. I instantly felt the warm California sunshine on my skin and smelled the salty air, and then with my next breath, it all changed. It went from day to night. It was extremely cold, and I knew then that God was not there. I could tell I was still at the beach. I could hear the waves pounding on the surf. It was pitch-black, and I could not tell in what direction to move. I knew it was over. I was never to choose to go back there again. I got the message loud and clear. I opened my eyes and immediately told Eddie I was ready to close the door to beaches and sheets.

Eddie helped me put into words what I needed to confess, and then Renee finished off by praying, and then we were done. No lightning from heaven struck down, nor did some superobvious sign that anything had changed. However, the spiritual sense that everything had changed vibrated through my soul. So much so that I knew it would take days, maybe weeks, before I could take it all in.

We all hugged, and I told everyone good-night. I was tired. It had been a rough few days. I felt a real sense of relief. Relief from knowing I finally did the right thing. I knew I could not be perfect, but in the spiritual sense, things were right. I knew God understood my habits better than I, and this was a journey we would have to do together like all the others we had walked through before. At least now I was back in full communication with God, and this, more than anything, brought me such wholeness. My focus was to seek God for insight before doing what I would now refer to as soothers. This is so I could make a conscious choice to seek Him for strength and walk away from any temptation that might come my way. God was going to have to be enough. It seemed risky, but I knew I just had to walk away from that old lifestyle. It was not an option any longer. It was not right. It was sin. I was no longer blind to it.

31

Accountability

In the early days that followed, I was able to start seeing how I lived life with a bit more clarity. Though I saw myself in the midst of a dark valley with no light from either direction, I somehow knew which way to keep on walking. When moments of confusion set in, I would stop, call on God, and follow His voice about which direction to go. I think the greatest realization was that though I desired greatly to leave the valley and wished for God to hurry this part of my life's journey along, I knew He was with me. I was discovering that it did not matter how long or what type of confusion tried to trip me up; I was not going back to where I had come. I knew my decision not to go back to mutilating/cutting was final.

Temptations came, and at times, they made me long for my old little-*g* god of relief. But the door had been shut, and I knew I could never let it become an option again. No longer was I going to be bound by the chains of mutilation/cutting, which had once been a part of my life.

I finally accepted that this process of healing from my past was not and will never be a one-shot deal. Though I had experienced incredible moments of healing, and I am forever grateful for them, I could see God taking me through many smaller and larger journeys. In those moments, I have found the need to recognize and then make the wisest choices. God leaves it up to me.

It is the same for everyone in life, not just those who have been sexually abused. We all react to things based on our past experiences, good and bad. Some things might be so tiny we think nothing of them, and others are so obvious to other people. We might have just been so used to things in our life—like I was with the mutilation/cutting and going off to sheets and beaches—that we become blind and see it as a normal way of life. With an open attitude and willingness to receive all that God desires for me to work in my life, I become a more usable vessel to Him and for the kingdom.

John (NIV) 6:28–29 reads, "Then they asked him, 'What must we do to do the works of God requires?' Jesus answered, 'The work of God is this; to believe in the one He has sent.'" These people who came to Jesus wanted to justify themselves for God's favor. I can understand that, for them, it is a form of control. One thing I had to be careful about when I decided not to return to my old habits was not to let my actions become small-*g* gods again and let myself think I was gaining favor with God. There is a saying that goes, "There is no right way to do the wrong thing." I had to be careful not to let control, overruling right behavior, be my righteousness. My good behavior or righteousness is, as the Bible states in Isaiah (NIV), 64:6, as filthy as rags. It is in Christ and only through Him that I find favor with God, as with all of us.

There is a great story in the Bible in the book of Philippians (NIV), chapter 3 verses 4 to 9, where a man named Paul talks about himself. It reads,

> If someone else thinks they have reasons to put confidence in the flesh, I have more: circumcised on the eighth day, of the people of Israel, of the tribe of Benjamin, a Hebrew of Hebrews; in regard to the law, a Pharisee; as for zeal persecuting the church; as for righteousness based on the law, faultless. But what were gains to me I now consider loss for the sake of Christ. What is more, I consider everything a loss because of the surpassing worth of knowing Christ Jesus my Lord, for whose sake I have lost all things. I consider them garbage, that I may gain Christ and be found in him, not having a righteousness of my own that comes from the law, but that which is through faith in Christ the righteousness that comes from God on the basis of faith.

Paul was spelling out clearly how he was the crème de la crème, the top dog, in his life. He had the résumé everyone would desire. He had the ranking, and there was no question he had the passion to carry out good works. This was how he was going to get into heaven/get good with God. It was all about the right performance and doing all the right moves. It was about what he could do. Yet, as you read the verse above, you can see that when his blinded eyes were opened, he counted all his good works as garbage. His right as a Jewish elite was nothing to him any longer.

In turn, I had to be extremely careful of trying to please God with all my righteous acts and not controlling my world; for when I would do this, I would be like a dog chasing his own tail and getting absolutely nowhere fast. I like that Paul could never be "good enough." My righteousness comes from God alone and no place else. We are to give ourselves over continually to Him and do as He commands; and through this, we will find contentment, peace, joy, and the incredible, engulfing love of God.

The first day after saying no more to my destructive habits was hard. Going through the following days, though a new freedom existed, was like building legs with muscles that had never been used. The second week was tough but not impossible. By the third month, I felt I was now on my way out of the dark valley. I still could not see beyond the turns on the road, but again, I knew what road to stay on. The muscles in my legs developed daily as they were used, and some days I got rest as I felt no resistance. This gave the muscles in my legs time to relax and regenerate. My confidence was growing. My relationship with God was thriving and maturing in a whole new area.

Temptations

In those early days, the stupidest things that never caused me trouble now became temptations. I can remember going to the kitchen to work on dinner and pulling out some fresh chicken out of the fridge. I then pulled open the knife drawer to cut the meat. A rush of thoughts bombarded me like never before. This was so new to me and very unexpected. These thoughts caused my stress level to rise quickly. At first, it was too hard to slow down my mind, and so I just said, "Jesus." My mind cleared. I continued to prepare the family's dinner. As I did, little thoughts came to me, questioning where the stress came from. I never before had any problems in all these years with the knife drawer. What made today different? Immediately the thought came to me, *What would it feel like to cut yourself with one of your kitchen knives?* It was a horrific thought, and I pushed it away.

Later that evening, I spoke to John and told him I would continue to make dinner but would appreciate if he could come be with me in the kitchen when I made it. Maybe just sit at the kitchen table and talk, read a book, or be on his laptop. I knew I was still at the point of not trusting myself. Asking for help like this was embarrassing, and I hated it. Yet I knew this was what God wanted me to do. I needed some sort of accountability till I was able to do this without it being a temptation.

John was glad I came to him. He told me he thought Eddie, Renee, and of course, Linda, who was still counseling me, should know of these moments as well. I knew he was right, though I was not thrilled to share this with them. I did not want them knowing the evil thoughts going through my head! Yet, somehow, just by sharing this information with John it softened the voices of temptation which were shouting in my head and made it easier for John and I to go to God. The secret thoughts were now crushed. Knowing all I had to do to crush the sinful thoughts away was call on the name of Jesus was also powerful for me, as well as reminding myself that God has promised never to leave or forsake me.

Two weeks later, I did not need anyone with me in the kitchen. Did any of those horrid thoughts of using the kitchen knives come back? Yes, they did. However, my response was much stronger now, and in the name of Jesus, my answer was a solid no. It may sound silly to some, but I knew that in the name of Jesus, there is power. I knew I needed not just to call on it but trust and believe in it. Slowly, over time, when I reached for a knife in the kitchen, I was tempted less and less, and I enjoyed my freedom in Christ more.

Silly things during this time, like being cut by a sharp can after opening it, would instantly fill me with guilt, whereas if this just happened by accident, there would no guilt. However, now accusations of my past behavior filled my mind. The accusations were true, but it was also true that I did not behave in that manner any longer. The other truth was when I did accidently cut myself on something, I felt pain. It was not like I lived life free from pain, but for the first time in my life, I did not displace the pain or deaden it. I actually stayed in the moment and felt it. In these moments, keeping my accountability partners aware and being open and honest with what was going on inside me helped me continue to crush what the enemy was trying to do, which of course was to lure me back into my old habits.

Other things, just like sitting back and watching a TV show, could be a trigger point for me. I remember watching the news, and they reported the police were looking for a rapist. It was when I was only about a month free from hurting myself, and a thought came to me about leaving the room, but I ignored it. It was then I realized I was chewing the side of my finger, but though I knew it was wrong, I struggled to stop. It was not like I was hurting myself, but in the next instant, I could taste blood in my mouth. Immediately I got up and was mad that this even took place. I was just nervously putting my finger in my mouth. This was so small! I knew I should have, at the first moment, gotten up and left the room, but it was too late. I went to God and apologized. Here He was trying to help me by making me aware that I should get up and leave the room, but I did not pay attention. What I was discovering was that some of my triggers could just be something as simple as watching something on TV. I made sure afterward to speak to John about what happened, not only for accountability but for him to know why I might just excuse myself during a TV show or conversation.

My hope was in the future. I would react to the promptings God gave me and get up and leave or stop doing certain actions before they went too far. That, over time, would become second nature. I prayed that my sensitivity toward the subject of sexual abuse/mutilation/cutting would be less and less. Thankfully, today I can say God has granted my request.

I am asked often when I share my story if I ever feel like cutting or hurting myself physically again. My answer is, "Heck no! It hurts too much." Since stopping the sinful behavior, I have encountered pain without using any of the methods of escape from my past. I think my first year was the hardest, but God helped me to remain faithful. It makes no sense to put myself in that position again. I see it as sick and horrid, something I will no longer do in my life. The second most-asked question is, "Am I ever tempted?" My answer is, "Very rarely these days, but I have learned that temptation comes to everyone, and I have no need to feel guilty just because I have been tempted." First Corinthians (NIV), 10:13 states, "No temptation has overtaken you except what is common to mankind. And God is faithful; he will not let you be tempted beyond what you can bear. But when you are tempted, he will also provide a way out so that you can endure it."

Sharing with Others

Only three months after I had walked away from the sins of mutilating/cutting myself, as well as using beaches and sheets as a way to play dead, I came upon a person who was hurting from a broken relationship. I shared how Christ had healed my broken heart and how much God loved her. Though she was extremely interested, she had a very guarded heart and wanted to take time reading the Bible on her own. After about a month, she accepted Christ as her Savior; but inside, I knew there was something more going on. It was then that God revealed to me she was involved in the same sin of physically hurting herself and was living in a life of bondage.

The next time I met up with her, I started our conversation with some questions about sin. I then moved on to telling her that I knew her secret, her secret of privately hurting herself, thinking no one in the world would know. I explained that God knew, and with Him, there are no secrets. I told her God loved her so much and wanted to set her free from the bondage she did not even realize she was trapped in. She then denied she harmed herself. Now I felt stupid bringing it up, but it was as if I immediately knew it was on her stomach. When I told her where she mutilated herself, she looked away.

She then sat before me, giving me all the reasons, including how she was not hurting anyone else and how she had it under control. Though she abused her body differently than I did, it was like hearing my old self giving reasons why I did wrong. It was like looking into an ugly mirror of my past, and I did not like what I saw.

In our conversation, I pointed out that she was a Christian now and that her body was not her own. I read her the scripture in 1 Corinthians (NIV), 6:19–20:

> Do you not know that your body is a temple of the
> Holy Spirit, who is in you, whom you have received
> from God? You are not your own; you were bought at
> a price. Therefore honor God with your body.

She heard me but was not ready to give up what had helped her keep her world in control since she was a little girl. She too started at a young age because of being sexually abused. Our conversation ended, and she promised she would talk to God about her actions.

I spoke to Renee, who was still interning with us at the time, and asked if she would please take over counseling this woman, for it was only three months since I came away from the same sin. I felt I knew nothing and did not want to mess things up. Renee tried to build a relationship with this young woman, but things were just not clicking. I spoke to John about feeling that I wasn't the right person to be working with the young woman. He agreed but was not sure who we could find to do it. We finally settled with me working with the young woman and keeping accountability with John and Renee. I also agreed to step away from counseling her if things became too much.

My biggest frustration with the young woman was her blindness to how wrong hurting herself was. Though I could understand her blindness, I just did not know how to get her to open her eyes to it. Her ways of protecting and soothing herself were wrong, but again, she felt it only affected her and no one else.

One day, I got frustrated with her attitude and told her she was wrong, that hurting herself affected more than just herself. It was reflected on many other areas of her life. I pointed to ways it invaded her marriage, friendships, etc. I told her I knew the ugliness of it all because I had just recently come out of it. She looked at me shocked and thought I must be lying. She told me I could not have been cutting, for I had known Jesus for so many years. I was a Christian, a pastor, and someone who loved everyone. I explained to her that you can be a Christian and still be involved in sin.

We both sat there in silence for a couple of minutes. I could tell she was confused. She shook her head no as though she was not going to accept what I told her. I then knew I had to do the unthinkable, something that, even in the last three months, I had not done for anyone since I confessed my sin. No one ever asked, not even John, Eddie, or Renee, and I did not offer! However, right here with this young lady, I knew God wanted me to reach out and not hold anything back. So I started to show her a few scars, and in that moment, I could see this young woman hurt for me. She started to cry. I asked why she was crying. She said, "I can't imagine why you would do something like that to yourself. I love you so much, and your hurting yourself is horrible."

I talked to her about how much God loved her as well and how He hurt for both of us as we mutilated our bodies, how He has always wanted to take care of our pain; but because we had kept it tightly in our own hands, choosing to relieve it in our own way, He could do nothing. He will not force His love or His will on people. I explained we were not created to carry such heavy loads emotionally, and God is there to comfort us in our pain, burdens, and sorrows if we will only turn to Him and not our own devices.

She then asked why I would do such harm to myself. I shared with her about my abuse and how I felt it only affected me, which in reality, was a lie. It affected the relationships I had with other people, including my own children. The insecurities from such horrid betrayal from those I trusted left me at arm's length with those I loved and adored so I would not get hurt again. The harsh, judgmental attitude I showed not just toward myself but toward others at times was a way of protecting myself and controlling my world.

I went on to explain that though I have grown in maturity in Christ over the years and have become less controlling, there were things that were viewable to my children. I told her I pray they are able to make better decisions than I have in my past and realize that I am far from a perfect example.

We began to take steps in walking through the tough issues of the sexual abuse from her past. Her stress level would rise, which was normal; but at times it became too high that it became her practice to leave for a few minutes and then return calmer. In those moments, I told her we were done for the day. I was not going to be part of her hurting herself in the bathroom to displace her stress and then come out calm. This, of course, angered her, which I could completely understood, but I was not going to budge on this issue.

When we were back at it again a few days later, she lasted for a little while, and then I saw her stress level rising. I suggested we stop and pray, but when we did, it was obvious she was not focusing. Her mind was elsewhere. She committed to not walking away, but her body started to fight her in other ways. Since she avoided hurting herself, her body turned on her and became ill. She would become sick to her stomach, and/or a horrible headache would come on. It was obvious we were dealing with a spiritual battle with tons of emotions crashing in at the same time.

Thankfully God opened my eyes to the little signs on her face or the mannerisms she showed as she started to feel stressed. I would be able to direct questions better in other areas till she felt more comfortable and then walk more toward the sensitive areas bit by bit. After three months of working with her, we went over the scripture 1 Corinthians 16:19–20 once more, and she finally got it!

There she sat, actually grieving that what she had been doing was wrong. However, her biggest dilemma was that she had no idea how she was going to stop her sinful behavior. She sat there in front of me in tears, confessing her sin out loud and asking God to forgive her. She admitted it was wrong, she felt completely hopeless about the whole situation.

I told her that was the best place to begin: admitting she could do nothing. This was going to have to be a God thing. I explained to her how repentance was a huge key. We prayed, and she sought God for the strength she needed not to go back cutting herself.

Each day of her not hurting herself was a victory. Like me, she had some setbacks when she did not even realize she was doing something; but when she did realize it, she stopped and sought God. She kept being honest with herself and God and kept accountability with others. I was so proud of her and thrilled to see God working in her life.

On tough days, her desire to go back to deadening her pain would be a great temptation. I helped her walk through the process of seeing her past actions as an unwise choice. For those who have been abused, it seems they lose themselves, and in turn, a part of them seems to die. Internally this seems to affect many parts of their life; the most important is "being in the moment." Staying in those moments, even if they are painful, living them without avoidance and discovering God through them, helps in making possible better choices in the future instead of playing dead to them.

A few weeks later in church, this same woman, when they asked for prayer requests and praises from the pulpit, spoke up. Softly at first, she spoke of how she used to hate herself. She did not go into details and kept it simple. She spoke of how she used to hurt herself in order to find relief. She mentioned the Bible verse in 1 Corinthians and how once she was a slave to this sin of cutting. But now she lives in a new freedom, one she never knew could exist. I was incredibly happy for her, as was everyone else in the room; for no one—except John, Eddie, Renee, and I—knew what she had been working through.

Though this was a moment I should be celebrating with great joy with the others in the church, my heart felt heavy. It was heavy with the knowledge that here was this brand-new Christian of three months willing to share her sin—which of course she was embarrassed with—unashamed to tell others what Christ had done for her. She was exceedingly happy and full of joy, and it was written all over her face, coming out like a song in her voice when she spoke of how good God was to her.

As for me, not even my immediate family except for John knew of my struggle over the past six months! This was a tough reality. I wish I could have done what she did, but shame kept me tied to the shadows of my old sin. Though I had confessed to a few others and was being accountable as well, it was still very much a secret.

I had several reasons for being quiet: One, I did not want my kids to worry and be burdened. Two, I felt I needed some time to understand and really comprehend what I was walking through with God before discussing this out in the open with others. Three, I was still very much embarrassed with being involved in mutilation/cutting, and I did not want anyone to know. I figured one day maybe I could speak to my family about it, but not now. Little did I realize that those three reasons were all linked to me still having to be in control.

One Sunday, I was given Matthew (NIV), 9:1–8 to preach on. I had just recently been healed of some growths that had developed in my vocal chords, and the verse I was to preach was about some men who brought Jesus a paraplegic to heal. As I studied the verse, I noticed in verse 2 —"Take heart son; your sins are forgiven"—Jesus proceeded to heal the man and told him to pick up his mat and go home, which he did. The part that stuck out in my mind was not the paraplegic being healed, but more than that, the man's sins were forgiven. Somehow I could relate. Though I was extremely grateful for God healing my vocal chords a few days beforehand, I was much more grateful for what God had healed in my soul from the mutilating/cutting situation months prior. I could have lived my life without a voice. Yes, it would have had its challenges. To live life as a person chained to the mutilation/cutting sin would have been extremely difficult.

It was on this Sunday, while sharing the message of the healing and reading Matthew 9, I shared with my family members about the heavy weight sin can be in one's life, how a person can become crippled by its ensnarling effects, and how only God can bring total and complete healing to the heart. I explained that the man in Matthew 9 could have gone on living as a paraplegic, but not as a free man from his sins, unless set free by Christ. The forgiveness of his sins was actually the greater healing.

I then slowly, and with not much confidence, shared what God wanted me to share. I told my present family members about the sin of hurting myself. At first it did not seem they comprehended what I was speaking about, for they had never seen me do any actions against myself. Then one family member said, "Well, at least you were not doing what some of the skaters do, as in actually cutting their skin." I wanted to disappear right there. I did not want to respond. Keeping my addiction a secret was so much easier than revealing its ugly truth. I quickly spoke up before I could chicken out, "Yes, I did."

John quickly confirmed that I did do this against myself, but he made it clear that I had repented and was set free. I sat there and fought the squirming sensation inside me that wanted to soften what John just said and, if possible, take it all back. However, it was out in the open now. It was the truth. My past sin was no longer private, and the shame that had held me captive was somehow released. It was good and healing to have the love and support of my family members. Though I did not sit and go into the details of the ways I used to hurt myself, it was the start of not hiding anymore, and at least my family knew I was open to talk about it with them.

Not hiding when I was exposed was extremely tough, but in the end, it helped kill the shame off so much quicker than keeping it a secret. The more I exposed the small-*g* gods I created, the more they became powerless over my life.

My freedom grew past my old shame in praise for what God was doing in my life. He pulled me from a tangled mess no one could free me from, not even myself. It took consistently being humble, trusting God in an area I had never trusted Him before, and then thanking Him for what He was going to do. Do I ever feel shame? You bet! However, it drives me to God, who guides me through the truth of the situation; and eventually we end up at the cross and what Christ did for me, and my shame is gone.

Accountability

It was about the six-month point after the incredible night where I said no to the sin of mutilating/cutting and giving it over to God that John and I received a visit from Greg Getz. He was the one, after my husband graduated and received his pastoral license, who encouraged me to go back to school and do the same. He and his wife, Sara, have been close friends and incredible prayer warriors for us personally and ministry-wise.

During the time I was walking through the process of facing my addiction, they were one of the couples we wrote to, asking them to join us in prayer. It was right at the beginning, and I had not really faced the sin issue in my life fully. I let them know John and I were going through a very challenging point in our marriage, and we would appreciate prayer. I made it clear in my request that I was not going to explain the situation by e-mail. However, I did say we would explain more in person when we saw Greg in six months.

By the time of Greg's visit, I had made it six months without mutilating/cutting. I requested time for us to be able to talk. Greg is not only our great friend but the person we regularly contact for the denomination in which my husband and I are licensed pastors. Because of this, I felt I needed time to share with him about the mutilating/cutting I had done in the past. I knew it was time to be open, honest, and also, turn in my pastoral license. It was tough, for I felt I worked so hard to receive it and that God was using it in our ministry, but I knew I also wanted to honor such a responsible role and did not want to shame it or the denomination by my actions.

As Greg and I sat, he listened intently as I gave a short outline of the abuse I went through when I was younger. I then brought him up to speed to the point where I was six months before he arrived here, telling him about the mutilation/cutting. I explained I honestly had become blind to the acts that I did to soothe myself, but when God brought them to my attention, they became a tough mountain to scale. As I was speaking, everything inside me felt he would just not understand. I still did not understand it all, but I knew I still had tons of trash and gunk to clean out, my *stinking thinking*.

Greg was the first person I told beyond my kids and the two couples who already knew. I hated every word that was coming out of my mouth and wished I was speaking about someone else. I then explained how, in the beginning, I did not want to repent because I had so many mixed-up feelings of not being sorry and being completely sorrowful for letting it develop as it had. I told him about my lowest point of actually taking the X-ACTO knife and cutting myself in the early-morning hours, how the trust between John and me was broken, how I now had accountability persons in my life and that John and I counseled still with John and Linda.

I shared about the incredible night of saying no to it all and walking away victorious. Lastly, I shared the great shame that though I was thrilled to be set free from the wickedness of the sin that held me by heavy chains, I realized I had been having this behavior as a pastor. If I would have seen those chains and sin clearly, I never would have gone to school to be licensed. I told him I was extremely sorry, and I was ready to turn in my pastoral license.

Greg sat there quietly for what seemed like an eternity, yet it was probably more like three minutes. He then asked me questions about those whom I was accountable to, how it worked, and I explained it the best I could by giving several examples. The silence resumed. He then finally said, "So it has been six months since you have cut or mutilated yourself?" Ouch! Those words stung. To have myself associated with those words still were sharp to my soul. Though I knew they were truth, swallowing the words when said by another sure was hard. I responded with a heavy, "Yes, it has been six months since I cut myself." The weight of that statement should have been a joyful-hallelujah victory statement, but instead it was filled with the weight of much regret and shame. I looked away and waited in silence.

Greg finally spoke, "I don't believe you need to turn in your license. You found yourself in sin, and you repented and turned away from it. Obviously it had been a habit for almost all your life and not something that had just come up. However, though you may be frustrated with yourself, in the end, you were obedient to God. I believe you will continue to walk victoriously. It seems you have an incredible accountability team and the Holy Spirit, which nudges you not to let things rest, including yourself, in sin. It has only been six months. Keep being accountable and keep me up to date on how things are going in this arena. I see no reason for taking away your pastoral license at this time because I see God doing great things with you, and you are not abusing yourself any longer."

Whoa, I was not expecting this kind of response at all. I was incredibly taken aback for the grace Greg offered that day. It was if he were saying he trusted me even though I blew it so badly. This bolstered my confidence in the work God was pouring into me. Shame and regret had to flee for the new strength and confidence that I was on the right road. I made sure to ask Greg, when he returned home, to explain all this to his wife and to thank her for praying for our family during this season. In turn, I got a beautiful letter of love from Sara stating that she believed God was continuing to do His powerful work in my life.

32

Guilt and Shame Knocking

After receiving the incredible freedom from the bondage of mutilating/cutting, the process of continuing to honor God has become incredibly important to me. I obviously like being the one in control, and the process of being accountable has been a learning process for me. I just was going to have to make accountability part of my life. Without a doubt, I know in my spirit this is something God wants me to hold on to. It does not matter if it has been six months or four years without any issues. The bottom line is that I stay obedient to God's directions, and I know He is clear on keeping my accountability partners. I am not saying everyone needs this accountability support, but for me, it has worked well.

It was incredibly hard in the beginning to go to my accountability partners, mostly because there was so much shame involved. As time went by, going to them about the littlest temptations, thoughts, or ideas seemed ridiculous.

However, God knows my mind, body, and soul better than I know myself, and I was to heed His promptings in any situation. To ignore, avoid, or put off these little things as insignificant would only give Satan a chance to tempt, oppress, and leave guilt or shame at my doorstep, knocking and just waiting for me to answer it.

One of these incidents that I felt was insignificant happened several years into being away from the sin of mutilating/cutting. I was getting a pedicure, and it was brought to my attention by the pedicurist that I had two bruised toes, and she was inquiring about what happened. I looked closely, and I could not remember any incident in which I had hurt my toes. She then pressed the top of each toe. It was obvious they were tender, but nothing superpainful.

From that day going forward, I tried to pay attention while walking in high heels or walking/running to see if my shoes were an issue. Since I had started working out three to four days a week, I figured it must be my shoes. Though I was paying attention, I did not feel any pain. To make sure, I bought new running shoes. However, this did not fix the bruised toenails. Of course, no one saw the bruises except me and the person who gave me pedicures. I wore dark-enough colors on my toes to hide the bruises, so it really was no big deal. At least that was what I thought at first.

Then after about two months, it started to bother me. My pedicurist kept asking me if I dropped something on my foot. She kept pressing to find out how I was hurting my two toes.

She also was concerned that it was causing me a lot of pain. I informed her I was good, and it did not hurt that bad. She then informed me that both nails were about to fall off. This was not going to look pretty. You can't put nail polish on skin! I asked the pedicurist to use glue to hold the nails on as long as possible, and she did as I asked. As I sat there, I was pelted by Satan with seeds of guilt from hurting myself, trying to plant them. Obviously I must have hurt myself, or I would not have two bruised toes with nails ready to fall off. This was frustrating. I had done nothing, and I knew it. Because this was all pressing into the mutilation/cutting issue, I really needed to just reach out and ask my accountability partners to join me in seeking God for wisdom. However, I did not. It seemed completely ridiculous.

Time went on, and about three weeks later, I was getting my nails done again, and of course, the pedicurist asked, "What happened to your toes?" I gave the same response as from the weeks past. Sitting there, frustrated and tired of questions from different pedicurists, I asked God, "What is going on?" This was the first time I brought it up to God. I realized in that moment that I talk to Him all the time during the day, but this subject just never came up. I waited to get some direction from God, and I got nothing. Well, as to the answer why my toes were bruised, I did, however, get a prompting in my spirit to speak to my husband, John, about it. I brushed the idea aside because it seemed so small and insignificant.

After that, it seemed the accusations of guilt started to seep in more often. Satan had a history of my sins, with many mutilating acts done to my feet. Those thoughts would come to me, and I would just remind myself that I was a new creation in Christ, and I was not going to do those types of things to relieve stress or pain in my life again. I was getting frustrated with these thoughts reminding me of my past. I went to God and asked Him again what was going on. I got silence. In the silence, I remembered that God wanted me to go to John and speak to him about the bruised toenails, but I thought it was silly. I knew now what I had to do.

I went to John and explained the situation. He asked me why I did not mention it before to him. I explained, "It was nothing. It seemed so silly and small." I continued telling him that I, at no time, was tempted to hurt myself, but it seemed guilt and shame hovered over me. John then asked what guilt and shame were doing to me. It told him it was like they were slowing me down from moving forward in my relationship with Christ. It was like an aha moment. I could see myself succumbing to the heavy weight of guilt and shame. This was why God wanted me to talk to John, so that I would be able to see what was happening, to have someone to pray with me. Or it might be as it was in the beginning: one small chain link, and then the next would find me in bondage. After talking with John, the burden of my bruised toes and the guilt and shame were removed. I was grateful for a husband who did not think it was silly and who again was thankful to be allowed to help me.

Though the guilt and shame were taken care of, I felt in my spirit that I needed to call Eddie, one of my accountability persons, and give him a heads-up on what had been going on. All I could think of was that this was going to be the stupidest phone call ever! I called Eddie and asked him to pray for me to find out why I keep bruising my two toenails and continually having them fall off. While we were on the phone talking, I did not realize he was googling on his computer. He had a hunch why the two toenails were having an issue. He then explained what he was doing and ran across something called runner's toe. This, he explained by reading to me, is the bluing or blackening of the toenails due to the impact of the foot on the shoe. Lots of things can contribute to it, as in not tying your shoes properly or just wearing shoes that don't fit. It was such a quick answer to prayer, and I was thrilled to take this information and share it with John.

The next morning, less than twenty-four hours later, I was in the shower and noticed something peeling off one of my bruised toes. Unfortunately it was one of the toenails. Though I was sad to see it fall off, I knew God had answered my prayers, and there was no doubt how it was happening. I was extremely grateful to God for clearing all the mystery up. I reached down without guilt or shame and tried to pick up my nail to throw in the trash. To my surprise, it was just my nail polish peeling off. It just neatly peeled off in one piece, and that was why I thought it was my whole nail. What I now saw before me was a healthy white and pink toenail. This was amazing! The week before, it was ready to fall off at the pedicurist being black and blue.

I touched my new nail several times. This could not be. Did God heal my toenail? I immediately grabbed the nail-polish remover and took off the polish on the other toenail, which of course was in the same ugly condition as this one once was. To my amazement, it was now a healthy pink and white. A brand-new nail was there. Wow, God!

I sat there surprised. It was such a little thing, and yet God healed my two toenails. I never even asked for healing, just for the information on the why and how they were getting bruised. I then went off immediately to John and showed him my toes. He then said, "Well, I prayed God would heal your toes. I was not like you. I was not consumed with how it happened." He explained that he knew I was not hurting myself. Oh, to hear those words come from him after such a rough couple of weeks being slapped with guilt for something I was not doing. It was like having a soothing ointment poured over my soul.

By the end of the day, I was still in awe of knowing that God healed my two toes. I could have lived just fine without two toenails. So many others need some serious health healings, and this was so small and insignificant. All it did was remind me how I have not even begun to scratch the surface of understanding my amazing, incredible, loving

God. I do not know why He heals some and others not yet. However, no matter what I see, He is always consistent. He is always good. When I removed the polish off the last toe to see if it was healed as well, it was as if God reached out and hugged me, a hug that let me know He cares so much about the little things in my life just as much as the big things. He truly loves me.

I discovered a lot of things through that lesson. I need to go to God no matter how small or large the situation is. Obviously He still desires for me to use the accountability partners in my life to join me in prayer. I'll be honest. I would still rather not have any accountability partners in my life. However, having a fellowship of prayer warriors, keeping me on track with more than just the mutilating/cutting issues, makes me stronger and helps me live a more successful Christian life. I learned John still trusted me, and this felt great! I also learned how to tie my tennis shoes correctly to prevent the bruised-toe situation in the first place, and this was a good thing.

33

Temptation
Fighting the Giant

Temptation comes to each one of us. Having a plan helps a person be prepared when those moments arrive. When I lived in California, I can remember in my parents' pantry a large supply of flashlights prepped and ready for use, as well as candles, in case the power went out. This, as well as extra water and canned items, made for a good earthquake-survival plan. While living in Houston, Texas, there were constant reminders each year on the radio and TV to be prepared for hurricanes. The same is true for being prepared for the moment when temptation comes.

Each day, we are all tempted over and over again. Saying no sounds pretty simple; but in the beginning, walking away from sin, such as an addiction, may be difficult. It is important to seek God for His strength in answering temptation with a solid no. Keeping a constant communication with God all day long to me is a huge key. Be honest. Let Him know how you are doing and when you are in need. Psalms 34:17 tells us that God hears our cry. Call on the name of Jesus! His name is full of power. Say it out loud! Philippians 2 says that because of the cross, every knee will bow at the name of Jesus. It is that powerful. I am not going back to mutilating/cutting with temptation overwhelming me. The name of Jesus is one of great authority. It is greater than any temptation Satan can throw at us.

For example, when I held many teacher-aid positions in high school in order to get extra credit at times I had to let a student know about a project they needed to get done and returned to me by a certain time. One day, a student looked at me with great defiance and said, "And just who is going to make me do this?" I, in turn, replied, "Your teacher, who sent me to tell you to do it." In that moment, the student changed his attitude from defiance toward me to complete compliance. He now knew where my authority came from. I now, with the power given to me, was in control of the student's grade and the fact he needed to pass this class in order to graduate in a few weeks. Just like I got my authority from the teacher, I am able to have authority over any temptation that comes my way by the ultimate authority of Jesus Christ.

Luke 4:15 speaks about how Jesus was tempted by sin just like us, but He did not give in to the temptation. Instead He used God's Word to confront temptation and crush the enemy. We too can do the same thing. Jesus had the same Holy Spirit that He has given to us today, those who have accepted Christ as their Savior, living in Him. Jesus said we will always be tempted. Because He has let us know this ahead of time, we need to use wisdom and be prepared. If you have no plans when temptation pops its enticing little head, you may begin to stumble.

Get in regular workouts in the Word of God, the Bible. Don't just take the time to read it; study it. There are so many great study aids out there to sink your teeth into to produce strong muscles in Christ. Douse yourself in the Word by hearing it spoken out loud regularly. With physical muscles, the old saying "Use it or lose it!" is true; so it is for our spiritual muscles. So keep lifting your Bible daily and read what pure truth it holds for you.

Get your hope muscle into action by flexing your faith and pressing forward to win the race God has placed inside all of us. Remember, we are never alone. God is always there with us. Trust Him. Hebrews 15:5 (AMP) reads, "For He, God himself, has said, I will not in any way fail you, nor give you up, nor leave you without support. I will not, I will not in any degree leave you helpless, nor forsake, nor let you down (relax My hold on you)! Assuredly not!"

If you are in the process of building up your spiritual muscles, or you have just gotten a little complacent and found yourself facing a temptation that is starting to look good, just call out the name of Jesus. Do not let the temptation go any further. Refocus and press on with the promises God has given you to use against the fiery darts of temptation that will come your way.

> No temptation has overtaken you except what is common to mankind. And God is faithful; he will not let you be tempted beyond what you can bear. But when you are tempted, he will also provide a way out so that you can endure it. (1 Corinthians (NIV), 10:13)

34

Effects and Influences

For those who are abused, there are numerous ways of dealing with the abuse apart from seeking God. Playing dead to emotions is very common, but there is always some sort of price to pay. In my case, physically taking it out on myself to quiet my screaming soul was one way. Others find that living their life with no boundaries at all works for them. They just can't say no to anything, and in the end, it leaves them feeling used and of little worth. There are those who find relief when they are liked by everyone around them. This includes perfectionism, as well as playing the martyr. There are some who just live life angry and don't need anyone else to do anything for them. Their emotions are guarded, for they will not be stupid enough to let anyone around them cause them pain. There are people who guard their virginity only to have it stepped on and now puts themselves in the mode of being used to fulfill what ugliness was done to them over and over again, purposefully choosing others for dates so they are sexually repeating the message that their heart sings with great pain, of a life out of control.

These are just some of the examples of what I have seen as the behavioral side affects of being abused, and I know there are many more examples and combinations.

Because of the past abuse and the bad decisions I made early in life, I lived my life on a weak foundation, pitted and mostly made of sand. It was an infrastructure laid with lies mixed with truths; so when real challenges or trials came my way, it seemed that another part of my foundation would just be washed away by life's storms. No amount of determination could hold it together. My constantly providing for my own foundation made for a poor-quality patchwork of cement that only brought temporary relief. The Bible verse in Matthew (NIV), 7:24 states, "Therefore everyone who hears these words of mine and puts them into practice is like a wise man who built his house on the rock."

Tearing down the old foundation was vital in my life so God could build a solid one in its place based upon His truth, His righteousness, and His hope so when life has its storms, I can withstand them with Him at my side. Only when I continually allow and give God access does He then faithfully pour in His liquid concrete, and it hardens to an impenetrable fortress in which the enemy is no longer welcomed.

The good news is we are able to live a life free from enslavement of sin through Christ! Romans (NIV), 6:11 reads,

"In the same way, count yourselves dead to sin but alive to God in Christ Jesus." Further in verse 14, it states, "For sin shall not be your master, because you are not under law, but under grace." The power of sin can be broken because our master is Jesus, and we live under this amazing gift of grace!

When I read the book of Exodus of the Bible, I am reminded of the dark journey in which I felt I was walking through, coming out of my addiction from mutilation/cutting. I can see it so clearly where in the story it speaks of how joyful God's chosen people were when they were leaving Egypt and walking freely away from slavery. These people rejoiced greatly! They did it with songs of praise, and their great joy flowed and lasted for a few chapters. Then all of a sudden, you start to read about their beginning to grumble. One moment they were celebrating their incredible freedom, and in the next—because they found themselves trapped against the Red Sea with Pharaoh, ready to pounce on them—they were in dismay. It is then you hear not their cry of praise to God but their cry with the question of, Why did we ever decide to leave Egypt? on their lips. Sure, they were slaves in Egypt, but at least they knew what life was going to be like, and there was no mystery. Here on the open road, reality came pretty quickly. When they realized there were going to be trials and testing of their faith, they wanted no part of it. I could sure understand where they were coming from.

I am so thankful for stories like this in the Bible, for it keeps me focused on the road in front of me and to remember that Egypt is no longer an option for me. The doors are closed, and even if I were to be foolish enough to turn back and bang on those doors, I know who is on the other side—Satan. He himself would be waiting there only to take advantage of my desperation for immediate relief. The Bible explains that going back to the sin I had been set free from would only leave me in a worse situation than I was in before. I can understand this, for it probably would take much more physical pain and openness to strange places in order to play dead effectively.

The last thing Pharaoh was going to do was welcome his slaves back. He was angry they had left, and he was going to make sure all of them paid big time if they returned. In fact, in Exodus, the story continues, and you can read how Pharaoh became angry with his decision to let the slaves go, and he took his army and went after them. I know the same holds true for Satan and the temporary fixes he offers. John (NIV), 10:10 states, "The thief comes only to steal and kill and destroy; I have come that they may have life and have it to the full."

Satan's desire is to steal my peace, kill my joy, and see me destroyed. Jesus says He has come so I can have a life that is full.

Unfortunately, if you read the book of Exodus, you will see it took forty years of wandering in the wilderness for the Israelites to reach the land of milk and honey. This journey could have been done in eleven days, but because of their disobedience and lack of faith in God, He would not lead them straight to the Promised Land.

We all have a choice in our journeys in the valley to keep our faith in God and get to the land of milk and honey sooner, or create our own stumbling blocks by our impatience or desire to do it our own way. I can't see the Promised Land filled with milk and honey, but I have God's promise He will never leave me or forsake me. He will guide me on the road of life, and all I need to do is trust in Him.

I'll be honest. There are days that are tough, when I feel I am only taking pitiful baby steps toward the Promised Land. However, though small steps or none at all, I am able to stay facing the right direction in His strength and in the hope He gives me in the darkest of nights.

What does a dark night look like for me? It is when I am asked in the face of adversity to keep on moving forward in faith without seeing or hearing from God, when I sense nothing from the Holy Spirit that gives me a clue He is even near, when I feel so very alone and yet could be surrounded by many. It is He alone I desire and want, and yet the stillness is engulfing, and no God-spoken words come to my heart. It is then I lean on the Word of God. The powerful Word of the Bible, is His very breath. Though I don't understand everything in it, I know my God created it to be an important part of my foundation. I take those words and eat them and let them stir me to stay facing the right direction, to take the next step, to keep on going. I then make sure I have on the whole armor of God described in Ephesians (NIV); 6:10–18:

> Finally, be strong in the Lord and in his mighty power. Put on the full armor of God so that you can take your stand against the devil's schemes. For our struggle is not against flesh and blood, but against the rulers, against the authorities, against the powers of this dark world and against the spiritual forces of evil in the heavenly realms. Therefore put on the full armor of God, so that when the day of evil comes, you may be able to stand your ground, and after you have done everything, to stand. Stand firm then, with the belt of truth buckled around your waist, with the breastplate of righteousness in place with your feet fitted with the readiness that comes from the gospel of peace. In addition to all this, take up the shield of faith, with which you can extinguish all the flaming arrows of the evil one. Take the helmet of salvation and the sword of the Spirit, which is the Word of God. And pray in the spirit on all occasions with all kinds of prayers and requests. With this in mind, be alert and always keep on praying for the saints.

When fed and clothed by the Word, I am then able to take the next step in the dark night moments. Small as it might be, with a whisper of the word *help* on my lips, I know the power in the faith, where the strength will come from. I keep praying as Ephesians speaks and hear my plea as it reverberates off my heart's walls. Has a light gone on? Has the situation changed? Most of the time no; it still looks just as dark as it was before. However, that does not matter because I know I am to take a step and then two more and find solid ground that will then fill me with much more confidence than I had before. I know now that by doing this, I will be right back into a full-paced walk in no time, even if it stays dark! I can do this because of faith, and this was only possible because I trusted and believed in the Word that is God.

In those beginning years, my faith was so tiny, and I needed to know God was there with me all the time. I needed Him to always show me He was near or in control of a situation. This time spent with Him increased my trust on our relationship, which then formed a strong foundation built on truths. As a Christian, I feel like there is walking-on-water moments, like Peter in Matthew 14:22–33. I got those moments of trusting God more and stepped out on the water. I learned early on like Peter that keeping my eyes on Him was the only way I was going to find myself walking on water; otherwise, I would begin to sink.

After a while, walking on water with God became more of a joyful act instead of a constant check to see how close the boat is in case I start to sink. Being back inside the boat would give my flesh the in-control desire it wants, but it does not satisfy the desire of my soul to grow in my relationship with my God.

Now, many years later, after getting out of the boat thousands of times, I find water-walking moments can truly be extremely pleasurable with God. In fact, I can say I have not only found myself walking but running and dancing on the water with Him. It might take, at times, reminding myself to keep Christ as my focus, but once the dance begins and my heart subsides from beating too quickly, I become at ease and find pure joy and freedom in His presence and where we are on the journey across the water.

There are times when the darkness threatens to keep me from seeing Him as we journey over the water-walking experience, but because of the relationship we have built over the years, I have found I don't need to see Him constantly. I know my love is not far away, and He will always be faithful. His Word, the Bible, promises this, and I find my feet on a solid foundation.

I have been asked if I have ever started to sink into the water like Peter and cry, "Lord, save me." You bet. I am not perfect. I am human, and each day is a learning experience and a relationship-building opportunity with God. I would say most days I see no growth at all or any foundation of truth added. However, it is the consistency of fellowship with God that develops, bit by bit, my strength in Him.

For example, it was a beautiful Sunday, and my husband and I were talking about what gift to give one of our daughters who was about to be married. Though we knew we would give a large gift, we wanted to give something special, which would have meaning in the years to come. Thankfully God gave the idea of taking our daughter's wedding invitation, which she customized herself, and framing it with a beautiful matting. Though the idea was good, we found there was no company who could get it done one week before the wedding.

I knew my husband was good with cutting and getting lines exact; I figured we could possibly do this project ourselves. I went to the store and put some beautiful contrasting matte colors for the framing, a gorgeous frame, some double-sided tape and an X-ACTO knife in my basket. When placing the X-ACTO knife in my basket, my mind was flooded with the last time I used one of these knives. It had been many years since the morning I awoke at 3:00 a.m. and ended up in the bathroom cutting the back of my knee. From that moment on, there had not been one of those cutting tools in our home.

I headed to the counter, determined to not let those memories bother me. However, they were coming fast and furious, as well as the emotions that were tied to them. I immediately started to feel condemnation and guilt, as if others in the store knew what I had done with the X-ACTO knife. I knew this was not from God, and I knew entertaining thoughts like this was not right. In my soul, I shouted so my heart would pay attention, "Shut up, Satan! I am forgiven and free. Thank you, God." Immediately my heart stopped racing with the guilt and memories that were flooding my soul.

Two days later, I walked into the kitchen to see my husband working on the gift project. He had a couple of questions about how I wanted the matting, and I came up to the table he was working on. It was then my eyes caught the shine of the X-ACTO knife just sitting there on the table as a tool. It was then I mentioned to John what happened at the store when I purchased the knife and how, in the end, I felt I had to protect something from being taken from me. He asked me, "What was it that you felt was being taken away from you?" It was a good question, but one whose answer I was not sure of.

After a few minutes, I was able to put into words what I was thinking. At first, I thought it was the joy of giving a gift to our daughter. However, I think it was more of my vision, my dream of a life of never going back to mutilating/cutting myself. To entertain the thoughts of being condemned and such heavy guilt would be what the Bible states as going back and eating my own vomit. Proverbs (NIV), 26:11 reads, "As a dog returns to his vomit, so does a fool repeat his folly."

This X-ACTO-knife situation was a little hiccup on the road, a bump, a stone that tried to get me off the straight and narrow path of living the freedom that Christ has given me. Thankfully it did not knock me off the path but fortified my foundation in reviewing what God has done in my life, which only made me stronger in moving forward.

God is extremely patient and loves me in spite of myself, just like I love my children dearly. My love does not change for them when I see them do things that are not pleasing to me. My heart hurts for them, for I desire the best for them, just like our Heavenly Father. Becoming a parent has helped me so much in understanding the unconditional love one person can have for another. I don't love my children for who they are going to be but for who they are today. Not because they are good enough but because they are mine, created by God, for whom He has great plans.

35

Playing Dead to the Truth

Recently, when turning on the TV, I came across an interview of a young woman who had been sexually abused for a long time. She, while being interviewed, spoke of how she was now free from the abuse and how there was no way she was ever going to let her past abuse impact her life any way in the future. As I turned off the TV, I knew the reality of what she wanted and what was to follow in the years to come would be very different.

The poor woman obviously needed control of her life again, and you could hear it in the words she used. It was obvious her freedom was taken away, and she had no control for a long time while being abused. However, pure determination in oneself is a false small-*g* god. This false god of self-determination and being in control was being congratulated by everyone around her in the interview. I knew in the end it gave her the ability to build incredible walls of security around herself, including moats with crocodiles in the water, ready at any given time to take on any intruders who may want to get close to her heart.

However, the walls she was building out of desperation for control would also keep out the nourishment that her heart needed to function as a human here on earth. The high-security walls she was engineering with the highest grades of materials in her soul would eventually become overgrown by moss and start to erode. The moat that she surrounded herself with for protection would be filled with smelly stagnate water, which eventually even the crocodiles would leave. All that would be left are mosquito-infested waters that will end up attacking her flesh, leaving her in utter misery when she least expects it.

Oh, how I wanted to reach across the TV set and let this poor woman know that being in control like she was trying to be was a false god of major proportions, how the lies and doubts love to creep in when she is not paying attention, how Satan plans this all out perfectly so a person reaches the moment of sheer hopelessness. I wanted to share with her the hope that only comes through Christ and how He can bring healing into her heart so she won't have to keep the world far away from her.

Sometimes life can be tough. I have experienced times when the valley floor I am walking on looks and feels like a treadmill, and I get incredibly frustrated. Each time I take an inventory of how far I have walked, it is obvious that I am on the same spot, looking at the same rock in front of me, the same tree beside the road, and the thoughts come, *This is stupid. I am going nowhere. In fact, I don't see you God at all!* However, Jesus promised He would be with me always.

Matthew 28:20 speaks about how Jesus gave us His Holy Spirit so we will never have to function alone again. It is imperative we build our relationship with the Spirit to discern right from wrong before we end up doing things we will regret later. We need to stay right in the moment we have been given, even if it feels like a treadmill, and persevere in trusting Him. To my amazement, I found that when I remain faithful, even though my eyes saw no differences, God did. He saw the muscles He was developing in me so I could go even further than I had ever imagined before.

Hebrews (NIV), 13:5 says, "Never will I leave you; never will I forsake you." This means even when we are in the midst of sin, He is there close by, ready to forgive, encourage us, and get us back on the road with Him. I love the verse in Psalms (NIV), 139:8: "If I go up to the heavens, you are there; if I make my bed in the depths, you are there." Basically it is stating that God is everywhere. He does not sleep, so it does not matter where or when we need Him. He is available 24-7 to us. This is the good news I have to share with people like the woman on TV.

36

Protective Instincts

One day I was walking, just talking with God; and out of the blue, the subject of abuse came up, not the side I relate to so well as a victim but from the side of the perpetrators. How does a person get to the point where they care more about themselves, to the point of potentially hurting another person? How can this be stopped or even prevented? God and I have never spoken about this subject before, so I was a bit surprised.

It was then I remembered something that most males have in common. I believe there is a natural instinct implanted in males to protect. I remember, when I was seven, my father fighting off a full-grown German shepherd, which was just ready to attack me, with no care for his own well-being. I have seen this instinct growing up with my brothers as well, the way they tried to protect us sisters. I can remember times when my younger brother would barge into a situation and be protective even though I did not want him there. I have seen it with my husband and know he would do anything and go anywhere to protect our children. I have seen smaller men walk right up to larger men to challenge them about how their child was being treated. This built-in instinct is very strong and at times overrides common sense. Of course, there is always an exception, but overall, males do tend to be protectors. I believe females have this instinct as well, but God was purposefully showing me the male side in order for me to understand something more fully.

God was speaking to me about the ability of men to grasp the protectiveness He has implanted into them and use it to ward off their fleshly desires. I could see He was talking about pornography in Web sites, films, commercials that devalue females. The advertisements that feature scantily dressed women—which are used to draw the eye and where men's eyes linger longer than they should—strip away the dignity of His creation. If the men could see pictures of those who actually need protection, their viewpoint would change.

The majority of fathers would never want to see their daughters' bodies sold, abused, or used lustfully. Women are not treasured as God's creation but used in sin to fulfill others' fleshly desires. So when you are presented with porn in any form, I encourage you to keep yourselves pure and use the protective instinct given to you. This includes us females as well, for we are not immune to pornography.

As I continued in conversation with God, I started to think of the Shadow Man. I remembered how he used to purchase pornographic magazines with pictures of women in all sorts of inappropriate poses. As I thought about this more, I could remember other men in my life, including neighbors and relatives, who had pornography in their garages (because their wives did not want those types of magazines or calendars in their home). I can't guarantee that the abuse originated from my abusers participating in pornography, but I can surely see a connection.

I started to think about prostitution and human trafficking, not the victims but those who by choice fulfill the lust of their flesh by using others as if they were *nothing*. It was a powerful moment of God showing me it really started with a first glance that lingered. Inside, the person knew it was wrong. One look led to another, and somehow it brought them to the point of it not being enough. First Thessalonians (NKJV), 4:3–8 states,

> For this is the will of God, your sanctification: that you should abstain from sexual immorality; that each of you should know how to possess his own vessel in sanctification and honor, not in passion of lust, like the Gentiles who do not know God; that no one should take advantage of and defraud his brother in this matter, because the Lord is the avenger of all such sins, as we also forewarned you and testified. For God did not call us to uncleanness, but in holiness. Therefore he who rejects this does not reject man, but God, who has also given us His Holy Spirit.

God is saying we are to stay away from sexual immorality. We are to live lives of purity, and when we don't, we reject God and His message of holiness.

I believe God was telling me to share with others how those bits of temptation are out there every day, but we can choose to live a life of purity. You know when images before you turn from purity to impurity. Honor God with your life by keeping your mind, body, and soul pure. The saturation of pornography is everywhere in America—not just on TV, movies, computers, books, and magazines but even on our cell phones. Sure, it is a challenge we obviously have to face every day everywhere, but God can give you the strength to turn your eyes and change your lust of the flesh to a heart of purity. Ask God to give you His heart, which sees those who pose in the pictures as His holy creation, and honor God daily with your choices.

Lastly, stop downloading porn. Stop buying magazines with scantily dressed persons on them. So many cutters I run into almost always use the line, "I am not hurting anyone else, so it is okay." Of course, that sounds crazy coming from a former cutter, but it is the same excuse by those who purchase pornography. In both cases, it is a sin against their own bodies, and they seem blind to it. Don't be blind. Be aware. Get accountability in your life. Let others see your Internet history records monthly if need be. Accountability is not a bad thing; it is a way of keeping yourself free from the bondage of sin.

37

Soothers

Are you—or someone you know—in the midst of dealing with life using acts such as mutilating/cutting, doing drugs, drinking alcohol, including eating disorders such as bulimia or anorexia to soothe yourself? Do you eat your way to feeling better, run to chocolate when your soul screams for a moment of peace, overexercise so the adrenaline soothes you? What about having fits of rage in order to relieve the stress inside, leaving trails of hurt people behind you? These soothing activities are always a temporary fix and make you blind to the shame you are trying so desperately to cram down and never truly face. They are also highly addictive and damaging for your life. Be bold; seek God. The longer you keep shoving it down, the more toxic they become over time. They steal away from not only your relationship with others but with God, who loves you so dearly.

When Jesus went to the cross, He took not only my sin but the whole world's. He also took away our shame. It is not enough to be forgiven in order to live a Christian life but to know we have been freed from the shackles of shame. Jesus knows shame. He was lied to, beaten, accused of being a criminal, spit upon, mocked, stripped of almost all his clothes, and crucified. Killing off the pain or stress in life with any of the abovementioned will only require more of those actions the longer you practice them. These vices are sin.

Jesus forgives all sin. First John (NIV), 1:8–10 reads,

> If we claim to be without sin, we deceive ourselves and the truth is not in us. If we confess our sins, he is faithful and just and will forgive us our sins and purify us from all unrighteousness. If we claim we have not sinned, we make him out to be a liar and his word is not in us.

It is time to say, "Here I am, and this is what I have done to Jesus." Be honest and transparent. We need, no matter how painful it might be, to let the light of Jesus' truth shine on our issues. It does make you vulnerable, but in doing so, He is able to come in and bring the healing you so desperately need. In turn, others will be able to see the hope you have in Christ. Christ died on the cross to pay for sin. It was serious. It was a big deal. He died for our sin. Jesus does forgive all sin no matter what it is.

Jesus takes all shame, as the verse above states. This is huge as shame for the sexually abused is like a heavy boulder chained around our necks, and no matter how we adjust in life to survive, it always seems to be tripping us up or holding us back. Jesus not only forgives us sinners but cleanses us from the shame of the sin that came upon us. I know from all the stories others have told me that I was not the only one who, after being sexually assaulted, went and took a shower. I scrubbed myself red and raw because I needed to be cleaned from all the unrighteousness, the unrighteousness that was done to me. What I found was that there was no soap or rough-enough scrubbing that cleaned off the shame left upon me. Jesus is the only One who can take it away.

Because of Jesus's taking away my shame, I was able to wear white on my wedding day because I knew Jesus washed it all away, all the ugliness done to me. I was not a filthy little girl. I am a woman of God running her race daily. Sure, every now and then, Satan likes to feed lies into my life and lay shame on me, but I remind myself what God has done and look at my identity in Christ—there is no shame to be found in my Savior.

As for the pesky sins we might have ensnarled ourselves in to relieve life's stress or the painful memories of the past, I remember this powerful verse from Romans (NIV) 6:6: "For we know that our old self was crucified with him so that the body ruled by sin might be done away with, that we should no longer be slaves to sin."

We were created to live in victory over sin. No longer are we to be Satan's puppet. If you are a Christian, it is time to grab hold of the truth. The chains of sin have been broken; you are no longer a slave to your old nature. If you find yourself saying, "I have failed before," you are probably right. You have failed. However, God has never or will fail. Let's be honest. Most use the failures to keep themselves from trying again. You are letting failures become a stumbling block of fear or just hopelessness. If you keep going in this direction, the pit of self-pity will suck you completely in its wide mouth. Falling into the pit is the easy part; climbing out is the hard part.

I now see myself living a life blessed beyond measure. I feel strong, and no longer is my spirit left on the pastor's office floor but alive and very well in Christ. I keep seeking to do His will and share with everyone who will listen—who is in bondage and desires to be free—how God is completely able and willing to set them free as well. I am no longer a slave to sin. I am free. You can be free too!

I feel healed. I really do. Well, to be honest, I felt healed ten years earlier. However, what I had to discover and allow was for healing to be a process, day by day growing closer to Christ, which means less of me and more of Him. Inside, I hope I have gone through the hardest stuff, but there are no guarantees. However, my confidence is so much stronger in God, in whom I have my hope and trust, for I know my Savior lives and loves me dearly. He will never leave me alone. This I can count on.

There are days that I am challenged to the core. On those days, the big guns come out. Sure, there are handguns and automatic machine guns; but with a bazooka, just aim and shoot, and the odds of hitting and destroying are at a full maximum. Even if I might be off by a little, everything in the surrounding area is still exposed and affected.

When I am challenged, I fire back with the ammunition of a full-powered bazooka, which is the Word of God. It speaks to my spirit like nothing else. When guilt starts to fill my soul, I pull out my weapon and fire with a 1 John (NIV) 1:9: "If we confess our sins, he is faithful and just and will forgive us our sins and purify us from all unrighteousness." When I need peace, I fire with Philippians (NIV) 4:7: "And the peace of God, which transcends all understanding, will guard your hearts and minds in Christ Jesus." When I doubt my beauty, I remind myself of Ephesians (NIV) 1:4: "For he chose us in him before the creation of the world to be holy and blameless in his sight."

These are some of what I use as my identity verses (weapons).

38

Power of Choices

As we live in the world, it can become easy to collect chain links. Usually it is by one small link at a time, so in the end, you never see you are being bound until it is too late. All of a sudden, you might find yourself in a heap of heavy chains shackled to some rusty old god. I was chained for over forty years to mutilating/cutting. I was blind to the one person I hated more than anyone else in the world—myself. That was until God opened my eyes. I was shocked and ashamed. I felt trapped in the sin, and worse, I felt like a failure. Here I thought my world was in control—it functioned as though it was—but it was only a delusion that would one day fall apart. It was only a matter of time before my weak foundation of lies collapsed, and I ended up hanging from the chain Satan used to ensnare me for so many years.

We all have the choice of who our god will be. At times, as you have seen in my past, I chose myself as my own god.

We all have. The Bible speaks of acting out in this manner as the "works of the flesh." The Bible does not mince words on this one. Galatians 5:19–21 in the Message Bible reads like this:

> It is obvious what kind of life develops out of trying to get your own way all the time; repetitive, loveless cheap sex; a stinking accumulation of mental and emotional garbage; frenzied and joyless grabs for happiness; trinket gods; magic show religion; paranoid loneliness; cutthroat competition; all consuming-yet-never-satisfied wants; a brutal temper; and impotence to love or be loved; divided homes and divided lives; small-minded and lopsided pursuits; the vicious habit of depersonalizing everyone in a rival; uncontrolled and uncontrollable addictions; ugly parodies of community. I could go on. This isn't the first time I have warned you, you know. If you use your freedom this way, you will not inherit God's kingdom.

The reward I earned for choosing to play god easily shows up in this verse. I had a stinking accumulation of mental and emotional garbage, trinket gods, and of course, uncontrollable addictions to mutilating/cutting. What acts of the flesh have you done that are reflected in that verse?

Jesus already paid the price for the freedom we so desperately need. This can't be a blaming game on Satan when it is up to us to hear the Word of God, the Bible, and respond to it. When the sin was revealed to me, I had to take responsibility for the choices I made. I might have once been blind as the song "Amazing Grace" states: "But now I see."

I sure did hate the fact that I could see this ugly sin. I knew the Word of God and knew I needed to respond, but I was frightened to live without the sin in my life. What would I do instead? We all need to answer this question when faced with the reality of God showing us a change we need to make in our lives. Ultimately our goal should be to submit to our Lord and King, our Creator God. We are to let Him lead, run, and guide our lives. When we do this, something amazing happens. God changes the desires of the flesh to fulfilling our needs, our ways, to a spiritual hunger, which is for Him.

Denial is part of the process of coming to terms with what sin is in our lives. I remember, during the first year, when I would be asked by one accountability partner about the mutilating/cutting, I would cringe inside just hearing the words mutilating/cutting. The sound of the word *cutting* was so harsh and cold. I had a really difficult time hearing those words used to describe what I did, and it was even more excruciating to hear the words flow from my mouth. It probably took two years before I could comfortably say the words without my stomach tightening.

The same is true about mutilating/cutting being associated with addiction. I pushed this truth far away from myself as I could. My friends and husband were patient with me as I grew in strength each day, facing the reality of what I was involved in. There was a lot of processing to do, and they gave me the much-needed space and time. Now, of course, I can easily see how addicted to the act I was, but back then, it was a real struggle to accept it.

There are many reasons for the fight of not wanting an *addiction* label put on a person. The biggest is that in today's society a person is tied to it forever. However, I got God, who is bigger than any addiction. We can surrender our addictions over to Jesus Christ and walk away, leaving them at His feet. You can go to programs and try to use willpower to make it through, but it is just like using sand for your foundation. When it rains, your house will be washed away, just like it states in Matthew (NIV) 7:26–27,

> But everyone who hears these words of mine and does not put them into practice is like a foolish man who built his house on sand. The rain came down, the streams rose, and the winds blew and beat against that house, and it fell with a great crash.

I have no problems with programs as long as they point to Christ as the strength and the Deliverer. We also need Him to put a new mind inside us to replace our old way of thinking.

> You were taught, with regard to your former way of life, to put off your old self, which is being corrupted by its deceitful desires; to be made new in the attitude

of your minds; and to put on the new self, created
to be like God in true righteousness and holiness.
(Ephesians (NIV) 4:22–24)

It always comes down to making a choice. I had to make
a choice of believing the truth of God's Word. In reality, it is
a simple concept, but living it out in our daily lives is where
it can turn complex. In doing this, I received the freedom I so
desperately needed in an area of my life I did not even know
I had a need. When I called out to God, I thought I heard
silence; but what I did not realize was He was speaking to me
through my good friends and family, who surround me daily.
I'll be honest. I did not want to be accountable to them or
anyone else. My pride shouted, "I am an adult. I don't need
anyone!" Well, I was wrong, and God was going to hold me to
it. Every time I wanted to push it to the side, the Holy Spirit
let me know if I needed to contact my accountability persons,
whether I think I did or not.

Though I may not be crazy about what my accountability
team has to say to me at times, I know God has provided me
this great support team of incredible friends. I can count on
their being honest. I can reach out to them to pray with me
anytime, day or night. These people walked with me in the
darkest of nights and stuck by me. I am now whole and free
from the addiction. It was not because I went into a program
but because I went to Jesus. Yes, He did provide me with
an incredible accountability and prayer partners, who have

been awesome. However, they could not deliver me. Only God could do this for me. My friends and family could not have pleaded or guilt-tripped me enough to walk away from something I had lived with for over forty years in one day; only God could do that. He is my Deliverer.

God is more than enough to take on whatever junk we have. This might sound harsh, but some people desire to stay victims for the rest of their lies. I have witnessed this countless times. They love the attention from being chained to eating disorders, mutilating/cutting, drugs, alcohol, porn, etc. If Satan can keep them focused on their issues, how trapped in sin they are, and give them the endless drinks of hopelessness, they will stay bound to their addictions.

In the beginning, because it was a struggle to ask for prayer or help, Eddie came up with an idea that has worked well for me. If I was struggling, just needed prayer, or just plain stressed—which could eventually lead to cutting temptations—I would send a picture of a key on my phone to my accountability partners. I purchased a yellow key with a picture of a cross on it. At moments like these, I would text the photo of the key to them, and then I would no longer be on my own. Just the physical act of having to send the picture made me stop and not brush my anxiety aside, to see I needed to call upon God for help. The agreement was that I would later follow up with them what I was struggling with. However, in these moments, I was not forced to do anything but ask for help in prayer. In turn, this gave me a sense of control, which I desperately longed for, and at the same time, an accountability I could live with. It really helped me to stop in the midst of a struggle or a downpour of Satan's lies and seek God. For some, this would not work; but for me, it has worked very well. Ask God what works best for you.

39

Attention

There are different kinds of cutters/mutilators, and lately, it seems more and more teens are "coming out," announcing they are cutters. It is important to note that there are those who confess to being cutters only for attention. Possibly they feel lonely or unloved. Their self-esteem and self-confidence are very low, and they are looking for validation of their self-worth.

People with attention-seeking behaviors are common in our society. Being the center of attention diminishes the feelings of insecurity, but the relief is temporary, and the issue of their low self-esteem and self-confidence remains. Those who have these behaviors don't realize that though they are using them in their minds temporarily, these behaviors become a highly addictive part of their life. Then the person needs to not only deal with their addictions but their insecurities and low self-esteem as well.

Knowing who one is in Christ builds one's self-esteem.

Who I Am in Christ

If you are a Christian, then the statements below are true of you. If you are not a follower of Christ and would like to know, go to https://www.ficm.org/handy-links/#!/who-i-am-in-christ

I am accepted…

John 1:12 I am God's child.

John 15:15 As a disciple, I am a friend of Jesus Christ.

Romans 5:1 I have been justified.

1 Corinthians 6:17 I am united with the Lord, and I am one with Him in spirit.

1 Corinthians 6:19-20 I have been bought with a price and I belong to God.

1 Corinthians 12:27 I am a member of Christ's body.

Ephesians 1:3-8 I have been chosen by God and adopted as His child.

Colossians 1:13-14 I have been redeemed and forgiven of all my sins.

Colossians 2:9-10 I am complete in Christ.

Hebrews 4:14-16 I have direct access to the throne of grace through Jesus Christ.

I am secure...

Romans 8:1-2 I am free from condemnation.

Romans 8:28 I am assured that God works for my good in all circumstances.

Romans 8:31-39 I am free from any condemnation brought against me and I cannot be separated from the love of God.

2 Corinthians 1:21-22 I have been established, anointed and sealed by God.

Colossians 3:1-4 I am hidden with Christ in God.

Philippians 1:6 I am confident that God will complete the good work He started in me.

Philippians 3:20 I am a citizen of heaven.

2 Timothy 1:7 I have not been given a spirit of fear but of power, love and a sound mind.

1 John 5:18 I am born of God and the evil one cannot touch me.

I am significant...

John 15:5 I am a branch of Jesus Christ, the true vine, and a channel of His life.

John 15:16 I have been chosen and appointed to bear fruit.

1 Corinthians 3:16 I am God's temple.

2 Corinthians 5:17-21 I am a minister of reconciliation for God.

Ephesians 2:6 I am seated with Jesus Christ in the heavenly realm.

Ephesians 2:10 I am God's workmanship.

Ephesians 3:12 I may approach God with freedom and confidence.

Philippians 4:13 I can do all things through Christ, who strengthens me.

https://www.ficm.org/handy-links/#!/who-i-am-in-christ

40

Paralyzing Guilt and Shame

The emotional baggage that clutters a heart that has been sexually abused starts almost immediately. From the first moments of being abused, the powerlessness and fear the victims feel become scary and overwhelming. Though it makes sense to be in this mode, it takes the abused person by complete surprise, and just breathing at times takes too much conscious effort. The trauma they endure puts them in a type of shock. They are functioning in a survival mode: get through the next minute. Though they make it through their first restless night, instead of relief waiting for them the next morning, shame and guilt are ready to chain their next victim.

With much debate, I have held off going into the next details of shame and guilt, but because I have dealt with so many victims struggling with the following information, I felt it necessary to add it. There, as I have pointed out, are all the mistrust, shame, guilt, fear, ugliness, etc., during and after the abuse. The humiliation and shame of others knowing you have been molested or raped is immeasurable, as well as different, for each victim. However, it goes to a different dimension when others witness the abuse of the victim. I have dealt with many who, for one reason or another, have experienced this other element, and it only compounds the shame. It could be a gang rape or being forced to watch another being abused. The ugly stories I have heard seem endless. Yet they are unfortunately common.

For the person being abused, it adds to the shame because someone else saw the event happen. When I was being abused at night, I was sharing a room with another sibling. I can remember it was always worse if I awoke to the Shadow Man undressing me and then seeing the shadow of my sibling on their bed across the room. Sometimes my sibling had already gone to my parents' room because of a bad dream, or maybe they were not feeling well. The sight of their empty bed would bring a form of relief. It meant the extra shame of their possibly watching me being abused was taken out of the equation.

The nights when I could see enough through the shadows my sibling's sleeping face toward me, I have no English words to describe what was going through my mind. The word *shame* could never be a strong enough word to express all that was flowing through me in those moments. To die at the hands of the Shadow Man was my deepest desire. To face the next day knowing just maybe my sibling saw me being molested made me pray the sun would not rise. This added element of someone possibly watching made it all the harder to mentally escape being abused. Moments I lay there loathing the fact my sibling might be watching, but what usually happened was worse. My sibling, while still asleep, turned and faced the other way, and I lay there feeling completely betrayed. It was a no-win situation for my sibling or myself.

For those who have experienced similar situations, realize you are not the only one. Others have found themselves in this horrid spot of being chained by these types of events, and I understand the humiliation and shame that can suffocate you. Though you may have never spoken or felt you can speak of these heavy chains you carry around since the abuse, the God who created you has heard your cries. He can and will bring healing into this area of your life; you can count on it. I also mentioned the above for those counseling with or married to the victims. It is important for others who witnessed the abuse to make sure this extra bondage of shame and guilt is addressed in order to bring healing to the brokenhearted.

I felt guilt, as I have mentioned before, in many ways, but one I was not ready to deal with or speak about was how my body reacted to the abuse. How could I express the disappointment and shame I felt for myself, which ran into my core? I wish long ago I would have tried to communicate this pain, but I could not even admit it to myself without being flooded with guilt and shame, so it was easier to play dead to any emotions or thoughts toward it. This avoidance only postponed the cleansing of my wounds in this area, and my soul became filled with sores that always became infected. These types of sores must be faced in order to receive the truth, good or bad. My puny thinking was that I had to forgive myself in order overcome the hate I had for my body, but I was wrong.

41

Why Me?

There are many questions that create stumbling blocks when a victim tries to open themselves up to a relationship with Christ. Most want to know the reason why they were the one chosen to be abused. Did they do something wrong? Are they being punished for something? Why did God not stop the abuse from happening? Why? Those may sound like selfish questions for the person who was abused, but they are desperate to know the answers so they can prevent the abuse from happening again in the future. Questions like these can consume a lot of energy when no one here on earth will be able to give you an answer that will suffice.

God knew about my grandfather hurting his granddaughter, the Shadow Man haunting my nights, the man at the amusement park, the blind date, and the pastor. He knew the lust that ran through their hearts and the sinful desires they chose to follow through. How can I see God as love looking at these facts? What I have learned is my questions are possibly put together wrong. Genesis (NIV) 1:27 says, "So God created man in His own image, in the image of God He created him; male and female He created them."

He placed them in a garden with one main restriction, and that was not to eat of the tree of knowledge of good and evil. As most of us know, they did eat from that tree. God did not stop them from doing wrong, for when He created man in His image, that image included the freedom to choose between good or evil. God loves His creation and desires to commune with them, but He leaves it as a matter of choice. Loving God would have not been a choice, and God is a God of love. Love is never an obligation; it comes from the free will of one's heart. This is the way God desired His relationship with His creation to be.

The opposite of good is evil, and unfortunately some will choose to sin and fulfill the lust of their flesh, which in turn hurts others. I do not believe God chose me to be abused; those who chose to sin picked me. They did it from the choice they were given. It was wrong, hurtful, and what they did should never be done to another human being.

Was God there when I was being abused? With great confidence, I can say He certainly was there. God is everywhere as His Word states. Do we always choose to turn to Him in our pain? No, not always. When I could take the pain no longer and called out to Him to let me die on the floor of the pastor's office, I know He heard my cry. I could not understand then why He would not answer my desperate prayer. However, from this vantage point many years later, I can see a God who hurt for me and grieved over the wounds I suffered from that terrible day. I can see this same God who hurt for me having a heart filled with great sorrow over the condition of the pastor's heart, which led him to violate another human being.

Though I turned my face away from God and lived in the shame that at times seemed to consume me, He did not leave me. Though I took matters into my own hands to soothe my hurting soul, He stayed by me. Though I did all this and other things—such as playing dead to my pain, which prolonged getting my healing from Him—He did not leave me. Even when I struck out against my physical body, which He created, He did not leave me. He waited in love. He knew I needed to come to an end of me before I could begin with Him. This free will goes both ways for the good and the evil. I would have hated God for forcing His love on me. Instead, He just waited and offered His love freely. I know many times I slammed the door in His face, but He is such a great and loving God who knows me deeply. He knew I was responding from the hurt in my soul and my great need to protect myself from being hurt again.

The message I desire to share is that God is greater than any fear, depression, thought, task, danger, sin, or wound you may be dealing with. He just asks us to give ourselves to Him. Follow His ways, and we will be in His hands. For those who have been hurt or abused, I understand that trust can be a huge stumbling block for you. Everyone has experienced some sort of betrayal, unjust anger, or plain old unkindness from others. Satan's goal since the beginning of time has been to keep us as far away from God as possible. John (NIV) 10:10 says, "The thief comes to steal, kill and destroy; I have come that they may have life, and have it to the full."

Satan is a thief. I believed in the seeds of lies from my past for so long, and those seeds sprouted into large plants that stole joy and life from me. As long as I listened to him, all hope was killed, and eventually I would be destroyed. Notice that the last line of the scripture above is so powerful. Jesus came for me to live, which is completely opposite to Satan's desires. The awesome part is it is not just for me to live but to live life to the fullest! The choices are, do I want Satan's way that leads to death or God's way that will make me whole and give life abundantly? For me, I choose abundant life and sticking close to God.

In order to live that abundant life, I had to stop settling for less. I started to embrace the fact that I have overcome the mutilating/cutting addiction that was once in my life by the power of Jesus' victory at the cross. I have heard from so many people who are addicted to alcohol, bulimia, gambling, cutting, etc., that this is the way it is, and they will always be addicts. I may have heard it, but I don't believe it. For I have seen with my own eyes others besides myself who have been completely set free by our Creator God. Do you know my

Jesus? The Bible says in John (NKJV), 3:16, "For God so loved the world that He gave His only begotten Son, that whoever believes in Him shall not perish but have everlasting life."

This amazing God who created everything desires a relationship with you and me. He sent His Son, Jesus, to earth to save us from our sin. Our sin separates us from God, but by accepting Christ into our lives as our Lord and Savior and asking for forgiveness of our sins, we can have what the Bible states in John (NIV) 1:12: "But to those that receive Him, to them He gives the right to become children of God, to those who believe in His name."

God is a forgiving God. Psalms (NIV), 103:12 says, "As far as the east is from the west, so far has He removed our transgressions from us." This means that once we ask for forgiveness, God does not consider us guilty anymore. We are free; we can live our lives free. Not that we won't suffer consequences for our sinful choices, but sinful choices don't have to darken our lives anymore, and we don't have to be chained to them. There is a trust involved when you choose God. God says in His Word that all we need is faith the size of a mustard seed in order to move a mountain. I love this verse in Matthew 17:20. The best way for me to describe the size of a mustard seed is to imagine the top of a pin that you use to sew with. It is just a tiny speck. That is pretty darn small.

Though I was crushed by the events that happened in my life, somewhere inside my being there was faith, maybe the size of a mustard seed, but that was all I needed. I am not saying it is easy to trust, but at least being willing to step forward in faith.

To me, all Christians are living miracles walking the face of the earth. They are not perfect, though they are a new creation, as stated in 2 Corinthians (KNJV), 5:17–18, "Therefore, if anyone is in Christ, he is a new creation; old things have passed away and all things have become new."

When I became a Christian, change was a slow process. Hope was the sound I could always hear in the distance, and I desired it greatly. It was the song of the hope of leaving my old self behind and walking more freely in trust, of letting God do His work in His new creation. Accepting Christ is letting God be the master and ruler of your life. Though it may be tough for those who have been abused or those whose trust has been severely broken, allowing salvation to come into our lives make a richer experience for us, for we know what true trust looks like. We know because we are very aware when we are hiding or pretending to trust others.

Each Christian has a testimony of how God made them new. I love the verse in Psalm (NKJV) 30:11: "You have turned for me my mourning into dancing; you have put off my sackcloth and clothed me with gladness."

My testimony is from a woman who danced for approval from a filled stadium. She stood and enjoyed, for a brief moment, the audience cheering and clapping. The applause made me feel accepted. Yet walking back to the dressing room, I would see a mirror reflecting the pain I hid inside my soul, and the approval of the world would evaporate just as quickly as it was given. I now dance to an audience of one in my relationship I have in Christ. The approval is not temporal, and with joy in my heart, I spin as I am clothed in gladness.

As you start your Christian walk, it begins to get easier to trust God daily. Psalm (NIV) 105:4 says, "Look to the Lord and His strength; seek His face always." Each day, as we seek God in our lives, He is there to offer His strength and guidance. This gives a person with low self-esteem courage to move forward in the joy He offers. For in seeking Him, we find our worth in Him giving His all at the cross to save us from our sins. And in this, we discover His grace and mercy.

As a woman, I do not think scars are appealing. I would rather have none. Yet scars happen when people get injured. People get wounded because we live in a sinful world. Sometimes we cause scars on others as well as on ourselves. This does not just happen because of something physical but emotional as well. The only place to run to is God, who can heal all our wounds and set us free from the prison in which we have put ourselves. Are you ready to dance with joy and be clothed in gladness? Then it is time you talk with God.

I wrote this story with many details to provide a possible springboard for conversations with those who have been abused, so they can bring these subjects up with those who are walking with them in their journey to healing. I understand the struggle to come up with words to express the specific areas of life such as the details of one's abuse. I have revealed much, my private life exposed, but I feel if I did not, you, the reader, would not understand to the degree of finding hope in Christ. For me, to find my beauty and worth in Christ is everything. I no longer have to play dead to the pain in my heart. I shared what I have so you who have been abused might understand that God is the only answer for your hurting heart, and He will answer you when you call out to Him. There is hope for the wounded heart!

42

Physical

One day, while reading *The Wounded Heart* by Dr. Dan B. Allender, I discovered some new truths. Though I was treated inhumanely and tortured for four hours in the pastor's office, my sixteen-year-old body functioned normally. I was created to function sexually, and when the genitals are touched, it is normal for the body to respond. Though my brain could not comprehend beyond the instinct of survival and the physical pain, my body naturally responded against my will. This left me conflicted mentally and not only powerless over my perpetrator but over my own body. From that moment on, I despised my body more than I ever had, and I did everything I could to combat the normal sexual feelings a woman might enjoy by shutting them down and playing dead.

I suppose the reason for needing to shut my feelings down was because the sexual feelings would stir memories, and the heaviness from the chains of guilt would become unbearable.

The bad news for those who have been sexually abused is that it can be incredibly difficult to have a healthy, normal, intimate sex life as our bodies were designed for in marriage. In fact, I have found most women have no issues until they marry and then start to have flashbacks so unexpectedly, for they blocked all those memories and emotions away when they were younger. Thankfully God can and will continue to free you, with trust in Him, of the chains of even that ugly guilt or the way you despise your body, which is His creation and which you have controlled so tightly for way too long.

God's grace did this for my husband and me. If I were to pick out one of the biggest growing seasons for us intimately, it would be when I repented of mutilating/cutting myself physically. I didn't completely understand how it connected with our relationship until we both realized it was something that was not with us any longer in the bedroom. I was blind to the fact I was wearing a heavy backpack filled with guilt and shame because I had been used to living with it my whole life. My husband was blind to it as well and thought the intimate part of our marriage was normal. And because he had not been intimate with anyone else, he just thought this was how life was to be lived.

Through the repentance, trust was built back between John and me. He learned to trust the God in me, and I learned to trust more in God to help me walk each day away from my sinful old lifestyle and in the freedom He graciously gave me. I think one of the most moving nights John and I shared together was when I opened up to show him one of my scars. This might sound hard to believe for those reading this, but John did not once ask to see any of my scars when he found out I physically cut/mutilated myself. He said he knew that when I was ready, I would open up this part of my life to him. Without pressure, I was able to heal much more quickly.

This may not seem like much, but for John, it was the first time he was let into a space I shared with no one except God. My fear was John would see my scars and reject me. This, of course, was a lie straight from Satan, but I knew the sooner I got it over with and crushed, the sooner John and I could move forward in our relationship. When I showed John one of my scars, he did not pull back or reject me. He simply loved me for sharing this part of my life with him. This brought a huge healing piece in our marriage. I know scars are ugly, and knowing I caused them only gives shame control. However, shame lost its control because I was able to experience unconditional love.

You have gotten a brief glimpse of the incredible people God has placed in my life to help me walk the journey of healing, but they could only get me so far. I count these people as a huge blessing. Though they love and care for me, there was nothing they could do to heal my hurt, which they did not even know existed in my soul. I had locked it away from them, God, and even myself. Thankfully no one can hide anything from God. He knew exactly, to the precise detail, the sinful acts perpetrated upon me as well as the sin I used to soothe my aching soul. God created me. He knew where to bring the healing and the exact moment I would be open to even receive it in my life. God does use people as vessels to bring healing, but He is the only one who can restore a person back to being whole in mind, body, and soul. Some of you reading this might be saying, "No, not me." I challenge you to give God just one inch of the space you have been keeping from Him from. If you think you have given God everything, do it again and ask Him to show you if there is more to walk through. God does want to see you living life to the fullest instead of being numb to some parts of it.

I am thankful to the authors Dr. Dan B. Allender and Dr. Larry Crabb for letting God use them to bring hope to the sexually abused. Their books definitely are not a light read and provide a great reference for victims, as well as for those walking the journey with them. I have found, working with victims, *The Wounded Heart* is an excellent resource.

43

Truth

It took a long time to write this book. When I finished writing what you have just read, I thought there was no more to write about. I even sent it off to begin the editing process. There was not one more word to add. I was done. I had told my story the best I could. I prayerfully gave as many details of my private life for the reader to possibly experience a sliver of how an abused person thinks and for those who were abused to relate to. What I did not expect was to be picking up my laptop once more to add to my story. Just three weeks after sending this book off to be edited, a huge bomb of revelation blew up in my life about the sexual abuse I experienced as a child. This bomb was filled with razor-sharp shrapnel, gathered and put together even before the day of my birth, information that not only impacted my life but every single one of my family members. All the verses I have given you, the reader, to find comfort in God I had to drink once again.

The revelation blew apart so much of what I thought of as true. I knew somewhere in the midst of all the debris lying everywhere was God. I held to this tightly, for I was left with a wounded heart that I could not soothe and an ache in my soul that I could not comprehend. The bomb of betrayal was delivered by a man I love deeply, and when I least expected it. The horrific truth exploded its ugly debris before my eyes and my family's and left us all in the state of grieving.

Bomb of Truth

In the ministry my husband and I are involved in, I travel about five to six times a year across the United States to speak and teach about sexual abuse, discipleship, and regular subjects. I do this with churches, pastoral staffs, counselors, victims of sexual abuse. Sometimes I get the blessing of returning to Southern California where most of my family lives. Though it has not happened very often over the years, it was the second year in a row I was blessed to go to do a few speaking engagements and be able to tie in seeing my family members as well.

As usual, I would stay at my parents' home for the majority of the trip. Though my visiting time is usually very limited, getting a hotel room in my culture would be an offense and just is not done. My parents have always treated me kindly as a houseguest and are so grateful for any time we are able to spend together. They are retired now and live in the same home I grew up in when I was a child. Though the rooms are empty, because it is rare for me to come to town, my siblings will head in, and the empty home will fill up for an afternoon of barbeque.

The last two years, my parents set up the "blue room" for me each time I visited. It is the bedroom right across the hall from my parents' room. It is always filled with many wonderful, welcoming soft blankets and pillows. Two years ago, I arrived from a later flight, so by the time I arrived at my parents' home, it was after 6:00 p.m. I visited with the family till 9:00 p.m., and then I had to excuse myself and head to bed. I had awakened early for my flight that day with a long layover as well. I came from a different time zone, two hours ahead of California, and I was tired. I said my good-nights to everyone and headed to bed.

I fell into a deep sleep right away. While sleeping, I started to hear the familiar sound of someone turning the old glass doorknob on my bedroom door. When the click engaged, I woke with a start and gasped loudly at the sight of the hallway lights flooding my dark room. My mother walked in and apologized profusely for waking me, for she thought I would still be awake. I looked at the clock, and it read 10:00 p.m. She said she just had a few questions about the following day's itinerary, and I quickly gave it to her, and she left. I lay there trying to slow down my breathing so that my heart would stop beating so rapidly. I was still very startled at being awakened with the door opening in the midst of my sleep. This rapid beating of my heart seemed so familiar, and I started to pray and ask God. That was when I realized for the first time where I was sleeping. Though I had slept in this room many times in past years with my husband when visiting, this was the first time I was here alone. Alone, in the same room I was abused in from the time I was a small child till about ten years of age.

I immediately reminded myself that those days were behind me. I was a new creation in Christ. God had walked me through so much healing, and I have so much to be grateful for. In fact, I started to thank God for bringing me to this point. Bottom line, there was nothing to fear in that room. It was just a bedroom that held old memories of hideous things a long time ago, but now it was going to be a place where I would lay my head in sleep and in peace. I quickly drifted off to sleep.

A couple of hours later, I was woken up by the familiar slow sound of the glass doorknob now turning once again. I told myself to calm down, that it was just my mind playing a trick on me. However, as I turned to check out the clock by the bed, which was by the door, I saw the door open up; and with the night-light from the adjacent room, I saw a man walked in. This time, I not only gasped in fright but sat straight up. Immediately I recognized my father's voice. My father apologized that he had awakened me. He said he thought I would still be awake. He then proceeded to tell me that he was glad I had come for a visit and he had missed seeing me for the last five years. I looked at the clock and said, "Dad, it is 12:30 a.m." With that, he apologized again. I thanked him for having me in their home and planning the barbeque the following day, but I really needed to get some sleep. Calming my heart after he left seemed impossible. However, I started to speak to God, asking Him for help; and the next thing I knew, I awoke the next day rested.

That event was over a year and a half ago, and now I was back in California for another ministry trip. On my first night there, I was prepared for my mother's entrance into the room after I went to bed; none came from her or my father. However, on my last night's stay there, I got home around 1:30 a.m. from a long night of visiting. I was exhausted but thrilled with the God experiences I was able to witness throughout my day. As soon as my head hit the pillow, I fell quickly asleep.

Then in the midst of my sleep, I heard the all-too-familiar sound of my bedroom doorknob turning. To be honest, I really thought I was just dreaming at first. However, it was the shuffling of feet that lit my brain into a hyperspeed of consciousness, and my eyes flew open. To my surprise, I saw a man standing right by my bedside with his robe open. It was dark, so at first my mind could not figure out who the person was. But it frightened me to the point, when this all came into view within seconds, of gasping and throwing back the bedcovers. In this process of haste, my body, without thinking, just wanted to get out of the bedroom; and so, as I threw back the covers, I sat up and turned my body, putting my feet to the floor and jumping out of bed. This caused the person standing by my bedside to fly backward because of the momentum of me coming toward him. The man stumbled backward and hit the wooden bedroom door, which in turn slammed with a loud bang against the plaster wall.

It was then I realized from the night-light in the hall that the man was my father. My father? Immediately, when I realized this, I went from running out of the room to protect myself to making sure he was not hurt. I asked him if he was okay, and he replied he was fine. Trying to find some sort of clarity after being awakened to such a fearful sight, I asked my father, as I looked at the bedroom clock on the bed stand, what he was doing in my room at 3:30 a.m. He replied he tripped while he was in the hallway and sort of fell into my room. Though my father was explaining this all to me, I really only heard words without comprehending any of them, for my heart was beating so rapidly and loudly in my ears. All I could think of as he spoke was, *I need out. I need a hotel room!*

Checking one more time with my father to make sure he was fine, I walked past him, leaving him in my old bedroom, and up the hallway to the far-end bathroom of the house. I needed air and time to think. As I walked up the hallway, I noticed my father's office light was on, as well as his computer. *Hmm,* I thought, *he must be having a hard time sleeping.*

While in the bathroom, I splashed water on my face to try to clear my mind and get my heart to calm down, for there was so much adrenaline still running through me. My hands were shaking. I immediately started to go through the logic of what just happened. Questions started to form. Why was my father in my bedroom? This was so strange. His presence reminded me of awakening to the horrific familiarity of a man by my bedside without ever hearing the bedroom door open. Immediately I told myself to stop it. This was my last night staying in my old bedroom, and I only had a few hours left before I would be waking up to start my next day, filled with things I needed to accomplish before flying back to my comfortable bed in Texas. Back home, no one would surprise me in the middle of the night, and I would be able to rest peacefully. I left the bathroom and walked back down the hallway. I noticed my father was back in his office, and he said good-night to me, and I replied the same back to him.

As I entered my room, I looked across the hall at my parents' bedroom door, which was opened halfway. I immediately wondered why my mother did not come running out to ask if everything was okay. She is a light sleeper like me, and when my father's body hit the door, it bounced loudly several times as it hit the plaster wall. My voice, as well as my father's, when I was checking on him to make sure he was okay was not soft but loud. This seemed odd. I then got back into bed and lay there like the year before, trying to get my heart and breathing to slow down so I could just go to sleep. I started to talk to God, but somewhere in the midst of our conversation, I must have fallen asleep. By 7:00 a.m., the alarm went off and woke me with a start.

No thoughts of the early 3:30 a.m. intrusion of my father's startling visit crossed my mind. I awoke fully focused on my day's appointments, which all had to be done by noon, including returning my rental car and catching a ride to lunch with a couple I would be traveling with to the next leg of my journey. If all went according to plan, by 1:00 p.m. I should be asleep in the back of this couple's car on the way to Arizona. I said my good-byes to my parents at breakfast and drove off in my rental car.

Because of the time change when I do trips like this on the West Coast, I have found contacting my hubby first thing in the morning is the best time for us to catch up. I slip on my earpiece, call him, talk about those I had been experiencing, and John will tell me about how his days have been going. I love hearing about his praise reports and his concerns, and the same goes for him with regard to me as well. In the end, we close in prayer, and then we go about our day. After about ten minutes of conversation, my husband, John, asked me, "So how have you been sleeping out there in California?" I told him I was sleeping fine because my days were long and I usually hit my pillow pretty worn-out. However, I proceeded to tell him that the strangest thing happened last night. He asked what happened. I told him at 3:30 a.m., I awoke to my father standing right beside my bed, and it scared me something fierce. My husband, in a very serious tone, asked,

"What was your father doing in your room at 3:30 a.m.?" I told him that he told me he fell in, that he tripped or something like that. John wanted to talk about it more, but I was only five minutes away from my next destination, and I could tell by my husband's tone that this would not be a short conversation.

To be honest, it was not one I was thrilled to explore. My insides were tight, and I started to feel again the anxiety I experienced the night before. I told my husband I would be home in a couple of days, and then we could talk about it. I could tell my husband was not thrilled with my response, for his silence spoke volumes as both of us listened to the tension-filled quiet over the phone. I knew right in that moment that I was wrong not engaging more with my husband on the subject. Something inside me needed to protect myself from going there with him in conversation. I not only needed to protect myself, but I knew I would not be able to move forward 100 percent with what the day had in front of me to accomplish if I was to stop and go there in conversation with him. I was wrong. With that, we said our good-byes; and within a few days, I found myself getting off an airplane and heading into a wonderful dinner to be reunited with my hubby. I am sorry now I did not honor my husband and take the time-out to at least discuss with him more the questions he had for me that fateful morning.

That evening, as we lay in bed, John asked me the question I had all but forgotten, "So why was your father in your bedroom at 3:30 a.m.?" I told him I did not know why he was there except for the reason my father stated. He then asked, "Do you think there is any chance your father was part of your abuse when you were a little?" I told him, "No." I reminded him that when I was around twenty-three years of age, we learned the identity of the Shadow Man, and the matter of who came in my room at night was settled. John did not seem settled with the answer I gave him. He then asked several more questions, for which I had no good answers to give. In fact, he was making me quite irritated by even asking these questions about my father. He then asked for more details about what happened when my father ended up in my room. Again I gave him all I could remember from my trip. With that, we then fell asleep and awoke to a weekend where we both had a lot of work to complete.

During the weekend, while passing each other in the apartment, John asked me to consider asking God about my father's being in my room during my trip in the early-morning hours. I told him I would, and while on a walk talking to God about it, the thoughts of my abuse and the details of the events started to float around in my mind. My thoughts came to who was there during the abuse. I was there, God was there, and of course, so was the person who was sexually abusing me.

Then, all of a sudden, an idea came to me. This book that you are reading right now was in the process of being edited. I included many details of my abuse in order to reach the sexually abused and those who are living with them or those who are trying to bring them the love of Christ and the healing only He can provide. This thought hit me, *What if I take the unedited manuscript to the person who revealed themselves to John and me at the age of twenty-three and have them read it?* This would give this person a chance to see if there are discrepancies in any story or a part in which he was not involved. As soon as I entered through the door from my walk, I spoke to John about this idea, and he liked it very much. We immediately contacted this person and discussed it with him. He agreed to read it and get back with us in a few days. I also spoke with our good friend Greg Getz if he could read my manuscript and see if there is anything in it that would point even to the possibility of my father being involved in the sexual abuse I experienced. He agreed to read it as well.

Greg got back to us pretty quickly and said he could see a connection with the timeline of when my abuse stopped at around age ten and when my parents became born-again Christians. I never noticed this before, nor did John. However, there was a huge part of me that could not go any further thinking of my father's being involved. It would hurt too much to have that be true. I held out for the person who said they were the Shadow Man to get back to me with his comments. My prayer: Greg would be wrong.

A few days passed, and I got a call from this person. The tone he had on the other end of the phone was not good. He began the conversation with an apology. He proceeded to tell me he had no idea how badly the abuse affected my life. I told him he had asked for my forgiveness many years ago, and it was given. I loved him, and we were good. He then told me that when I sat in the car with him and he admitted to being the person who came in my room at night he only told me part of the truth. There was another involved; but because everyone was older and he loved this family member so much, he just felt it was best not to mention him and take the hit for being the one who abused me. However, he explained it was obvious he couldn't take the hit for all I had written about in the manuscript. As I listened to him, I could not comprehend what he was talking about. I heard him take a deep breath, and then he tried to explain so I could understand completely.

He then told me that when I was young, around probably four years of age, I stayed in the blue room, which was at the far end of the hallway, away from the major living areas. The youngest children, it seemed, were given that room due to the fact it was the closest to our parents' room. He said that because I was little, I went to bed earlier than others in the home. And my room being so far away from the major living areas made it easy to just shut the door at the main end of the hallway, and the little ones would not be easily awakened.

He proceeded to tell me that he was walking down the hallway one time to use the restroom on this side of the house and heard a noise coming from inside my bedroom. He thought I was being disobedient and, instead of going to sleep, was up playing in my room. He noticed the door was open a crack, so he thought he would open the door quickly to scare me; but when he did, he found my grandfather molesting me. My grandfather waved him to come in the room and shut the door. He stared at my grandpa, trying to figure out what was happening. He then told me that Grandpa said, "This is what little girls and women like." He said he just stood there in unspeakable shock. He stood there for a brief moment and then turned and walked out of the room.

He proceeded to explain to me that his mind was racing as to what he was to do next, for he loved Grandpa and he loved me. He could not figure out if he should go tell someone what Grandpa was doing. What if he told someone and then they questioned him why he just stood there and watched? It was like he was damned if he did and damned if he did not. In the end, he did nothing. He proceeded to tell me this happened a few more times when Grandpa visited. He was drawn in to witness what was done, and then somehow it stopped.

Meanwhile, I was on the other end of the phone, overwhelmed with this new information. It was all too much to take within just the few short minutes we had talked over the phone. The whole time he was telling me these things, my soul was crying out to God to help me hear the truth and not run from it. This was such a huge hit, and each piece of information he shared was like a boxcar on a train. And for me, it was as if the train was coming down the tracks too fast.

It was all becoming too much, and there was no way I could comprehend it all.

Without stopping, he continued to tell me something that completely took my breath away. He said it like it was a known fact: "Annette, it was no mystery to others that Grandpa was in your room or that Dad went in and out of there at all different hours of the night." Hearing this information, I felt as if there were too many train cars slamming into me from behind. The pain became insurmountable to the point that I became numb. I literally felt myself detach from the conversation. Thoughts of betrayal tried to flood my heart, and the sharp arrows of each word he spoke were now flying all around me. It was a lot to take in.

By now, you, the reader, need to know that the person who admitted to being the Shadow Man is my oldest brother. I have never given this information out freely because I wanted to protect his identity, and as I have said several times, he asked for forgiveness, and I had forgiven him.

My brother kept speaking that when he read the manuscript, he noticed immediately some actions of my sexual abuse that were not of his doing or my grandpa's. Going into details with my brother was not something I planned on doing that day over the phone, and it was detestable identifying which actions were his, my grandpa's, or my father's. However, as we talked, I felt God right there with me. I knew I was not alone. I knew His love toward me had not changed. In fact, my brother talked to me about how moved he was by the faithfulness he could see God had shown throughout my life.

I then proceeded to share with my brother my concern and what had just transpired with my father at odd hours of the night during my past two visits in California. He went on to explain to me how it was not possible for him to be the sole abuser for all those years. He mentioned reading in the manuscript about some of the times when, after the abuse was over, I would wait till the house was perfectly still and the Shadow Man's footsteps were gone then get up and vomit in the bathroom between my room and my parents'. He then asked me, "When you vomited, weren't you noisy?" I laughed and said, "Yes." He then went on to ask, "When we were little and we were vomiting, what would happen?" I told him Mom would run to help us out, pull back our hair, clean us up, put a cool cloth on our foreheads, and get us some clear soda. He then pointed out that in my manuscript I never mentioned Mom coming to my aid. He was right. I never realized this before, and this did seem odd. He then pointed to the part where, after the vomiting was over, I would go to my parents' room and found them both in bed and climbed in for safety. I told him, "That is correct." He said, "When Grandpa and I were in your room with you, everyone in the household was awake. It was only the little ones like yourself who were already in bed. When we finished, you did not get up and go to find Mom and Dad in their room, for they were not there."

It was like a light clicking on. I somehow was now able to separate the intruders in my mind.

For the first time in my life, I realized that I gave the name Shadow Man to the person who came and molested me because though it was extremely dark in my room, I had not yet mastered detaching myself from my body and escaping to my fantasy worlds, and what I saw was a man and his shadow—which, of course, was now explained to me as my grandpa and my brother. This was a piece of the puzzle that, as an adult, I could never put together; yet at that very moment, over the phone, all the pieces seemed to start fitting into place. The abuse happened to me at such a young age. As a child, what I saw before me in the darkness was the shape of a grown man with a shadow. I was only four years of age, and because of this, I named the person like a four-year-old would. He became the Shadow Man.

Talking through the hideous details of the patterns and behaviors of the abusers with my brother, I was able to get a clearer picture of who they were. It was in that moment I realized it probably was not my brother who sexually abused my two sisters. I interrupted him to ask about my sisters, and he said he had never done anything to them. This was shocking news. It was then I had to ask for his forgiveness, for after he admitted many years ago that he was the Shadow Man, I went and asked my sisters if they had been sexually abused. These two sisters went through the same abuse that matched the behavior of not my brother or grandfather but that of our own father. I explained to my brother when he admitted he was the Shadow Man that so many years ago, I had gone to my sisters and asked if they had been touched. When they told me they had, I told them what happened with my brother, how he was truly sorry for his actions and had asked for forgiveness. I also told them that he probably would be contacting them soon to ask for their forgiveness. What I was finding out on the phone was he never contacted them because he had no taken part in their sexual abuse. My brother understood why I asked my sisters and told them the man who came in the dark was him, and he graciously forgave me.

This was a ton of information I had no idea would be given to me over this phone conversation. Obviously there was more to discuss, but both my brother and I needed a break. Our phone call ended, and I sat on my bed trying to process the things I just heard. I breathed the words, *Help, God* and started to walk from the bedroom, where I was talking on the phone, to my husband's office to try to explain to him what just transpired over the phone with my brother.

Though in reality my husband's office is not far from the bedroom, thoughts flooded my soul. The thought of my own father having a part in my abuse was just too big of a bite to process in such a short amount of time. To hear my grandpa and my brother involved together was overwhelming, but the most painful to hear was that others knew and had done nothing. I did not know how to drink in this information. I tried to remind myself that I am God's special creation, and immediately I felt an arrow stab me. *See, you were created for this! You are a throwaway and a piece of trash. You are not loved and have only been created to be used by others. You are a worthless, dirty old rag. No one cares about a worthless piece of trash.*

Wow, I felt such a darkness start to creep around me; but immediately, though it hurt, I knew this was not God's thinking, for He would never speak that to my soul. He would never mix truth with lies. The truth was that I was created, but not to be sexually abused. I am by no means a throwaway piece of trash, though Satan knew I have felt like it a thousand times. This makes a person feel unloved; so when the next line came to my mind—*You are not loved, and you are created to be used by others*—my soul knew it hit a core, as in their was a piece of truth in it, but most of it was a lie. I know I am loved by God and was created by Him. I know I was used by others, but combining the two in a sentence makes one feel worthless. I knew I could easily just start agreeing and feeling sorry for myself or speak the truth to my heart so I could drink in relief. I started with, "I am God's child (John 1:12). I am His disciple, and that makes me a friend of Jesus Christ (John 15:15). I know I am chosen by God, and I am dearly loved and holy in His sight (Colossians 3:12). God loves me unconditionally. It does not matter if one or one hundred persons have used me for their pleasure. It changes nothing about how He sees me. I am loved (John 3:16)." There is nothing more powerful than knowing God loves me. I reached my husband's office and spoke to him about the phone call.

After a time of John and I talking, he called my father. John asked my father what he was doing in my room in the early-morning hours. My father responded that he had not been in my room. John asked, "Not in her room at all?" My father said, "Yes, that is correct." At this point, I just got up and left the room where John was making the phone call. I could not stand to hear what was being said. I felt as though I would be painted as a liar or a person with an over-active imagination, just like while growing up.

John continued with the phone call, asking my father if he could please get my mother on their other phone extension. When my mother got on the phone, John asked my father again if he had been in my room on the last night I stayed with them in California. My father denied being in my room. John then pointed out that when I told him the story of what happened, I mentioned that my father and I did create a lot of noise due to my father's falling back into the bedroom door unexpectedly when I jumped out of bed. He then asked my mother if she heard anything. Before she could answer, my father said he remembered he stumbled into my room because, for some reason, the hallway was darker than it normally was, and he must have run into my bedroom door accidently. My father's reason did not match my version of the story, for I can remember seeing his office light on as I passed it on my way to the far end of the house's bathroom. With his office door open, it lit up the hallway very well. The phone call was going nowhere, and it was obvious my father was sticking to his story of accidently falling into my bedroom.

John and I prayed for the next twenty-four hours about the situation. We came to the conclusion that we needed to let our children know about the events that took place while I was in my parents' home. All our children are grown and live all over the United States, so this was going to take some time. Our goal was to prevent further incidents with them, as well as their children, if they visited my parents. Though we would have rather spoken to them in person, this needed to be handled as soon as possible, so it was done by phone.

44

Telling

In the midst of telling our children, I realized I needed to speak to my siblings as well. Many of my siblings, as well as their children and grandchildren, live close to my parents' home. Those who do not live close, when coming to town, usually stay at my parents' home.

First on my list to contact were my two sisters whom I misinformed about our brother saying he was the man who came at night. I explained to each how sorry I was that I really thought he was our brother. They understood, and I was grateful. However, I pressed each one a little for more details of the abuse they experienced. We never spoke details, and this, I was finding, was of utmost importance. I explained to them that I needed to compare some information. What I found was the actions of this same person matched my father's. Though my sisters experienced it at different intervals—one, only a few times; and the other, over a period of about six months—all they experienced matched mine from a young age till I was ten years old. Because I was abused for many years, I believe that is why my abuse involved much more and was more aggression. But it does not matter if a person is touched inappropriately once or for years. There is damage done to that person's soul, and only Jesus can make it whole again.

As I continued to speak to my sisters, sharing many tears, I finally mentioned why I called. I shared with them my concern and told them about what happened in California just a few weeks beforehand. They both understood why I needed to share this with the family and coming out to speak with my father in person since he seemed unwilling to admit anything over the phone.

My sisters said they wanted to be there when we met with our father, and I told them we would inform them how we were going to put things together. Obviously my father was dealing with some sin in his life, and John and I wanted to set up basically a Matthew (NIV) 18:16, which reads, "But if they will not listen, take on one or two others along, so that every matter may be established by the testimony of two or three witness." John had already talked to my father over the phone, and he denied it. However, now I had my two witnesses, two persons who had been put through many of the similar sexual acts perpetrated against me in the exact, same manner.

I then finished calling the rest of my siblings. Most just listened as I presented the facts. I sent them all a copy of my unedited manuscript so they would be up on what happened while we grew up. Many did not know any of the details I had written about. This was a hard bit of news for all to swallow.

Unfortunately I could have never been so right. Speaking to family members about why we were going to California, I found another victim of my father. To my unimaginable horror, I found he had molested one of his granddaughters. She had kept it a secret for almost two decades, and in one painful phone conversation, her silence was shattered. At the end of our dialogue, she made it clear she never wanted to speak of it again. The pain of knowing the abuse had moved to another generation of children in our family was distressing. John and I did not want, for one moment, to take a chance on another person getting abused by my father. We had to go to California as soon as possible so that our family could understand the seriousness of this situation.

John contacted my parents to set up a time within the next week for us to go down. My father felt like all this was being blown out of proportion. He made it clear he had plans, and though my mother tried to get him to change his plans, he was determined not to. We then set to travel to California the following weekend and meet not only with my parents but with my two sisters, as well as any other siblings who wanted to be present.

45

Facing My Father

Thankfully my boss gave me the time off from work, and John was able to travel around his work schedule. We contacted all my siblings, and it looked like all, as well as their mates, were coming to meet us at my parents' home. We also were able to schedule my parents' pastor to be present to not only provide support for them but, after all had been said, to provide counseling if requested. It was obvious it was going to be a tough meeting for all of us, but the most important thing to me was getting help for my father and mother and possibly seeing my father repent and seek God to help him overcome his sexual addictions.

We got into town on a late flight and stayed at a hotel about an hour away from my parents' home. We woke up the next morning and had some time to really seek God before heading to meet with our friends Pastor Bob and Sherry Reeve from the Cause Community Church at a small sandwich shop. We were grateful for their agreeing to meet with us on such a short notice, and it was so good to see them. We talked to them about why we came to town and gave them the details of other family members, as well as my parents' pastor, being present. They both were very encouraging to us, but then Pastor Bob looked at me and said he wanted to be honest. I told him to go for it!

He said he did not believe my father at his age would admit to any of the horrific things I and my sisters were accusing him of. He explained that if my father were to do that, then he would think this to be the legacy others would remember him by. I disagreed with Pastor Bob immediately. I explained to him that coming forward and repenting and seeking forgiveness would be the most incredible legacy my father could leave his family, my father truly showing he was a man of God caught in a horrible trap of sin and seeking to be set free. I also made it clear to him that my father loved us, all of us in the family; and when he would see we were coming to him in love, he would want to take that moment in time to make things right.

Pastor Bob looked at me and tried again to get me to see things from my father's point of view. He again reminded me of my father's age, his numerous grandchildren, and great-grandchildren. The odds were that my father would not want to be remembered as a child molester. I looked at Pastor Sherry, and though she said nothing, her eyes told me she regretfully agreed with her husband. Pastor Bob finished by saying that he desired with all his heart for my version to take place—that repentance would be the first action, and grace and forgiveness from all would flow freely as the family rejoiced. I knew he meant it, and it was good to know there was this hope to hold on to for my father and for those who had been wounded over the many long years. We all prayed together, seeking God for His will to be done and to prepare hearts for the meeting with the whole family the following day.

John and I woke the next morning and met my older brother and a couple of sisters at a restaurant not too far away from my parents' home for breakfast. It was good to see some of my siblings whom I had not seen in a while, but the mood was definitely somber as we all knew why we were there.

My two sisters went over the letters they wrote ahead of time at the table with those present. These were the letters they were going to read to my father in just an hour from now. It was incredibly hard to sit there and listen. They spoke about some of the abuse they went through and then proceeded to explain how it had affected their life from that time forward. They spoke of how crushing it was for them to find out it was our own father who had come in our rooms at night. (For them, it was only my father, not like mine, which included my brother and grandfather.)

Normally I hear these types of stories or letters in the ministry I work for pretty regularly. However, these were my own sisters, and it was our father. I so wanted to just get up from that table and return to our home in Houston. The pain was great, and the grief at the table was crushing. Our family, which looked perfect from the outside, was anything but. We were suffering from a horrible infection of generations sexually assaulting children, and who knows how many generations back it went. Today was the day we would be brave enough to uncover, to bring out in the open, the hidden wound. Though knowing it would be incredibly painful, we believed it would start the process of healing for us all and stop such a horrific sin from going forward to the next generations.

We waited patiently at the restaurant for my parents' pastor to arrive at my parents' home. This way, it would be easier for everyone—it would feel very uncomfortable sitting around and waiting to begin. I had some siblings at my parents' home who were going to let us know when the pastor arrived. About an hour later, we got the text the pastor arrived, so we all headed over to my parents' home.

Unfortunately, when we arrived, we found that the text message we received was misunderstood and the pastor had not yet arrived. I met a few of my siblings whom I had not seen for a while, and I was informed by one of them that they could only be at the meeting briefly, for they had a wedding they needed to be, which was not close by.

Because it had been years since all my siblings were together all in the same place, someone thought it would be grand to take a picture of us all together in the front yard. I understood the idea, but this was anything but a fun event. I went out in the front yard where they wanted to take the picture, and some of the mates of my siblings took out their phones to take pictures. All of us huddled close, and then a person saw my parents walking around in the front yard in the distance and called them over to join us. This was a horrible idea. I felt so uncomfortable. How could we stand together as a family and smile at a camera when I was standing there, along with two of my sisters, to accuse my father of sexually abusing us as children? What were these others thinking? At this point, I had not even said hello to my parents since I arrived and was waiting till we all gathered in the house when I would see them.

It took a couple of times of my sisters calling over my mom for her to come over and join in the picture. However, my father, seeing what was happening, started to walk further away, and this was when some of the family members started to shout to him to get him to join in. This was wrong in so many ways. My father obviously wanted people to stop shouting and came on over. He did not look at me, yet all I could do was look at him. All of a sudden, I realized they kept calling my name; they were asking me to look up and smile. It was as though I was on some sort of autopilot, and I looked up and smiled. Instantly I realized what just took place, and I walked away rather numb and went inside the house to be far from everyone.

Thankfully, as I was walking in the front door, I heard people saying the pastor had arrived. This was great news. We could finally get started. We all gathered in the family room.

I sat on a couch with one of my sisters. My mother sat on a single chair between me and the pastor (the pastor was close to her, which I believe was a good thing). John sat at the main table at the center of the room my father sat across from him.

We opened with prayer and tried to bring the pastor up to date as best we could. It was a tense beginning, but the family member who was in a rush to make it to the wedding pressed forward and wanted his questions answered. He asked my father and brother straight out with an incredible emotion of pain, "Did you do what Annette said was done to her in her book?" He was referring to the unedited manuscript of this book, which I gave to each of my siblings so they could be up to date about my past. My brother answered, "No." I believe he was answering the question as though it was phrased, "Did you do all the actions Annette spoke about in her manuscript?" Not all were his doing as I mentioned before. This family member got their answer and walked out of the house. They were done. They had already spoken with my father; now my brother and I guessed reading my manuscript was enough for them to make their decision. They asked me nothing, nor did he look at me. I was crushed.

My two sisters wanted to read their letters. They both got a chance, and it was incredibly heartrending. Immediately there were family members present telling us we needed to forgive our father. In my sisters' letters, they did mention they were working on the forgiving part, but for now, they were grieving. It was so painful to see such insensitivity toward these victims, who were so brave to come forward only to have others jumping on with, "You need to forgive, or you will just end up bitter."

My father spoke and said something like this, "It is obvious there has been abuse happening under my roof. I had no idea Grandpa was doing what he did. I had no idea what was going on with my son. However, I never did anything you three girls are accusing me of. However, I take full responsibility for what had gone on under my roof and apologize for not being there for you or protecting you. As for Annette, let's face it. You have always had an overactive imagination, and your mother and I were just so thankful that John came along to marry you." At that moment, John spoke up and said, "How could Annette imagine the same exact sexual acts which were perpetrated upon her sisters?" I had no words. I was crushed.

My father, my dad, the one I thought loved me, said the words I heard over and over again as a child from not only him but my mother as well—"You have an overactive imagination." I looked over at my mother, who had not said much since we started. She just sat there as though she were praying, looking at her hands on her lap and never looking up. She obviously was not going to affirm anything.

Some older siblings mentioned being molested by my grandfather. At this point, my mother spoke up, acknowledging she did know about it later after it happened, and mentioned it to our father. However, my father denied ever being told. Other things were mentioned by my siblings about my father's brothers, and my mother agreed those things did happen.

When it came to me, she said the only thing she could remember was passing by my bedroom one time and finding my older brother with me when I was lying there in bed asleep. She said nothing more.

I pressed her why she did not come and see if my dad and I were okay just a couple of weeks ago when I was staying at their house. She had to have heard the banging of the bedroom door and my freaking out loudly because my father was in my room. She had no comment. She resumed looking down at her hands and softly mumbling, praying.

My father changed the subject and said he knew nothing about the pastor who sexually assaulted me in his office, which he read about in my unedited manuscript. My mother spoke up and said, "We could not tell you." Over and over again, it was painful to see my father denying and trying to put the blame of the abuse of my sisters on anybody but himself, as well as pretty much painting me as mentally unstable and having an over-active imagination. From that moment on, my mother sat on her chair, not having eye contact with anyone and praying in small whispers, basically shutting out the rest of what went on around her.

I was done. I knew there was one thing I needed to speak out, and then I would be ready to leave. There was no molecule in my heart that desired to do what I was about to do. However, I knew the scriptures. I knew what God was asking me to do even though I did not feel like it. With a silent prayer in my mind, I asked God to help me mouth the words. I breathed and told my father that even though he was not admitting to anything, I was going to forgive him. It was obvious we didn't agree, but what happened, happened. I did not make up being abused as a child; others in the room experienced some of the abuse I did. It was not because I had a over-active imagination. When I knew both parents could hear me—though it seemed my mother was still in some sort of a buffered world of her own—I said, "I forgive you both." I was done. I did what my heart had to declare, and now I was emotionless.

Had I really forgiven my father? I would honestly say I did with my words, and I knew it was something I wanted to do from my soul. However, I knew I was still so numb from the past few weeks. I still could not put the obvious together: my father had a part in my abuse. This was going to take time, but I knew doing this face-to-face with my parents at that moment was what God wanted from me. Experience has taught me forgiveness would come easily if I just trusted in God and did things His way. For now, it was words with great intent, the intent of waking up daily and—when thoughts of betrayal, anger, or anything else came up about my father and the horrid things he did to me, to my sisters, to his own grandchild, when he made me look like a fool with a over-active imagination—saying out loud, "I forgive you." Not just for me to hear it coming from my lips in faith but for him and all of my family.

My experience with God has shown me that I only need to be faithful, and somehow, bit by bit, God will walk me through the forgiveness process. I can count on that. I knew eventually I would wake up in the morning and have no thoughts about my father and what he did. There would not be any bitterness toward him, only prayers that one day he would be set free.

After I spoke, the suggestion was made for the women to stay in the room we were in presently and for the men to go to the living room and pray and finish up for the day. Us women joined in prayer to confirm we were all in agreement that this curse of sexual sin would not continue to other generations ahead. We prayed for my father and all our families going forward in this now-uncovered news of our past. My prayer was short. I prayed for wisdom and forgiveness to flow freely.

It was time to leave. I could hear the men leaving the living room from a distance. John came in, and we prepared to leave and later meet a few siblings for dinner to chat. Mainly all had been discussed, and it was time to go. I told my mother good-bye, who was now chatting normally with everyone. In fact, she seemed like a woman who was really happy to have all her children at home and visiting. It was odd, but there was nothing anyone could do. You can't force persons to wake up and be in the moment if they choose to protect themselves and not engage with others.

I thanked the pastor for showing up. We talked for a few minutes, and it sounded like she was going to be a good support for my mother and father if they desired it. The pastor told me to keep walking in forgiveness and that she would be praying for my parents.

I saw my father in the dining room, and though it would have been easier to slip away and not say good-bye, I knew it was something I needed to do. The word *forgiveness* came to mind, and if I was going to start walking in it, maybe this was the first step. I walked in and told him I was leaving. He said okay. I then reached and side-hugged him, and he did not hug back. It was hard. It was as if for the first time I saw my father in a different light. It was the first time in my life I felt a crushing rejection of that kind from my father, and it hurt me greatly.

As I walked out my parents' back door and heard the familiar slam of the wood against the door's metal hinge, I thought about all the times I ran out that door to go play, hang laundry, open it for neighbors, go out to the garage to see what Dad was doing. I loved this old house. It held so many memories for me and my family, good and bad. I felt sadness as I walked down those steps, as though I was walking away and would never be welcomed there again. I was going to miss it. I think, more than anything, it was a good-bye to the naïve child I had been and a hello to the devastating reality of an adult living life in the aftermath of the truth revealed about her father and mother, whom she loved.

46

Going Forward

John and I attended church the following day. The message at church was all about forgiveness. My heart ached. Though personally it seemed like the worst timing for this type of message, it was actually God's just loving me more, reminding me to continue staying focused on walking forward free from any bitterness, hate, and thoughts of trying to plead my case—that He, the Almighty God, had this situation in His hands. When I said less than twenty-four hours ago that I forgave my parents, it was done. Though it might take my emotions and my mind much more time to process it, God wanted to remind me that unforgiveness was not something I should walk with even for one moment. For all it would do is weigh me down, cloud my thinking, and plant seeds of bitterness that would be incredibly hard to remove.

Overall, I was blessed by going to the Sunday-morning service and seeing friends we had not seen in years. The following day, I was back on my job, as well as working with those God had me coaching and discipling, which kept me relatively busy, and that was good. However, I can easily say that each day when I woke up, my heart ached from what took place that past weekend. My father sitting there and denying what he had done not only to me but my sisters replayed there in my memory. As soon as I arose and started to remember those familiar memories, I would say out loud, "I have forgiven my father. God, I pray he will receive the healing he needs to be free from the sin that has kept him bound. In Jesus's name, amen." Daily I kept doing this, and each time, no unforgiveness nagged at me or dragged me down.

As the days turned into weeks, I noticed I did not awake to the pain in my heart. Truly God was being faithful in helping me forgive the betrayal that stung so deep within and, at the same time, start to process and connect the dots of the truth of my parents and their actions.

I was talking to one of my friends at work about what happened in California. She was sorry for what my family and I were all going through. She then asked how I comprehended all this truth at this time. I told her it was hard to grasp that my father had anything to do with my abuse, though it was obvious with all the facts. However, my mother not participating for almost the entire meeting, refusing to make eye contact, disengaging from us and pulling into herself, and praying in her inaudible mumbles about her painful realization was easier to comprehend. Her actions spoke so loudly. Though it was still a horrendous, painful revelation of truth, I was able to understand she was part of this evil. She was a silent witness to the evil carried out upon her children for over a decade. Many, but not all of us, females went to her with cries for help, and they were not met with a follow-up of protection. Though she did say at the meeting that she spoke to my father about my grandfather, my father said he does not remember her saying anything; and if she did, why did she continue to let us be in my grandfather's presence alone? Unfathomable. I think my mother not protecting us and then letting the abuse continue from one generation to the next is heinous and incomprehensible.

My friend asked if my mother had been sexually abused. I told her I was told that my mother had been approached by my grandfather to have sex with him, and she did not. It was also obvious to me that she had the traits of one who had been sexually abused. My friend then asked my permission to share a story with me about a friend she grew up with. This friend came from a large family like I did and had been sexually abused for many years. I told her to go ahead and share it with me.

She said her friend, later in life, found out that her mother knew about her father sexually abusing her. When she asked her mother about it, her mother reasoned that in those days, married women rarely worked outside the home. Even if she did work, she would not have enough money to support the family. If her mother spoke up and went through a divorce, it would put her and the children in poverty. She said the mother weighed and balanced the options and went with the decision she felt at the time was the least of all evils. Let the sexual abuse continue in order for her and the rest of the children to survive.

My friend then explained that she did not condone the mother's decision for one minute but was just trying to give me some perspective. She then asked if my mother would have left my father if she had a parent to go to with all eight children. I told her, "No, my grandfather on one side was already sexually abusing the grandkids and wanted her to sleep with him, and her own father was an alcoholic, whom her mother was ready to divorce." My friend then asked about our religious views back then, and I told her we were Catholic, and divorce was not something that was done. In fact, when there were divorces, the men, for some reason, were not looked upon badly; however, the women were looked upon horribly as harlots. As we talked, I came up with so many reasons why my mother let the abuse continue. All of them were horribly wrong, but I now had some sort of compassion leak into my soul for her.

Moments would arise, after the day my friend shared that story with me, when I wondered about the times my mother drove me to countless counselors and psychiatrists. Even after I tried to end my life, she still never came out with the truth. It was just blamed on my overactive imagination.

It was in these reflective moments that I realized my mother had become just as sick with the sin perpetrated against not only me but others. On the day our family met, looking at her sitting in the family room, detached from all that was going on around her, I saw a woman who just could not take it anymore. She was lost in the grief, sorrow, and unfortunately, the oppressiveness of my father, and she chose to stay there with it playing dead.

Pastor Bob was right when he said the odds of my father admitting he did any of the sexual abuse in our home would be slim to none. For that would be his legacy. For my mother to admit she let the abuse happen would be the same. Sad. Sad for all involved. Not only for us victims of the crimes but for our mates, our children, and our grandchildren. I pray one day my mother will be set free from the chains that she does not even realize have her shackled.

As for my father, I traveled back to California eight months later. I had some mission, things I needed to get done. While I was there, I did see my mother and father very briefly in passing. My goal not be with my father alone. Unfortunately we ended up alone for no more than two minutes, but it was enough for him to let me know he was unhappy with me for not coming and spending time with them on this trip. I told him I felt very uncomfortable with the way things left last time at the family meeting and wanted to give all parties involved time and space. He told me the meeting should have never happened. I had an over-active imagination and needed to get it under control. I responded by reminding him about my sisters who read their letters for him, speaking of how he abused them, out loud to all those in the room. He stood there in front of me. He looked at me and, in a calm voice, said, "I don't remember any letters being read." I replied, "You've got to be kidding me." He then said, "Look, do you see any changes? All the family still comes here. Nothing has changed. Nothing." He then looked at me with such great satisfaction and pride. His words and actions caught me by surprise. He was right. The family still gathered with him and my mother once a month for a giant barbeque, and siblings still came with their mates and spent their nights at the house. He took my siblings still coming over and life moving on, with him and my mother still going to all the celebrations, as everyone being fine with it. I had to leave before I said something I would regret. I turned and just walked away.

As for my siblings, they do still go to my parents' house, and those who live out of town still stay there with my parents. What he said was correct. The personal relationship my siblings chose to have with my father is their decision. My goal was to let others know the truth so no one would be put in the position of being hurt in their home anymore.

The ones who have surprised me the most, with the news of what my father did, and acted with great caution around my parents are the grandchildren, and at least I can be extremely grateful for this. My goal was not to humiliate my father and mother but to protect others by not covering up the truth. These grandchildren have chosen bravely to keep the light of truth burning brightly and not put up with having their children grow up in the dark. They have drawn the line in the sand and are saying, "No more!" Some have even taken steps to make sure others are provided the education they need to teach their children, and some run the 10K to promote ministries against child abuse and human trafficking. I am so proud of these young adults. It is now up to those who have the knowledge of the truth how they will proceed with their lives.

My daughter Rickie wrote me a letter during the time I was working on this book, and I included it below:

Dear Mom,

I want to encourage you while you are finishing your book with some things in my heart.

With all of the grief caused by the actions of family and the denial of truth by some, it is easy to overlook how God has brought beauty from pain in our family.

The denial holds strong with Grandpa and Grandma while they continue to lie not only to themselves but others. Yet there has been repentance and forgiveness with my uncle, which has brought reconciliation. This has shown that great healing is possible if we are not afraid to confront such darkness. Many in the family have chosen to close their eyes and turn their backs to the truth brought forward, but others have stepped up and have put a foot down. No longer will this run down the family line! This is something I have seen with many of my cousins. It saddens me to see some pretend nothing happened, but I see God's work in their children.

I am glad you have spoken up and continue to allow God to bring beauty from your pain. With so many of my cousins and me being parents, we see the urgency of making sure our families are open and honest with one another so such darkness is cut from our family line. It is so important that we have help in confronting the shames of our past, and I hope you continue to help others along that path. God has shown me the pain some sins can cause, but also the healing if we trust His guidance.

Love,
Your daughter, Rickie Eastis Baker

47

The Family Factor

Not more than thirty days after I returned from my last trip to California, I was working with a sexually abused woman in Houston. She was talking to me about her children going to their grandfather's overnight. I thought I heard her wrong the first time she said it, so I asked her to repeat herself. I then asked if this was the same father who raped her teenage sister, and she answered yes. I looked at her rather shocked and asked how she thought it would be okay to leave her four-year-old daughter and fourteen-year-old son at his home? She explained he had not sexually abused anyone for many years, not that she knew of, and gave me a few more excuses. She then looked at me, realizing she really had no good excuse except the one reason that meant everything to her. She stated, "You don't understand, Annette. Your children have a grandfather. If I don't let my kids stay there, they won't have him in their life! He is the only grandfather they have. How can I not let them stay with him?"

I then had to share with her that my own children and grandchildren could not safely stay at my parents' home, and I did understand. I then had to explain that the testimony she had heard many months beforehand did not include the information that the abuse I endured at home as a child was done by family members. This was huge for her. She then asked how I could forgive those who were supposed to love me. I said nothing changed when it came to all I have shared on forgiveness. Yes, finding out my family members were involved in my abuse hurt like crazy. It was as if a whole new forgiveness needed to happen. But like all forgiveness, it happens with God. His example of unconditional love and forgiveness toward me speaks volumes of what I can give others.

That night, when I drove away from the meeting with this young lady, I realized there was no way I could finish this book and let you, the readers, not know about the "family" factor. More than 90 percent of the sexually abused I work with have experienced it at the hands of a family member or a close family friend, people who are supposed to love and who should have been trustworthy. In fact, I have found my testimony more powerful to those I share the family piece with.

As for my relationship with my father and mother, it is a work in progress. By the time this book goes out, I don't know how it will be; but for now, it is what it is. I told this part of the story, though very personal and painful, to reveal the God of love, hope, and grace, who can reach into the darkest of situations. It makes my relationship with my parents not so dark, and I am filled with hope that they will receive God's love the way they need Him in their lives.

Sure, it is embarrassing to shed light on such things in my family's past. However, the sexual abuse that took place in our home was not all that took place. Much love and caring went on. We made fantastic relationships, and memories of fishing trips, washing the car, and dancing in the backyard with stage curtains made from our bedsheets fill my mind with laughter. I treasure those memories. No family is perfect, but Jesus came here to earth and sacrificed His life to make us perfect in God's sight so we can spend eternity in His presence. I love Revelation (NIV) 21:4: "He will wipe every tear from their eyes. There will be no more death or mourning or crying or pain, for the old order of things has passed away."

I look forward to that day.

Was it hard to reveal so much ugliness about my family? Yes, it was. In fact, it still is hard for my family members. The one person who left early that day of the meeting, who had to go to a wedding, has not spoken to me since that day. I have tried writing e-mails and letters, only to get no response back. I miss them greatly, but I am entrusting this relationship in God's hands for Him to be glorified in it. I have been asked how my family will react to this book. I suppose they will not be happy about it. Many of the people mentioned here are alive. However, again, this message of hope for those sexually abused by family members could not be told without my speaking the truth. So with much love, I say, I shared to set the captives free from the bondage of their dark family secrets, from which they have never been able to break free.

48

But Then God

The first prayer I can ever recall saying was asking—no, begging—God to take away the Shadow Man. He did not. For the next seven years, I endured horrific visits by him in my room. My bedroom where, as a little girl, I should have felt safe became a place of dread, panic, and terror. I lived a life knowing from the age of three that no one was ever going to protect or rescue me. When the warm blankets were pulled back, my clothes removed, and I awoke to the feeling of the cold night's air upon my skin, I knew what was about to begin, and I had to escape as quickly as possible. My choice of escape was to play dead, and this became a way of life.

I had no relationship with the Shadow Man, for I did not know his identity till I was an adult. However, I knew pain. I lived with physical pain for days after a visit with the Shadow Man, reminding me he truly did exist. It was not my mind's imagination, and I knew his return was only a matter of time. Like a cruel friend, pain would always show up to remind me emotionally of how unworthy, worthless, and horrid I was to think such things at night would happen in my room. Pain greeted me every morning and was always the first to greet me when the Shadow Man showed up. The game began with who would win. I fought the emotional terror as quickly as possible by blocking every nerve and pain sensor in my body so not even the slightest touch caused me to flinch. I then mentally detached myself from the situation. In the beginning, this was so incredibly difficult. I would be in the midst of a dream only to wake so often in the middle of being sexually abused. It became a horrific game of who would win. Winning was everything. Over time, I became the victor; and though there was great fear when I heard the doorknob turning and knowing full well what was about to happen, immediately I would shut my eyes and play dead.

In the end, it caused me to hate myself and in turn hurt myself to kill the pain screaming for relief in my soul. I might have gotten my physical body to play dead and suffocated my emotions from surfacing, but somewhere inside me, my soul was alive, and it kept a record of the trauma.

Along life's journey, I did not lose faith that there was a God, though He did not answer my prayer. I knew He existed. I just knew I would never be worthy of Him ever wanting anything to do with me. When I said that prayer so many years ago as a small child, I figured I prayed too late. I prayed in the midst of being sexually abused, and He must not have answered me because I was already a filthy, dirty rag. If I had worth, it was already gone.

I still prayed to Him for other things as I grew up but did not expect anything to come of it. I really did not need Him or anyone else. My strong will got me through, and it would keep getting me through till I decided to end it all. I regularly dreamed and fantasized about suicide since I was nine years old. It was freeing to imagine not living in a world with so much pain, and the idea of being able to choose it at any time gave me a great feeling of control in a world that, to me, was spinning out of control.

But then God—God showed up when I least expected Him. Though I thought I was just going to give Him a tiny try, I opened the door enough for His unconditional love to find my heart. I can remember telling Him I just wanted salvation, nothing more, a way into heaven; and if He let me in, I would stay anywhere He had available in heaven, as well as try not to ask too many questions. I explained to Him what He was getting. I was not the girl in the story "Cinderella" who needed rescuing. I was more like the ugly, selfish stepmother who was incredibly bitter toward the world she lived in. In fact, I made it clear to Him I would not be His virgin young girl but the tramp who had no value at all. God, who should not have given me the time of day after all I told Him, still loved me. He gave me the gift of hope, and if I could see with my spiritual eyes, I bet He knocked Satan unconscious that night when I accepted Christ as my Savior.

From that moment on—though I have to admit I did not give in easily, for I had a pretty strong will and personality—that night when I accepted Christ, I started to live. The hope inside me started to scream louder than the hell trying to consume me. At times I did become afraid and fell back into being my own god. I still played dead when pain visited, but that did not stop God for one moment to continually love me unconditionally. What I found was that God had become much more faithful and reliable than pain. And in His love, I was slowly able to see the truth of who I was in Christ.

Before, with my wounded heart and with my soul playing dead, I could never hear the cries of others hurting, but now I do. I can now share the incredible blessing of how God brings His healing to hard and broken hearts and make them see complete recovery. God really did have a plan for my life. What Satan meant for my destruction God turned around and made a blessing in my life.

I am more blessed now than I have ever been in my life. God has healed me and, yes, is still healing me, making me more whole every day. He can do this for you. This I am sure, for God's Word is true. He loves you, and there is not one thing you can do to make His love go away. It took one breath of saying, "I believe, and I am willing to try." Will you give God a chance, step in faith, and open a tiny portion of your heart to Him? God is no fool. He knew full well what He was getting into when I came into a relationship with Him. Yet He was willing to look at my pain, my scars, willing to be patient till I was ready to trust Him with more of me. The beginning was slow, for I did not trust Him. I just could not understand why He did not answer my prayer way back in my bedroom as a little girl. How was I supposed to trust this God who did not take away the Shadow Man? I'll be honest. I don't know why He did not. This question would have to be one of those asked in heaven, but by then, it will be as it is right now: I really don't care. From the perspective I have now, I can see God taking the heart of an incredibly bitter and defiant teenager and deciding to love her no matter what. I can remember the first time I felt His love flowing out of the Bible, where it states, "'For I know the plans I have for you,' declares the Lord, 'plans to prosper you and not to harm you, plans to give you hope and a future'" (Jeremiah (NIV) 29:11).

I remember my breath could barely come as I wondered what kind of world it would be to have God, the ever so powerful, have plans for me at the age of twelve. It was pretty exciting.

Though there were so many trials and tribulations to still walk through, God never left me. I know He was there when I lay and begged Him to let me die on the office floor of the pastor who tortured me, and again, God did not answer my prayer. There was no greater desire in my heart that day than to die; He knew it. Yet God, with all the power He had to take my life, chose to have me live another day. Oh, the pain in my soul to wake the next day. Oh, the question of, *Does God really love me, or is this what He calls His plans for me? If they are, I do not want them for one second.* What I did not realize was that my blessing was just around the corner.

When I was around five years of age, sitting on the ground playing with my Barbies, I prayed God would bring me a good husband who would love me. By the age of nine, I prayed my husband would never show up, for I did not want him anymore; but more than anything, I did not want him to want me. I was fine on my own, and I never wanted to be touched by a human being ever again. Who would have thought one day God would bring me a husband, a gift who would wear patience as though it was a custom suit made just for him, who would love me beyond the fears, bitterness, and scars he saw upon my body and heart? Who would have thought we would be blessed to be part of the lives of five beautiful, beautiful children, their wonderful spouses, and so many precious grandchildren? None would exist today if my prayers were answered on the office floor. I was only thinking of the moment, but God was aware of my future. I thank God He did not answer my prayer that day to let me die.

Who would have thought that, as I grow in my relationship with God, I would be learning to wield a sword (the Word of God) and learn how to use it so effectively? Not that I have been a master student, for God has been incredibly patient with me as I wandered off into places I should not have gone or just up and ran in another direction out of fear, only to return to His presence and pick up the sword once again. In doing so, now I have found I have skills in being able to help set others free from the bondage in which they find themselves. I am on a quest, one where I am to bring the healing message of hope to the brokenhearted and to wake those who are playing dead. God really did have a plan for my life. What Satan meant for my destruction God was turning it around and making it a blessing in my life. Genesis (NIV) 50:20 says, "You intended to harm me, but God intended it for good to accomplish what is being done, the saving of many lives."

Playing dead was a huge part of my life that I said good-bye to. At times, like most victims of abuse, I have suffered from some PTSD (post-traumatic stress disorder) symptoms. Normal, everyday activities can be interrupted by sounds, smells, words, or actions of others that remind us of the trauma. It is like freezing-cold water thrown on you when you least expect it, and the moment I feel it, my old nature immediately desires to choose to play dead and go numb to protect myself. No more! I may stumble and trip as I shake off the shock of the cold water, but I am choosing life.

All I know is if I had not traveled the road before me, I would have never known the depth of unconditional love to its fullest, which I have been able to experience by God giving it to me as a gift and my giving it to another human being. I would have never understood the intensity and extent of forgiveness if I had not been forgiven and had not experienced such deep betrayal. I would have never been able to hope if I were not given the gift of salvation. I would have not known how deeply I am valued and treasured. Even when I had been so resentful and ugly, God still loves me. I would have never known that God placed others along the journey of my life to help me learn all these things and more so I could not only be set free but set others free as well.

Writing this chapter, I was drawn back to my first prayer as child, and I wondered what I really desired. My little mind said the words, "Take away the Shadow Man," which meant to me, "Make him just disappear. Poof! Gone forever." If he would have just disappeared, I would have grown up with a grandfather who probably would have looked like he, as well as my father, just up and abandoned their families without a good-bye. I would have missed out on the relationship I have with my oldest brother. People would have missed out on the other parts of their lives where these persons are a blessing. Music, which always forms some part of my day, probably would not mean as much to me as it does now. All three men adored it. They brought much joy to our home when I was little, playing endless songs; and I remember as a child, all of us danced to the beat of the Latin rhythm mixed with jazz with the soles of our feet to the beating of our hearts. The world would have been left with songs that were never to be written if my older brother would have disappeared. His incredible wife and their beautiful sons would not exist, as well as their children now. For this, I am grateful my prayer was not answered. I am not excusing their bad choices in life. I am just stating that there is more to them than those moments in my room.

Who would have thought I would come to the point in my life where I can make such a statement: "Thank you, God, for all of my past, for *all* those who played a part in it, and for your incredible wisdom to answer prayers that will not only bless me but the world where everything you have created lives." Certainly not me. Today my prayer is to live, experience, learn, love, forgive, and wield the sword that God has given me to set the captives free, bring healing to the brokenhearted, and wake those who are playing dead.

In the end what I have discovered was this story was not about my family, not even really about me. It is about God and His story being lived out in front of me. His story is the one that needs to be shared.